I ALWAYS SIT WITH MY BACK TO THE WALL

Managing Traumatic Stress and Combat PTSD
Through The R-E-C-O-V-E-R Approach
for Veterans and Families

Dr. Harry A. Croft, M.D.
Rev. Dr. Chrys L. Parker, J.D.

I Always Sit with My Back to the Wall

© 2011 My Back to the Wall LLC

AUTHOR CONTACT AND ORDERING:

To place individual or bulk/institutional orders for this book by check or credit card or to make inquiries regarding lectures, presentations, or workshops by Dr. Harry A. Croft, interested persons may use any of the following contacts:

Website: www.mybacktothewall.com
Telephone: 210-692-1222 (US)
Email: hcroft@drcroft.com
Postal: 7434 Louis Pasteur Drive, Suite 101
San Antonio, TX 78229

Produced for My Back to the Wall LLC by
Stillpoint Media Services

Editor: Lillie Ammann

Cover Designer: Ann Pressly

ISBN: 978-1-890498-43-6

First edition March 2011

Second Printing 2015

Printed in the United States of America

DEDICATION

The dedication of any written work, especially one that has been years in the making, has great significance for us as authors. It isn't merely a statement of thanks, but rather a recognition that our lives, our careers, and even our gifts and talents do not belong to any of us alone. They are joint endeavors that are inspired, nurtured, and supported by loving people with whom we each have the good fortune to be in close and abiding relationship. We dedicate this book to them.

CHAPLAIN PARKER

To five extraordinary men in my life. Because of you it has been an incredible journey.
To Peter Lambros, my late father, who showed me unbounded love.
To Joe Parker, Jr., my devoted husband, who showed me steadfast belief in all that I am.
To Glenn Sammis, my colleague, who showed me what it means to be a soldier.
To Ben Durr, who showed me that all men may live in the grip of grace.
And to Harry, who showed me the joy of a friendship that was meant to be.

DR. CROFT

To Buddy Bradshaw, my colleague, friend, and mentor, who taught me of all the lessons that can be learned around a dinner table.
To Charles Garrett who pushed me to "write the book."
To Chrys, my teacher and friend who shared the book's incredible journey with me.
And to my wife of 46 years, Benay, who is the love and inspiration of my life, and without whom I would not be complete.

Chaplain Parker walking the T-wall, Victory Base Camp, Iraq, with her colleague, Dr. (CH LTC, USA, Ret.) Glenn Sammis

ACKNOWLEDGMENTS

This book could not have been written without the contribution of the thousands of men and women who, over the course of thirty years, permitted us to walk with them upon the sacred ground of their most painful and traumatic experiences. There is not a day that goes by that we do not pay homage to them in our minds and hearts for the generosity of the trust they have placed in us, for the insightful lessons they have taught us, and for the depth of the sacrifices that they and their families have made in order that we and all other citizens of this country might continue to enjoy the blessings of a more secure land and a free society.

We wish to acknowledge the extraordinary men and women of the US Army Chaplaincy Corps and the inspiring leaders and spiritual heroes within its ranks. Special appreciation is extended to CH (MAJ GEN) Douglas Carver, the US Army Chief of Chaplains; CH (COL) Michael Lembke; CH (CPT) Michael Spikes; Dr. Steven Jordan, Ph.D. (CH LTC, USA Ret.); CH (COL) Michael Dugal; and CH (LTC) William Barbee.

Chaplain Parker extends special recognition to Dr. Darla H. Bejnar, M.D.; Dr. Donald Currie, M.D.; Dr. Steven Wolf, M.D.; and Dr. C. Leon Sims, Ed.D.; through their support, advocacy, and clinical mentorship, her career in medical and psychotherapeutic services to the traumatized was made possible.

Dr. Croft acknowledges the following great people who played such a significant role in his understanding of PTSD and its treatment: Lee Alley and Hector Villareal, war heroes and inspirations for this book; Col. Mykle Stahl, who taught him about war, the military, and the VA; former Veterans Administration Secretary James Peake (Lt. Gen., USA Ret), who, while medical director of QTCM, helped him with the evaluation of many of the veterans he saw; and the wonderful personnel of QTCM, the company that referred those veterans to him.

Finally, we would like to give a special acknowledgment to our super editor, Lillie Ammann, for her eagle eye and her knowledge of what it takes to make a book complete, and to our publisher, Charles Garrett, for taking the respective expressions of two authors and—much like a wise and capable counselor—melding them into one cohesive vision, through which we truly found our literary voice.

TABLE OF CONTENTS

A no-nonsense look at the realities of PTSD as it is really experienced by vets and their significant others. Without benefit of sugar coating and using the words of both the authors and of vets themselves, this chapter provides an honest and accurate description of the serious and life-altering effects of PTSD in every aspect of the veteran's life, including
• marriage, divorce, and the destruction of family life;
• PTSD-related effects on the ability to maintain stable employment;
• the experience of noxious PTSD symptoms such as nightmares, flashbacks, and reactions to posttraumatic triggers;
• inability to maintain stable interpersonal relationships and enjoy healthy personal intimacy; and

• the deterioration or destruction of spiritual relationships to God and one's faith community.

What mother, society, and the military never told you about trauma and PTSD. Authoritative yet understandable explanations of the dynamics of traumatic events, signs and symptoms of PTSD, and its relationship to the life history of the sufferer, the changing nature of combat-related traumatic exposure, the connection between the psychological and the biological aspects of PTSD, and (most importantly) why PTSD is definitely not "all in your head." The chapter concludes with a detailed examination of the full range of diagnostic criteria for the illness, what they mean, and how they are encountered in the day-to-day life of the veteran.

PTSD is not, as is widely assumed, merely a problem of inappropriate behavior. This chapter reveals the biological roots of PTSD in survival-based psycho-neurological and endocrine processes of the body. The reader will learn the essential elements of the "HPA Axis" (or survival-based stress response), the "Locked and Loaded" vs. "Hunkered in the Bunker" profiles of traumatic reaction, which types of reactions are under the conscious control of the sufferer and which are not, and simple ways to understand stress-related brain functioning through the "Upstairs/Downstairs"© model of comparing your brain to a common office building.

"Feeling bad" should never be accepted as "good enough." In this chapter, vets and family members receive clear, simple, and understandable step-by-step explanations of the various kinds of care available for PTSD, beginning with a self-inventory of symptoms and extending all the way through psychotherapeutic, psychological, pastoral, pharmacological, and psychiatric modes of care. Vets are empowered to take ownership of their mental health care and are given the tools needed to become conscientious and well-informed consumers, capable of proactively organizing both private and governmentally-based approaches to their mental health care.

R-E-C-O-V-E-R-Y begins with the vet himself or herself. This chapter examines the connections between perceptions, attitudes, and systems of interpersonal support on the one hand, and the capacity for posttraumatic resilience and recovery on the other. Included are sound strategies for increasing self-awareness and self-management of PTSD triggers, as well as bio-medical reasons why living a life in right relationship with others is actually nature's most powerful medicine.

By their very nature, human beings were not designed to go it alone. In this chapter, the authors explore the wealth of research that has demonstrated the importance of social and spiritual support in the pursuit of personal wellness in the wake of trauma. They also examine the essential principles of resilience and their determining effects upon the posttraumatic recovery of the human person. Sound advice is provided about how to locate and access these critical forms of pastoral, spiritual, and social support.

Recovery from trauma is not merely a challenge; it is an opportunity. In this chapter, the authors examine the critical role of meaning making in the fashioning of a healthy and resilient life, the relationship between meaning making and the expansion of old limitations upon our view of the world, distinguishing between what we do and who we are, and the importance of value systems in sustaining positive concepts of self-worth, as well as healthy relationships with others.

ABOUT THE AUTHORS

Dr. Harry A. Croft, M.D.

Dr. Harry A. Croft, identified in the text as Dr. C, has been a psychiatrist in private clinical practice in San Antonio, Texas, for more than thirty years. He is board certified in Adult Psychiatry, Addiction Medicine, and Sex Therapy. In addition to his private practice, he also serves as medical director and principal investigator in the San Antonio Psychiatric Research Center, where for the past twenty-five years he has participated in the development of many of the psychiatric medications now available for the treatment of depression and anxiety disorders.

He is well known in psychiatric medicine with publications in *Psychiatric Annals, JAMA, Psychiatry, American Journal of OB-GYN,* and others. He has given presentations to over one thousand groups of physicians and mental health professionals in all fifty of the US states and in seven foreign countries. He serves as medical director of HealthyPlace.com, the world's largest consumer-driven mental health website, and has appeared on commercial TV news with his award-winning mental health feature, "The Mind Is Powerful Medicine."

Dr. Croft's interest in PTSD started in 1973 when, as a major in the US Medical Corps, he served as medical director of the Drug and Alcohol Treatment program at Ft. Sam Houston, Texas. During the next three years, Dr. Croft took care of thousands of military members returning from Vietnam with not only substance abuse problems but also with what is now recognized as PTSD. Since 1998, he has evaluated more than six thousand veterans with PTSD and has become an advocate for those suffering from the disorder.

He is a Distinguished Life Fellow of the American Psychiatric Association and is the recipient of numerous awards and honors, including The US Army Meritorious Service Medal, The President's Award from the APA, and The National Mental Health Association Recognition Award, as well as more than fifty other national, state, and regional awards.

Although his biography has appeared in *Who's Who in America* since 1976, his proudest accomplishments are his forty-six year marriage to his wife, Benay; his two children; and his two granddaughters.

Rev. Dr. (Chaplain) Chrys L. Parker, J.D.

Rev. Dr. Chrys Parker, identified in the text as Chaplain P, is a clinical chaplain, clergywoman, pastoral counselor, and trauma therapist specializing in the spiritual and psychological care of PTSD experienced by individuals as a result of combat, critical burn injury, and sexual assault. In addition to mental health, her practice embraces the fields of theology and spirituality, trauma research, nonprofit care for the indigent, and allied medical services to individuals and families. She has served as pastoral director of numerous hospitals and medical facilities and is a former volunteer field medic.

Rev. Parker is the Executive and Clinical Director of the Burn Recovery and Research Foundation in San Antonio, Texas. From 2006 to 2010, she served as a member of the Allied Medical Staff of University Hospital in San Antonio, where she was affiliated with the hospital's pediatric burn team and directed what is believed to be the nation's first comprehensive program for the long-term, integrated medical, spiritual, and psychosocial care of PTSD-affected burned children and their families.

Chaplain Parker's career expanded to embrace service to the U.S. military in 2007, when she became a postgraduate instructor of combat and medical chaplains for the Pastoral Training Office of the US Army Medical Command Center and School of Allied Sciences. In 2009, she received appointment as Adjunct Assistant Professor lecturing in trauma studies and medical ethics at the University Of Texas Health Science Center, San Antonio, where she provides interdisciplinary instruction to medical providers concerning the psychological, medical, and spiritual impact of traumatic stress disorders and their connection to the ethical treatment of the medically ill and injured.

Licensed to practice law for over thirty-three years and now retired from active practice, Rev. Parker devotes her notable legal expertise and experience to legal advocacy for victims of trauma in state and federal courts and is a consulting expert on trauma for the Center for Legal and Social Justice of St. Mary's University School of Law (her alma mater). Equipped with the unique perspective that she has derived from her interdisciplinary training, she has rendered care for over 2500 traumatized individuals since 1998, including adults, children, and warriors, while providing consultation to physicians, surgeons, and psychiatrists. As a nationally recognized academic educator of military, medical, and civilian professionals, Rev. Parker has authored or co-authored more than sixty academic and professional courses in trauma and has provided training to over 4500 clinicians, including physicians, surgeons, chaplains, nurses, social workers, and therapists.

In 2010, in response to the invitational order of the Office of the Commanding General, CENTCOM, US Forces-Iraq, Chaplain Parker and her colleague Rev. Dr. Glenn C. Sammis (CH LTC, USA Ret.) voluntarily deployed to the Iraqi theater of operations to initiate (in military terms, to stand up) the Spiritual Fitness Initiative, a new and paradigmatic model of care for warriors, and to train US Army Chaplains in the use of spirituality as an effective vehicle for wellness maintenance, traumatic stress management, and human resource protection. In so doing, Chaplains Parker and Sammis became the first civilian chaplains in the 250-year history of the US Army Chaplaincy to be inserted downrange during wartime in service to US military forces.

As a recipient of numerous professional honors and awards, Rev. Parker remains active in civic organizations including the FBI Citizens' Academy Alumni Association and the Downtown Rotary Club of San Antonio. She and her husband Joe (a fourth generation Texas rancher) have been married for over twenty-six years. They are the proud parents of a daughter, two sons, and have a daughter-in-law and two beloved grandchildren. They live beneath the broad southwestern skies of Uvalde, Texas.

ABOUT THE ILLUSTRATOR

Chaplain (CPT) Stephen L. Dicks, D.Min.

CH Stephen L. Dicks has served with the XVIIIth Airborne Corps based at Ft. Bragg, with which he did his first overseas deployment to the Iraqi theater, serving at Victory Base Camp (Baghdad) and at the Combat Support Hospital in Mosul, Iraq. Later assignments took him to Ft. Sam Houston for advanced Clinical Pastoral Education and to Ft. Leavenworth, where he served as the Chaplain of the Army Disciplinary Barracks.

Everywhere CH Dicks has served, he has fused his artistic talent with his spiritual sensibilities, poignant and often humorous observations of human nature, and practical knowledge of Army life by drawing cartoons for local military publications. CH Dicks' drawings have enhanced not only this book, but also the programs conducted by Chaplain Parker in the combat theater. CH Dicks and his wife Jennifer are the parents of Ashley, Kaylee, Tina, and Stephen. As this book was being published, CH Dicks was on his way to another tour of duty in Iraq.

AUTHORS` NOTES

We (Dr. C and Chaplain P) met by accident in 2008, in a cellular phone store that we both happened to patronize. While striking up a conversation in this unlikely setting, we learned that each of us shared the other's all-consuming interest in the study and treatment of Posttraumatic Stress Disorder (PTSD). We agreed to continue our professional discourse at a local pancake house. There began a series of regular breakfasts at which our respective ideas and concerns—especially for the sufferings of traumatized warriors and family members—were shared over biscuits, pancakes, and steaming mugs of hot coffee. Our backgrounds could not have been more different, yet we shared a common interest in clinical issues of diagnosis and treatment that was so strong as to make us kindred spirits. Most important, however, was our common interest in the *human and social* casualties of PTSD. Each of us had worked with thousands of traumatized patients. We found that we shared a deep mutual concern and sorrow over the ways in which trauma survivors have too often been left to suffer in silence and informational darkness. More than once, we thought, "If only we could spill this information out to people the same way we talk about it at breakfast, it would be of such help to so many." Out of our accidental intellectual "collision," a great friendship, as well as new ways of thinking, conceptualizing, and talking about PTSD, began to take root. This book is the result.

This book is the outgrowth of countless conversations. In our estimation, PTSD can never, and should never, be borne alone. Like good conversation, it must become the stuff of mutual understanding between the people whose lives it affects. It must not be reduced to an unfeeling announcement of a clipboard diagnosis. If its effects are to be overcome, it must become the springboard for much mutually supportive dialogue between warriors, physicians, therapists, spiritual providers, and—very importantly—family members. It should also include the experiences of those who have traversed the hell of trauma, emerged on the other side, and survived to live an abundant life. We have written this book in such a way that the voices of many of these individuals can be heard.

We hope that you will make your way through the pages that follow as if you had joined us for breakfast at your favorite local diner. Think of this book as plain food and plain talk, of the kind we ourselves share on a regular basis. Most important to us is that you see yourself reflected in this book, as part of an ongoing dialogue comprised of many voices. We believe that PTSD should, and can, become the subject of a conversation that can be honest and empathic, not burdened by shame, judgment, blame, or guilt. It's time that this potentially devastating illness, which affects the lives of so many and prematurely ends the lives of some, should be demystified and explained in terms that are both clinically accurate and also simple enough for all to understand.

There are many fine books that have been written about PTSD in the decade of America's War on Terror. We list many on the www.mybacktothewall.com website, and frankly, we hope you have the chance to read them all and to take from each whatever is of value to you. But we believe that this book serves a unique purpose that is, quite simply, to *give voice* to multiple perspectives on a series of topics that are often overlooked or unexplained, but which may have deep significance to those who have suffered, and continue to suffer, from the effects of trauma.

So, each time you open this book, think of yourself as one who is joining us for breakfast. Listen to the conversation; don't just read it on the page but *hear* it in your head and feel whether or not it resonates in your life. Above all, feel free to contact us and contribute your two cents worth, for the value of that contribution is beyond price in our eyes. As authors, we want to be part of a continuing dialogue with our readers. We don't just want to speak to you, we want to listen back.

One way in which we have sought to make this possible is through the construction of a website (www.mybacktothewall.com) associated with this book. There are many things that we hope to accomplish through the website. The first is something you don't usually find in a printed work—the ability and desire of the authors to continually update it *without* requiring that you buy a new edition. We have shared the most up-to-date information available to us today; however, knowledge about PTSD is constantly increasing, and what is current today will be outdated in a few years. Affording our readers access to an associated website will help ensure that what you receive from us, as authors, is always as up to date as possible.

In addition, in order to make this book easy to read and understand, we have sought to provide our readers a broad overview of the topics we address. You, however, may want more in-depth information about some of the things you read here. Therefore, we have designed the website in a manner that will allow you to find the latest news, current research, and information about new and improved treatments. Clinicians who read this book will also find special sections of interest to the professional, through which you can link to other sites and resources and also find tools that may be useful in your own work with trauma-impacted warriors and family members. Do not be surprised if, at some time in the near future, you discover that you can receive continuing clinical education on trauma-related topics, for professional credit, through our website.

You now know something about what this book **is.** Now, permit us to say a few words about the people it is **for.** This book was written in honor of every man or woman who has ever gone to war and for every person who has ever lived with or loved a warrior. It is also written for their children, their friends, and their battle buddies and comrades in arms. We hope that the voices raised in the pages of this book bring you comfort, restore some measure of hope, and embrace you within the membership of an understanding community. Above all, we hope that in the voices of this book, you may hear the echoes of your own story.

Dr. C and Chaplain P in their "satellite office"

INTRODUCTION

DR. C's Reflections:

Over the past nine years, I have had the honor of performing psychiatric evaluations on more than six thousand veterans, including about three thousand Vietnam vets and more than two thousand veterans of the Gulf War, Iraq, or Afghanistan. Most of these vets have suffered from Posttraumatic Stress Disorder (PTSD), but many didn't realize that this disorder was the cause of their volatile emotions and behaviors. Although the numbers are important, the people those numbers represent are even more important.

Back in the early 1970s, I didn't understand PTSD. Virtually no one did. The disorder didn't even have a scientific name until 1980 (long after the Vietnam War ended in 1975). Prior to that time, it was called shell shock, war neurosis, or battle fatigue, terms that often connoted cowardice and were therefore rarely used. In 1973, when psychiatry was still ignorant about PTSD, I came to San Antonio to serve as chief of the mental hygiene clinic (outpatient mental health clinic for the active duty members) and medical director of the Drug & Alcohol Program at Fort Sam Houston, Texas. My term of service began toward the latter part of the Vietnam Conflict, and I then treated hundreds, if not thousands, of soldiers returning from Vietnam with substance abuse problems and most of them also suffering from what we now know as PTSD.

After listening to these vets' stories in the early 1970s, I gave them the standard-form advice I'd been taught to give. "Stop being angry all the time. Stop smoking all that dope or drinking all that alcohol. Mellow out. Get a social group, get a grip, and get on with your life." Tragically, I now realize that these suggestions weren't helpful or even appropriate, but they were similar to the recommendations being doled out at various medical facilities to countless other vets by perhaps well-intentioned, but not well-informed, mental health professionals. Many of the Vietnam vets I've interviewed told me, "I went to the clinic at the VA back then and explained the way I was thinking and feeling and behaving, only to go away believing that they just didn't understand—or even care."

But I cared then. And I care now. In the process of my present-day evaluations, I have been humbled and amazed at the willingness of these veterans to open up to me about their war experiences, as well as their life stories since returning home. For me, it has been like walking into a part of their lives that is sacred ground. The willingness of these men and women to be vulnerable for the hour or so that they are with me is an enormous gift, from which I have gained great insight.

Quite often, my exam is the first time that they have talked to anyone about their actual combat experiences and the thoughts and feelings about those experiences that may have lain inside them, like sleeping giants, for years or decades. In addition, in 2008, I was privileged to be invited to attend a reunion of the 5th Battalion, 60th Infantry of the 9th Infantry Division vets (more about the reunions later in this book) and learned from the 200 or so who attended how helpful it was to finally let out all those feelings they had worked so hard to hide from everyone, including themselves.

Over the years, I've become very sensitive to the negative stereotypes that society has created about these veterans. But *stereotypes* did not sit in the chairs across from me in my office and share their deepest feelings—*people* did. And, contrary to prevailing myth, these people were, by and large, not nonfunctional down-and-outers.

Although many were willing to admit to me that they had abused drugs or alcohol upon their return from Vietnam, most had significantly reduced or alto gether stopped their substance abuse over the years. A lot of them had married (often more than once, the record being nine times!) and had worked hard at holding down long-term jobs at some point since their return. In the more than thirty-five years that have passed, many have retired or have had to quit working due to age or physical and emotional problems. But, for reasons that our society is only now coming to grips with, most are justifiably angry and embittered, and many have lost hope that they can change or be helped to live life more fully.

In virtually every evaluation I have conducted, I've posed the same question to these warriors of conflicts past. "How are you different now since you returned from the combat area where you were stationed?" And it is then that the vets begin to open up to me and answer questions I ask about their lives in the years since their deployment.

The purpose of this book is to share some of those answers, as well as the insights I have gained in the course of my work. My goal is to reach the vets, their family members, and others who care about them who want to understand the whys of their thoughts, feelings, and behaviors since returning. We have written this book to help all these vets—those from conflicts past and conflicts present, those who have suffered in silence for decades and those who have recently begun to suffer from PTSD symptoms, and those who love and care about them and for them.

Many years ago, I resolved to never again instruct a veteran to "get on with your life." In this book, armed with insight I did not possess thirty-five years ago, I hope to open a new chapter in your life as a trauma survivor, as I have opened a new chapter in my life as a physician. I won't tell you to "get on with it." Instead, I hope to equip you with knowledge, understanding, and—most importantly—tools with which to reshape your life. This is one journey we can walk together.

Chaplain P's Reflections:

Thirty-three years ago, while Dr. C was busy treating traumatized warriors the best way he knew how and decades before I became a clinical professional, I was still a young lawyer fast-tracking my way to a promising career. Posttraumatic Stress Disorder (PTSD) was not so much as a blip on the radar screen of my life; indeed, it wasn't even an acronym in my vocabulary. A future career in medical services, mental health, and trauma ministry wouldn't have commanded my attention. Having entered the legal profession filled with grand ideals, I had set my sights on a life in politics or perhaps the judiciary. Finding a life of purpose among soldiers would have seemed an unlikely destiny.

I won't recount the many unanticipated life experiences that changed those plans over the thirty-three years that transpired since I stood in front of the American flag in the federal courthouse in San Antonio, Texas, and swore the oath required of every newly licensed attorney. What strikes me as ironic, in retrospect, is how similar that oath was to the one that has also been sworn by every soldier I would ever come to know and care for. Just as the mission of every soldier is to serve as a caregiver to the nation, my mission was to become a caregiver to the warrior.

There are critical differences that have always separated our worlds. While I have been blessed to render my service in an atmosphere of safety, the soldiers I serve have endured unimaginable hardships and terrifying traumas so that others might live in freedom. I always understood and honored the fact that their sufferings had served as the ransom that bought and paid for the liberty all Americans enjoy. No one who has not walked into harm's way in combat can ever truly say that they have walked in those soldiers' shoes. That being the case, my journey has been to walk beside soldiers and abide with their pain. Slowly, over time, I found myself becoming not only accepted, but absorbed, into the fabric of military life among those I serve. I was honored to receive the comradeship of the extraordinary men and women of the US Army Chaplain Corps. Many of them became my students; others became my colleagues and collaborators; all profoundly changed my life. I have seen a great deal through the lens of their experiences, as well as those of the many other warriors who have come under my care. And thanks to them, I was fortunate to go downrange and see yet more of their experience through my own observation.

If there is one thing that my experience tells me is true, it is this: that those who wear the uniform have indeed suffered greatly, but that they are not the only psychological casualties of the wars in Iraq, in Afghanistan, or in any other armed conflict in which America has been engaged. In fact, I believe the number of soldiers who are traumatized in connection with their service is at least equaled and probably greatly exceeded by the number of wives, children, and other loved ones who themselves acquire secondary PTSD or who suffer greatly from the consequences of living with those who are afflicted with the disorder. This book is written as much for them as it is for those who swear the oath and wear the camouflage.

Dr. C (as a psychiatrist) and I (as a pastoral counselor and psychotherapist specializing in trauma) share only a six-year difference in age. But we did our clinical training roughly three decades apart. Clinically speaking, we are members of different generations. Yet surprisingly little has changed in that span of time. To be sure, we now know what PTSD is and how to more effectively treat it. Yet, the remorse Dr. C felt thirty years ago in working with newly returned Vietnam vets is virtually the same remorse that I myself feel today each time I am called upon to care for a new patient who has wandered in the wilderness for years without adequate information about PTSD, let alone access to proper care.

To this day, graduate level counseling programs teach psychiatric trauma treatment only rarely. When I am called upon to provide clinical education about PTSD for physicians, surgeons, or other medical professionals, it is frequently the first instruction they have had in the subject. How could we have made so little progress in such a long period of time? How can it be that so many lives continue to be so tragically affected, when we now know better? Those are the questions that drive my contribution to this book.

As a psychotherapist, I see all of PTSD's casualties. In addition to providing care for traumatized warriors, I see many of the unseen victims of conflicts past and present, including their spouses and children. Whenever I am attempting to unravel a complex problem involving mental illness that has made its way through all members of an entire family, I frequently find that there is an old, unresolved combat trauma lurking in the background. Often, veterans—who never got proper care for PTSD—and their spouses—who gritted their teeth and tolerated the vets' disordered behavior for years—unknowingly created dysfunctional environments in which their children became severely affected. So now we must include those children who are traumatized by a parent's service-connected death, violent behavior, emotional detachment, or mutilating disability. Even the constant separation caused by a parent's repeated deployments may, in and of itself, have a traumatic impact on children and subject them to enormously high levels of fear and chronic anxiety.

Some of the military personnel I work with are now old enough to have worn colonel's wings for many years. They tell stories about when they came home from Vietnam and watched their comrades ditch their uniforms in airport bathrooms so they wouldn't have to endure the taunting of the crowds gathered outside the airport. But, by and large, I am working with a new breed of warrior whose traumas—both the ones they suffered before their military service and the ones they have taken away from it—are of a different sort.

13

As the wars in Iraq and Afghanistan stretched our military's human resources ever thinner and over multiple theaters of operation, the recruitment demands of a volunteer military began to grow. In the wartime military, many young men and women have found an opportunity for employment, education, and a bright future. But many of these young recruits are already the "old veterans" of what I call the social warfare that goes on in our nation. Their lives are often already scarred by years of childhood abuse and neglect, sexual assault, exposure to gang violence, neighborhood crime, and rampant drug abuse among their peers and family members. Just the trauma of the daily lives from which they have come runs many steps ahead of, and may be even more severe than, the traumas of war that await them.

Once they are downrange, today's warriors are less likely to be affected by single-event catastrophes and are more often impacted by multiple and ongoing traumatic events that constantly pound on their central nervous systems like a perpetual jackhammer. Unfortunately, the medical research on PTSD that was done during the first two decades after Vietnam was largely geared to single-event military traumas. Not until many years after Vietnam did research begin to focus upon the traumas suffered by non-military combatants (e.g., assault, rape, auto accident, hurricane, fire, flood, etc.), nor was it oriented to the types of chronic, or multiple-event connected, traumatic stress that has become the hallmark of our most recent military conflicts. Medical research notwithstanding, it is still largely up to individuals to navigate their own way through terribly complex systems to get the care and information they need. That experience, alone, can be traumatizing.

For this reason I, like Dr. C, am committed to giving people straight talk about PTSD in language that is clear, understandable, and usable. Trauma is, by definition, rooted in helplessness. Knowledge, by contrast, confers power back to the individual. In this battle against PTSD, knowledge is the first and most important medicine anyone should access. So put this book and the information within it to good use. The quality of your life, or that of someone you love, may depend on it.

HOW TO MAKE APPROPRIATE USE OF THE

"R-E-C-O-V-E-R"

APPROACH TO POSTTRAUMATIC STRESS

DR. C AND CHAPLAIN P:

This book has a multitude of uses. But by far, its most important purpose is to inspire you, the reader, to begin a pathway to recovery from the effects of Posttraumatic Stress Disorder. To assist you in achieving this goal, we have sought to provide you with information (l) that is clinically and medically sound, (2) that is expressed in understandable language, and (3) that outlines a specific pathway to guide you on this most challenging journey.

In order to undertake that journey, we both believe that veterans with combat-related PTSD require four essential things:

> (1) Veterans need to know that the thoughts, feelings, emotions, and physical symptoms that they experience are *not* unusual, nor do these symptoms indicate that the warrior is "crazy" or weak willed. They do, however, signal the presence of a dysregulated stress response, which is a treatable condition.

> (2) Veterans need accurate and understandable explanations of how PTSD starts, develops, and progresses. They need to know how it affects the brain, body, and central nervous system, and how it contributes to the creation of the thoughts, feelings, emotions, and physical symptoms that result.

> (3) Veterans need a source of straight talk about the many ways that PTSD commonly affects the lives, families, and careers of military members. This includes areas of discussion that are often bypassed or avoided by other writers.

(4) Veterans need information about concrete strategies that they can use in their own self-assessment, in the effective self-management of at least a portion of their PTSD symptoms, and in pursuing satisfactory professional treatment.

For many who read this book, the journey toward more effective management of Posttraumatic Stress Disorder may be the most challenging of their entire lives. Why, therefore, do we focus on recovery from effects of the disorder rather than upon its cure? There are several important answers to this question.

First, the story and history of every person who reads and uses this book is different and unique. Some readers will have experienced PTSD symptoms for three months, while others will have suffered its ravages for more than thirty years. For some readers, therefore, the time is still ripe to alter the pathways in the brain and central nervous system (CNS) in a way that will permanently remedy the symptoms of the disorder. For others, stress pathways in the brain and CNS have been laid down, like ruts in a road, for so long that it is not possible to eliminate them, but the road may still be useable. Each PTSD sufferer is different. We emphasize, therefore, that *only your doctor or mental health or medical care provider can diagnose you.* We cannot, nor does this book seek to do so.

Second, many people have made life-long adjustments to their PTSD symptoms that involve not only their own habits but those of spouses, children, friends, and loved ones. For these people, changing habits that are the products of decades of accommodation to a disorder may be as challenging as the effects of the disorder itself. Our goal is to assist people toward wellness in a gentle manner rather than insisting that they dismantle their lives. In our view, if people experience improvement in the way they manage and experience their lives through the use of a simple and gradual approach, that is a goal well worth pursuing.

Finally, we are clinically responsible practitioners who do not believe in making false claims that any particular course of action can lead to a cure for something which, it must be remembered, is a *medical* disorder. Instead, we advocate an approach to the development of life skills and lifestyle management that will help you become a better teammate, both to yourself and to your physician, counselor, or health provider.

Our goal is to help *all* people who suffer from PTSD, not only those who are potentially "curable," live more successfully with the condition. We believe that "cure" is not necessarily the appropriate goal for everyone when dealing with PTSD. Rather, we believe that management, improvement, and the restoration of a more abundant life are goals toward which every person can advance. Our view is that depending upon the unique circumstances of each individual (including his or her own motivations and desires) these goals are, to a greater or lesser extent, attainable by almost all people who will adopt the R-E-C-O-V-E-R approach.

R-E-C-O-V-E-R is a seven-step method through which warriors can take an orderly approach to their traumatic stress. It is an approach that keeps vets from becoming overwhelmed and instead empowers them and their families to identify the issues that are affecting them and to take appropriate action to improve their lives.

Each of the initials in the R-E-C-O-V-E-R acronym stands for a step that readers can take in understanding and addressing the problems of traumatic stress and PTSD, and we have devoted a chapter to each topic. We pray that the R-E-C-O-V-E-R approach may open doors for you toward that more abundant life that all human beings deserve.

Dr. Harry A. Croft, M.D.
Rev. Dr. Chrys L. Parker, J.D.
March 2011

THE

R-E-C-O-V-E-R

APPROACH TO PTSD

R   Recognizing   When PTSD Is in Your Life

E   Educating   Yourself about PTSD's Effects on Your Thoughts, Feelings, and Behaviors

C   Connecting   Your Biology to Your Psychology: Physiological Roots of PTSD

O   Organizing   A Care Plan to Manage PTSD

V   Viewing   Your Issues in a New Light

E   Empowering   Yourself through Useful Systems of Support

R   Redefining   The Meaning of Your Life: Seeking Posttraumatic Growth

NOTES CONCERNING ABBREVIATIONS AND GENDER USAGE

Throughout this book, the male gender refers to both men and women and vice-versa. Female soldiers, as well as wives of service members, also experience PTSD, especially in the current wars.

For convenience, the acronym *TFB* refers to "thoughts, feelings, and behaviors" of PTSD sufferers. "Middle East veterans" includes veterans of the First and Second Gulf Wars, the War in Iraq, and the War in Afghanistan. "Vietnam veterans" refers to veterans of the Vietnam War.

The words "Vietnam" or "Middle East" can just as easily be replaced with World War II, Korea, Bosnia, or any other war or military action—veterans with PTSD from those wars will benefit from this book as much as Vietnam and Middle East veterans.

Reference to one branch of the military (e.g., Army) is usually equally applicable to all the other branches (Air Force, Marines, Navy, Coast Guard) as well.

Personal details that might lead to the identification of individuals who spoke with us have been omitted in order to protect their privacy. Interestingly, we found that many veterans related similar stories, often using almost exactly the same words to express their feelings. One method that we employed to protect their privacy, therefore, was to consolidate the actual stories and identities of several individuals into a single entry.

Comments from each author are identified both by a distinct font and by a specific heading: Dr. C (for Dr. Harry Croft) and Chaplain P (for Rev. Dr. Chrys Parker). Text that is not attributed to either author was written jointly. The authors' joint literary voice appears in a third font. Vets' stories are set off in quotation marks or boxes.

Chaplain P asking soldiers,
"How does life after combat really feel to you?"

CHAPTER ONE:

RECOGNIZING WHEN PTSD IS IN YOUR LIFE

I once asked the wife of a veteran who was my patient, "When you go into a fairly empty restaurant, where does your husband sit? Without hesitation, almost as if it should be perfectly obvious, she answered, "In the farthest corner of whatever place we are in, with his back to the wall." When I asked if she understood why, she had not a clue; all she knew is that sitting in any other place was disastrous. She had no idea that, in the traumatized mind of her husband, sitting in that corner was like adopting a safe position in combat—one that allowed him an unobstructed vantage point of the lurking danger that he always expected to enter the place at any moment.

DR. C AND CHAPLAIN P:

Today, millions of Americans feel their lives have gone terribly wrong, but they don't know why. Statistically, if they are veterans, it is likely that many of them have Posttraumatic Stress Disorder, or PTSD. For most of them, it is a problem that will go unrecognized and therefore unresolved.

Resolution of a problem begins with its recognition, not just by name but in terms of how it affects one's life. If a person suffers an amputation or contracts a chronic disease or loses some significant physical function, for example, he or she can usually tell you right away how their medical condition has impacted their life. Strangely, PTSD seems different. PTSD is a disorder that causes either significant emotional distress or impairment in the day-to-day functioning for the persons who suffer it. However, it is like a ghost that one knows is present but cannot quite see or touch. Even though the lives of almost all of the veterans whom we have seen with PTSD have been radically changed by it, few of them can express in words exactly what has happened to them as a result of their disorder. Like the veteran in the

Dr. Harry A. Croft, M.D. and Rev. Dr. Chrys L. Parker, J.D.

story at the beginning of this chapter, they spend their lives with their backs to the wall without ever understanding why. All they know is that they are, now, somehow very different.

For many people affected by PTSD, the symptoms of the disorder are unrecognized, simply because they may have been present for so long that those who suffer with it—as well as their families, friends, and co-workers—have come to accept their posttraumatic behaviors as normal for them. Many Vietnam-era veterans became aware of their symptoms almost immediately after their return home from the war. But others, including many of the veterans of the Iraqi and Afghanistan wars (in this book called Middle East vets), suffer a slow kindling of the disorder, in which the process starts slowly and worsens as time goes by, producing more and more severe symptoms. Known as late onset PTSD, it builds with time and chronic exposure to multiple traumatic stressors and multiple deployments.

Still others, it is now known, had PTSD before they even enlisted. During periods when recruitment requirements were pressing, waivers of the traditional standards for enlistment were conferred, in order that many might be permitted to volunteer. Today's volunteer military became a Mecca for young men and women seeking to leave social environments and family lives marked by abuse, neglect, drugs, or domestic and gang violence.

But this emotional baggage continued to burden them throughout their military careers and made it more likely they would develop combat-related PTSD. Whatever their personal situation, many veterans and their families have learned over the years to shape their lives around the illness in ways that were usually intended to gloss over and deny the major impact it was having upon them. The illness has made them strangers to their families and—what is worse—strangers to themselves.

> *"John went to the war," said Cindy, a pretty strawberry blonde woman with sad eyes. "Some other man, masquerading as John, returned home."*

As difficult as it often is for people to explain why they are different now, it is rarely difficult for them to remember what they were like before. Often, the memories of what life was like *before* PTSD developed provoke tears and recollections of a way of being and of living that have slipped like sand through the fingers of affected people and disappeared.

> *"You know Doc, BEFORE I went to Vietnam, I was happy-go-lucky. I was social. I was in athletics. I loved people. I was active in church and a lady's man. Now it's all different. I'm not the same person. I just go through the motions of life. I have few friends and get little joy from life. I keep everything inside and don't feel much of anything anymore except for the anger. Sometimes I feel so depressed that I wish my life was over. I wonder if my family and everyone around me wouldn't be better off if I just wasn't here."*

Of course, the answer to that question is decidedly "No." They would *not* be better off with you dead. But they *and* you would both be better off if your PTSD were treated effectively. So we begin this chapter with one strong and sincere admonition:

> IF YOU ARE EXPERIENCING SUICIDAL THOUGHTS—EITHER WITH OR WITHOUT A PLAN FOR KILLING YOURSELF—PLEASE PUT THIS BOOK DOWN AND GO TO YOUR NEAREST EMERGENCY ROOM, VA CENTER, OR MEDICAL CARE PROFESSIONAL AND GET IMMEDIATE HELP. YOU ARE ENTITLED TO IT. YOU NEED IT. AND YOU DESERVE IT.

We like to think of this book as everything you ever really needed to know about PTSD that you should have been told in the first place and probably weren't. Just because PTSD has become a common term doesn't mean that people are any better informed about it now than they were forty years ago. At best, most members of the public are familiar with one or two common symptoms of the illness. But that is certainly not an adequate base of knowledge to tell if a person has the condition. Let's look at another kind of illness as an example to see why this is so.

If you were to go to a physician and say, "Doctor, I'm suffering from recurrent headaches. Does this mean I have a brain tumor?," we are pretty sure that almost any doctor would say to you, "Well, *it depends.*" That's because all illnesses result from complex processes in which one or two symptoms, standing alone, are not necessarily the determining diagnostic factors. For example, there are probably many illnesses in which headaches are a symptom, but most have nothing to do with a brain tumor. Migraines, allergies, or even stress might cause the headache.

Different causes may produce the same symptom, and each may be representative of different conditions and require different treatments. In the same way, some of the more common symptoms of PTSD—such as difficulty with sleep, anger, and irritability and discomfort with crowds or new situations—may be symptoms of many different conditions and not just PTSD. So in answer to the question of whether YOUR symptoms are attributable to PTSD, the answer is, "*It depends.*"

Every person who reads this book comes to it with a unique story and personal history that we, the authors, do not know. For that reason, we cannot and do not seek to diagnose you. What we *can* do is help you to begin recognizing if there is a problem in your life that may be connected to PTSD.

We believe that the best way for people to begin recognizing a potential problem is not with one- or two-word symptoms that may be meaningless when described without context. A better way to help people become educated and recognize if they have a problem is to begin by familiarizing them with the kinds of *circumstances* that frequently accompany PTSD. If, in reading this chapter, you see something of your own life mirrored back to you, then we encourage you to read further, as we discuss PTSD, its causes, symptoms, and treatments, in greater detail.

This chapter, like the entirety of the book, is a dialogue between the authors in which we hope you'll join. One of us (Dr. C) is a psychiatrist who approaches PTSD from the vantage point of a medical doctor who evaluates patients, diagnoses their illnesses, and prescribes medication. The other (Chaplain P) is a combat and medical chaplain, a trauma researcher, and a trauma therapist, who creates and implements the actual plans of interpersonal care that are designed to help trauma survivors recover. So we each view the same subject through a slightly different lens. But on one thing we agree: there are several major life issues that we frequently see as creating the circumstances, or *context,* of PTSD.

In this chapter we will present four such life issues. Interestingly every one of them is a *relationship* of one kind or another. Why? Well, because no human being is an island. We are conceived, both biologically and socially, as the products of relationships. Virtually everything that significantly impacts our lives owes its significance to the fact that it affects one or more relationships in which we are engaged, including relationships with *others* and with *ourselves.*

The relationships in which PTSD most often and visibly rears its head are

(1) marriage and family relationships,

(2) employment, work, and school relationships,

(3) other interpersonal relationships, and

(4) spiritual relationships.

Let's take a brief tour of some of the ways in which these critical relationships are affected by PTSD and examine the way PTSD looks, acts, and feels to many people who experience it within the context of those relationships. These, after all, are the interactions you can see and relate to most readily. Then you will have a better idea of whether PTSD has your relationships by the tail and whether this book may positively influence your life.

1. RECOGNIZING PTSD THROUGH ITS EFFECTS ON MARRIAGE AND FAMILY RELATIONSHIPS

Racking up your divorces or getting ready to start?

DR. C:

For many vets, the symptoms of PTSD have caused the alienation or even the ruination of their relationships with spouses, children, and even extended family. I often say that PTSD affects those who've been married many years, as well as those who've been married many times. Although there are definitely veterans with PTSD who have stayed married to the same person for many years, I observe a common factor that often causes the apparent success of these marriages. It is that the spouses of the PTSD suffererers have committed themselves to tolerating or even suffering with the PTSD symptoms of their partners, sometimes at huge emotional cost. This is particularly true of couples who married during the Vietnam era, in which divorce was still less frequent than it is today and people felt compelled to stick it out once they had gotten hitched and had children. Other veterans have seen their marriages dissolve again . . . and again . . . and again. The record, among patients whom I see, is nine times! They continue to marry and divorce without success, because they either aren't aware of their PTSD or aren't aware of the way it affects their relationships with others. They continue to believe that "this time it will be different." They don't recognize that nothing will be different as long as they and their PTSD symptoms stay the same.

CHAPLAIN P:

Well, I must admit that the course record in my office practice is "only five" marriages, held by a Vietnam vet. I sometimes call vets like him "serial monogamists." But, in all seriousness, I agree totally with Dr. C. Those five marriages came equipped with multiple sets of children and multiple abused spouses, all of whom suffered horrific emotional and physical consequences as a result of the untreated PTSD of the father. He was both verbally and physically aggressive, and instead of

getting help, he drowned himself in denial and booze, which only exac-
erbated his abusiveness. Despite the fact that this led him into conflicts
with the law, the infliction of mental illness on four of his six children,
and the loss of his parental rights, he denies, to this day, that anything
is wrong with either himself or his kids—a classic example of the unrecognized problem leading to unresolved relationships.

On the other end of the spectrum, I have for many years known
a couple who are held up to the public as a symbol of what a great
marriage should be. Because I know them well, I have seen how they
behave toward one another in private, and it is a less harmonious image
than the one the public sees. I was aware that the husband, who was a
disabled Gulf War vet, had a hair trigger, was over-controlling of every
situation, and would explode at the drop of a hat. His long-tolerant
wife appeared to let it all roll off her, like water off a duck's back, but I
sincerely doubted that this was the case. This woman deserved her own
Purple Heart. Her deep loyalty and love for her spouse had caused her
to endure many hidden wounds of her own.

Although we often tend to assume that the PTSD-affected soldier
husband is responsible for the breakdown of the marital relationship,
that is simply not the case. It is also not true that the person whose
dysfunctions initiate a breakdown in a marriage is always the one who
is deployed. There is an increasing number of military families in which
the service member is the wife or in which the PTSD-impacted person is
female. I have also witnessed the pain experienced by many soldiers who
worked diligently to support their marriages while deployed, but who
became aware that their marriages were breaking down "stateside."

I have repeatedly observed the frequency with which soldiers—especially those affected by prior trauma—become too quickly entangled
in marriage relationships without the time and opportunity to build
the type of foundation on which sound marriages are based. I see the
pain of many warriors whose prior life traumas have left them feeling
isolated, alone, and desperate to be loved by someone. This often leads
to either a marriage based on neediness or one based on sex, rather than
on the positive attributes that each spouse may bring to a relationship.

Once a combat deployment occurs and the parties to the marriage are at an enormous distance in time and space, they no longer receive the quick fix that their relationship was intended to provide. In this sense, traumatic stress may contribute not only to the breakdown of a marriage, but also to the inception of an unstable marriage in the first place.

Are you often absent from family activities?

DR. C:

I find that some of the greatest damage is caused by physical and social absence from family functions and special occasions, like weddings, graduations, birthdays, reunions, and funerals. It can lead family members to believe that the spouse or parent doesn't care about others, and it causes the veteran to miss the shared experiences that are the fundamental building blocks of family life.

Even in situations in which some vets are physically present, they are not emotionally present. This can be devastating. To have a parent be present and ignore you may be much worse than having the parent not attend a function at all. I can't count the number of adult children I know or have seen who are no longer willing to associate with their PTSD-affected parents because of the hurts inflicted during their upbringing. Worse yet are the adult children who blamed themselves for the unusual behavior of their relatives. The first thing that children do in the face of dysfunctional behavior is to look for a cause. And the closest cause that is always conveniently at hand to receive blame is the child himself—the one who is always saying to himself, "I don't matter enough for Dad to go to my games, my award ceremonies, my parties, my graduation . . ."

CHAPLAIN P:

What is so tragic about this situation is that family members usually think that a PTSD-affected parent doesn't care about them. The feeling that one's parent is emotionally unavailable or dismissive can be as damaging as physical abuse. In actuality, the PTSD-affected parent often cares a great deal but uses their detachment as a way of camouflaging fear: fear of embarrassment, fear of humiliation, fear of ridicule.

One vet whom I worked with put it very well:

> *"I'll never forget the day . . . I'd been under fire about 90% of the time, had stepped on an IED and survived, and had been home about a month. I was so happy to be at a soccer game with my thirteen-year-old son. Suddenly a helicopter flew up from behind a tree line, and I hit the ground. Everyone stared. My son was mortified. I had totally embarrassed him, and I was determined never to do it again. I didn't go out in public for almost three years after that."* ~ *Middle East vet*

Even if the veteran-parents don't know the exact cause for their responses, they may nevertheless sense that they are more likely to behave strangely in large gatherings, such as important family occasions, and may be deeply afraid to cause a scene or embarrass themselves or others. They don't realize that large gatherings, especially in noisy or crowded situations, can affect the central nervous system in ways that trigger traumatic stress. So they simply stay away. Their social absence, unfortunately, usually leads to an emotional disconnection that soon becomes difficult or impossible to repair.

I hasten to say that although my invitational deployment to Iraq did not expose me to combat-related stress of any kind, even I noticed a sense of "disconnectedness" in myself following my return home. My time in the Iraqi theater had been spent rendering care to soldiers and chaplains in settings that were very emotionally intense and physically exhausting. I was also very impacted by the sights, sounds, and smells of the theater. It was as though my senses had been bombarded by more than my words could possibly describe. When I returned home, friends and loved ones naturally wanted me to tell them about it, and I found that I lacked the words, even though words are the primary tools of my professional life. Making the attempt to explain my experience became impossible and, finally, exhausting. I noticed that I actually started to avoid the phone calls of close friends rather than face their questions about what I had experienced.

One of the things to which my deployment made me sensitive is the radical change in focus that occurs in a theater of operations. Focus becomes incredibly narrow. You eat the food that you are fed, sleep where you are billeted, and perform the mission that you are assigned. Although the life of a soldier may become incredibly hard, it at the same time becomes incredibly simplified. A huge number of the ordinary day-to-day tasks and concerns that face the spouse who remains stateside simply drop out of the soldier's existence. No grocery shopping, no midnight runs to the corner store for diapers, no battles with the landlord or the auto mechanic, no fighting for a parking place, no deciding how to cope with missing work because one has a sick child. In this sense, not only does the family understand less about the soldier, but the reverse is also true—the soldier may lose touch with the everyday concerns that drive the practical and emotional functions within the family.

Are you experiencing nightmares, flashbacks, and discomfort with certain smells, sounds, sights, places, and activities?

DR. C:

Spouses and family members don't understand vets' reactions when they have an episode in which they are re-experiencing their traumas through their senses of sight, smell, or hearing. These episodes are called nightmares, or sometimes "night terrors," when experienced during sleep and "flashbacks" when experienced while awake. At best, seeing someone in the midst of a night terror or a day flashback can be very frightening. At worst, it may be a source of physical danger to which spouses, children, or co-workers can be exposed. Vets will frequently mistake their family members for "the enemy" when in the midst of a flashback episode. They believe they are back in the jungle, the desert, or wherever their combat theater happened to be.

Similarly, family members are often confused about the cause of the discomfort or distress displayed by vets when they smell, see, hear, or go to places that remind them of their time in the combat zone. Vets often appear to be reacting to things that are "invisible," or that just flat don't exist as far as their family members are concerned. Because family members have not shared the vets' experiences, their nervous systems are not sensitive to these cues in the environment. As a result, certain environmental stimuli may go completely unnoticed by family members, but may be very real, very powerful, and extremely disturbing to the vets.

CHAPLAIN P:

Many people don't realize that, clinically speaking, there is a significant difference between the hypervigilance displayed by vets with PTSD, on the one hand, versus the paranoia displayed by people with psychotic disorders such as schizophrenia. The paranoid thoughts of a schizophrenic are truly irrational, e.g., they have no basis in fact. By contrast, the suspicious and security-conscious behaviors of the returned veteran are VERY logical, when understood in their own way.

These hypervigilant behaviors are: (1) the outgrowth of *real* experiences that the veterans have had and (2) are the result of real primal biological survival-oriented reactions that nature has preprogrammed in the human body. As if that weren't enough, the suspicious and security-conscious behaviors displayed by PTSD-affected vets are often magnified by the intense combat training that they have undergone in the military, which is designed to help keep them alive in battle! That's hardly "irrational." Most people wouldn't dream of applying the term "paranoid" to someone who had survived a traumatic natural disaster like the earthquake in Haiti, for example. But society applies that term all the time to military personnel who were traumatized *in the very same type of incident.* The unfortunate misuse of the term "paranoid" simply pounds another nail in the coffin of stigma about PTSD.

These hypervigilant symptoms don't happen only to armed combatants, but also to unarmed personnel. Doctors, cooks, office workers, chaplains, and many others are subjected to the same threats and incoming rounds as combat personnel, but may feel even more vulnerable because they typically perform their functions unarmed.

> *A combat chaplain once told me about the night that he was sure that a home invasion was taking place. Without thinking, and in a surge of strength, he picked up a huge, flat screen TV and threw it at the intruder, whom he observed in his wife's dressing room. His wife—who was terrified by the ear-splitting sounds of crashing glass—had to dive for cover to protect herself from flying shards that could have inflicted lethal injury. Only when the dust settled did this vet realize he had thrown the TV at his own reflection in the bathroom mirror. But the fear caused by the incident hung in the air for years thereafter, affecting not only the veteran, but also his wife, who became highly anxious and unable to sleep in the same room as her husband.*

Do people complain about your irritability and sudden anger?

DR. C:

If there's one symptom that impacts families and marriages more than any other, it's irritability and sudden, unexplained anger. Most PTSD-affected patients and families know exactly what I'm talking about. It's the hair-trigger temper, the intolerance for even small problems or infractions, and the determination to make major issues out of minor ones. It leads to arguments and fights that can destroy a family.

For some it is that their "fuse is too short" (they react too quickly—often without thinking it through), while for others it is that their "explosion is too large" (they overreact out of proportion to the situation). Spouses and children may feel that their husband or father doesn't love them or may think he is even hostile or dangerous to be around, leading to a lingering sense of unsafety in a family in which it becomes difficult or impossible to relax. Family members can really be upset by the behavior of a PTSD-affected adult who reacts inappropriately and out of all proportion to the situation, thereby causing spouses and children to avoid bringing friends home for fear of what unexpected behavior will confront them.

CHAPLAIN P:

Trust is essential to build and maintain healthy family intimacy. But trust is based, in part, on predictability. We must believe, and be able to predict, that an adult family member can be depended upon to act in certain socially acceptable ways. A person who, because of the PTSD symptoms of a parent or spouse, doesn't have that assurance is on guard all the time, walking on eggshells and fearing the next moment when "the other shoe will drop." This is one of the primary ways in which the posttraumatic anxiety of the parent can lead to anxiety disorders or even secondary trauma in a spouse or child.

Do you feel apathetic or avoidant about your life?

DR. C:

We talk a lot about the explosive or aggressive PTSD-affected veteran, as if this were the only way in which the disorder is manifested. In actuality, there appears to be a second, and significantly different, behavioral presentation. To the best of our knowledge, Chaplain P was the first to identify this symptomatic pattern in 2003, during her conduct of a two-year program of treatment and longitudinal observation of the life histories and symptomatic patterns of PTSD patients. This pattern, which Chaplain P later came to identify as the "*hypo*aroused" profile of PTSD, represents the complete opposite end of the behavioral spectrum. Instead of being "hyped up" and security conscious, hypoaroused PTSD sufferers are fatigued, withdrawn, lethargic, and often disengaged. We describe this profile in greater detail in later chapters of this book. For now, it is enough to say that some marriages and families are damaged or destroyed by this type of PTSD-induced apathy. Often spouses of affected vets see their loved one as "detached, distant, or unemotional, or worse—uncaring." This pattern of behavior can be as damaging to a relationship as the explosive and angry type. Either extreme upsets the balance we need in life in order to feel safe and secure in our relationships with others.

CHAPLAIN P:

That's absolutely right. There are some veterans who cope with their fear and terror by becoming immobilized and doing absolutely nothing. As we'll describe in later chapters, this is actually a very primal biological reaction. Unfortunately, however, that kind of helpless and nonproactive behavior displayed by a PTSD-affected parent affects not only that person but every other member of the family. Then real trouble ensues, and for obvious reasons.

We all must feel that we can depend upon our family members to do the right, or needed, thing that ensures our ability to function day to day. Helplessness in adults spells danger to children, and they know it. They depend upon their parents to protect and support them. Watching a parent dissolve into helplessness can instill real terror into a child. And that is exactly what happens. For some PTSD-sufferers, life grinds to a halt, and the needs of spouses and children may be totally ignored. In reality, the traumatized person is experiencing intense *freeze* responses, which we will discuss later. But in the minds of family members, they may appear unloving and uncaring.

> "I went to war feeling confident and like my mission had meaning. After about six months, everything changed. Although I was an administrative clerk, I wound up with an M-4 in my hand standing guard duty and working very dangerous situations. I was exposed to a great deal of suffering, death, and wounding. My tour was extended twice, and as a result, my kids didn't know me when I returned. I felt completely overwhelmed, like it had all been for nothing. Finally, I just shut off from everyone emotionally, like I have nothing to give them. I don't touch them. It's just the saddest part of my life." ~ *Middle East vet*

In this book, we call special attention to this reaction of emotional apathy and physical exhaustion because not only is it a symptom of PTSD in some veterans, but it is a frequently seen pattern in family members as well. There are countless veterans (usually men) who have come to me out of concern for their spouses, not realizing how entrapped these women have become in an unseen, private war zone. They often become ensnared between the military, which "robs" them of their spouse (often at the very worst time of life), and the spouse himself, whose PTSD may leave a wife feeling as though she is being held prisoner by a hostile actor. We will speak more of this later. For now, it is important for wives and family members to know that that they, too, can develop and display symptoms of PTSD.

2. RECOGNIZING PTSD IN WORK RELATIONSHIPS

Did your military service seem to affect your search for employment?

DR. C:

I didn't become truly and fully aware of how many returning vets could not find or hold jobs until more than twenty-five years after the Vietnam War ended. In the course of doing psychiatric evaluations for the Department of Veterans Affairs (VA), I heard the same stories over and over, so often that they were obviously not a figment of one person's imagination.

> *"Doc," my patient would say, "I had me a good job working in a warehouse before I went to 'Nam. When I came home, I thought I was real lucky to find an ad for a job that was perfect for me. I talked to the guy, and he was real happy when I told him about my experience on the old job. But when he asked me why I left, I told him that I'd got drafted. Then, all of a sudden, he decided my experience wasn't good enough after all."*

CHAPLAIN P:

Vietnam was the "other war," whose unpopularity stuck unfairly to veterans like some sort of toxic social lint. The troops who have served in Desert Storm and others who continue to serve in more recent conflicts in Iraq and Afghanistan enjoy a much better public opinion. So it surprised me to learn that, at the time this book was written, unemployment among veterans is still more than 24%—two to three times the national average—and is reaching crisis proportions. Unemployment creates terrible effects on individuals and families, especially families of warriors in the National Guard and Reserve forces. Many of these warriors were forced to leave stable jobs when they were reactivated, were required to serve multiple tours of hazardous duty, were awarded Combat Action Badges for "getting shot at," and then came home to no active-duty paycheck, no active-duty benefits, and no available employment through which to support themselves and their families.

This situation has very serious implications. The military is like a family in which people are trained to believe they can count on one another. So when activated Reservists and National Guardspersons are treated so very differently than active duty personnel, even though they have fought the same battles in the same war, it's a terrible situation. Just as if someone in the family had been deserted, the activated Reservist or Guardsperson may experience feelings of intense betrayal, abandonment, and discrimination. Substance abuse, depression, suicidal ideation, and marital destruction can all follow in the wake of this situation.

"Our Reserve unit commander knew that our unit was being disbanded and deliberately didn't tell us. He promised that we'd have a year's transition time within the unit after we returned from the war. Instead, all of us got an automated robo-call voice message the day after we got back, telling us to out-process within twenty-four hours. Poof! That was it. After risking our lives alongside the active duty personnel and getting Combat Action Badges for getting shot at, we were left with no pay, no medical or psychological benefits, and no advance notice. It felt like a huge betrayal." ~ *Middle East vet*

Are you afraid that people will think you're crazy?

DR. C:

Three and a half decades of hindsight have helped me to shape new perspectives on the relationship between PTSD, the warrior, and the workplace. My first observation about the effect of PTSD on employment is that employers and co-workers don't understand, and often don't tolerate, the veteran who experiences flashbacks while on the job. Depending on how severe the flashback is and whether the person screams out or acts in a chaotic or so-called paranoid way, observers in the workplace tend to think the person is bizarre at best or just plain crazy at worst. They do not recognize (I) that the person's central nervous system has been triggered, (2) that the individual is reacting through no fault of his or her own to something that may have taken place years ago, and (3) that the flashback is experienced in a way that is totally real and "here-and-now" in the mind of the veteran.

CHAPLAIN P:

Having had years of experience working with patients who experienced intense flashbacks—sometimes in my office—I've gained a significant degree of empathy for the problems that this creates for vets on the job. I have done my fair share of full body take-downs of clients who were experiencing flashbacks, in order to protect them from injury caused by their own thrashing about. They truly are experiencing a completely different world that others cannot see, and may disbelieve.

Among the burned patients I work with are individuals who may frequently re-experience themselves as being in the midst of a fiery inferno in which the body is being consumed alive by flame; they may even hear the sounds and smell the noxious odor of burning flesh. The horror and the terror they endure is truly moving to me.

Equally saddening is my observation that the same disbelieving or intolerant attitude toward flashbacks that is displayed by employers is also a problem in the medical environment. In such venues, I have worked with physicians and surgeons who provided superb medical care, but who did not seem to understand their patients from an emotional perspective at all. The surgical treatment for burns is excruciating, terrifying, and traumatizing—sometimes more traumatizing than the fire itself. Burned vets who return to the hospital for follow-up at a later date may become terror-stricken at the mere sight of a burn surgeon, as if they're experiencing the pain of treatment all over again. I once cared for a patient for whom the "whooshing" sound of the electric doors at the entry of Brooke Army Medical Center was enough to trigger a full blown posttraumatic response. Others are triggered by the mere sound of the metal cart coming down the hall, announcing the impending and excruciating daily ritual of wound care.

And that's just it—the activity that is so terrifying to the patient often has the word "care" built right into it. Because medical personnel think of a hospital as a caring and protected place, they are generally unable to appreciate how threatening and retriggering it may be to the patient. I have observed more than a few well-meaning doctors and nurses become resentful, personally offended, and angry at the patient who becomes terrified or experiences flashbacks during treatment. Like well-meaning employers in the workplace, they assume that the patient ought to recognize and be grateful for their benevolent efforts and cannot imagine the terror that is being relived in the mind of the patient who is also a PTSD sufferer.

Those who do understand are a special breed, regarded as absolute angels by their patients. These caregivers are possessed of a certain kind of empathy that comes naturally from the heart and which no medical school can teach. I have noted some of these "great hearts" in the dedication. Their heart for working with the traumatized has been a personal inspiration to me. I hope other medical providers will follow in their footsteps.

Do you feel "over-controlled" by your boss?

DR. C:

Wherever there are PTSD sufferers who experience flashbacks, triggering, or posttraumatic reactions on the job, one will also find employers who, quite understandably, attempt to manage the way in which these behaviors affect customers and co-workers. Let's face it—some workplaces are just triggers waiting to happen. They may be crowded and noisy. They may involve close contact that invades personal space (e.g., authorities, such as employers or supervisors). Not surprisingly, many vets with PTSD don't function effectively in work environments like these.

Vets may get angry at colleagues or other workers whom they feel do "stupid stuff" or don't take things seriously enough. Ironically, it is the vets themselves who violate the rules by becoming insubordinate and getting angry at supervisors who "don't know what they're doing when it comes to making decisions that will affect others."

These vets often react as though they are still in combat and their welfare is being jeopardized by troops not doing their job correctly or an incompetent company commander. In other instances, the sense of invasion and loss of personal control that some people experience can render them more vulnerable to stress reactions on the job—reactions that may be too much for them to handle. Once this begins to happen, they may seek to avoid the situation by not showing up for work or by disappearing from their work station.

Not surprisingly, after Vietnam, veterans in general suffered from social discrimination that often caused job opportunities to mysteriously disappear as soon as the employer discovered the job applicant was a war veteran. As a result, many vets went to work wherever they could find a job, especially in government and civil service positions where they were granted preference (rather than penalized) in connection with their military service. Many other vets sought employment in jobs that allowed them to work in quiet or solitude, simply to avoid the stress of the larger workplace.

> *"Working at the post office was kind of a perfect job for me,"* one vet related. *"Although there were others around, I really worked alone. Most of my supervisors accepted my temper outbursts and roller-coaster emotions and didn't fire me."*

My gut instinct tells me that some of these tolerant supervisors probably had PTSD themselves and were therefore more accepting of fellow vets with the disorder.

CHAPLAIN P:

Dr. C, I agree with you. I've known vets who were highly skilled, but took unskilled and low paying work just in order to avoid personal contact with others. This is also a chronic problem among military members who continue on active duty while they suffer from PTSD. Can you spell I-N-S-U-B-O-R-D-I-N-A-T-I-O-N? Superior officers typically, and justifiably, demand a high level of compliance and obedience to instructions and military orders. Military ROB (rules of behavior) is strictly observed. Depending upon whether a veteran has been captured, immobilized, pinned down in a combat situation, or has experienced circumstances in which forced obedience was part of the trauma, the requirement of having to submit to the control of others can evoke a very strong stress reaction that causes people to get in the face of their supervisors. Among military members, this can result in particularly serious consequences.

Does your work suffer because things distract or trigger you?

DR. C:

We've talked about how co-workers perceive the PTSD-affected vet and also how the vet perceives the work environment. The third factor I notice is the potential for PTSD-related decrease in job performance. If a vet with PTSD is hyperaroused, he or she may become easily distracted or startled by things which others wouldn't notice. Likewise, if a vet is hypervigilant, he may spend a lot of time scanning his environment and keeping a constant watch on things instead of attending to his specific job function. Before long, he will find that he no longer has that job function.

CHAPLAIN P:

As if all this weren't enough, PTSD is known to cause cognitive impairment (trouble with memory, concentration or clear thinking— sometimes temporary, sometimes permanent), especially in reading, language, and decision-making. None of this is helpful on the job.

DR. C:

Exactly. I seriously doubt that many employers know the actual medical facts about PTSD and its effects on employees. My personal opinion is that what they do know about is the common gossip on the street, which may imply that veterans are more likely than others to have PTSD, that they will behave erratically, and that it is better just to steer clear of them. If so, then it is a very sad, and even tragic, repetition of old stereotypes and prejudices from the Vietnam era.

Has a traumatic environment come to feel "safe" to you?

A similar pattern is seen among some veterans of the conflicts in the Middle East who sometimes "re-up" in order to become reunited with their unit. This was depicted vividly in the 2009 Academy Award winning film *Hurt Locker* in which the film's hero (an explosive ordnance tech) returns home to wife and family, walks into a grocery store cereal aisle, and is instantly unable to cope with the reality of ordinary life. Suddenly, the film shows him back in Iraq, disarming IEDs, and satisfying his craving for the danger that has actually come to feel "safer" to him than family life in suburbia.

This last phrase speaks volumes about the way in which the PTSD-affected brain seeks the familiar. The brain exercises a distinct preference for well-worn patterns of response that have become imprinted (or hard-wired) in the neural circuitry, causing the repeating old "default" behaviors that take less mental energy and effort than crafting new ones. The "ease" with which this happens is deceptive and feels comfortable and normal, even when it is not. Familiarity masquerades as "safety" and lulls people into situations and relationships that may be dangerous or compromising.

CHAPLAIN P:

In regard to the way in which PTSD keeps many people "locked" into unhealthy or even dangerous relationships, I have observed that this is sometimes as true of love and marital relationships as it is of workplace or military situations. There are thousands upon thousands of unhappily married couples in which both parties suffer from PTSD. The husband may be a vet, and the wife may be a rape survivor. Or the wife may be a vet, and the husband may be a survivor of gang violence. Whatever their background, they are each in a search of safety. And whatever feels predictable and familiar feels safe, even if it isn't safe in reality. Ironically, many of these marriages erupt into domestic violence. But relatively few of these relational partners will leave one another because they become co-dependent upon each other and the familiarity of their behaviors.

Their brains confuse familiarity with safety. As one woman put it: "Yeah, he beats me up pretty bad; but it's been going on so long that I've learned to see it comin'. I'm just used to it, is all." As a result of this tendency to become "habituated" to the familiar, some people with PTSD become "toxically bonded" to situations in which they may be over-controlled, exploited, or endangered.

3. PTSD AND INTERPERSONAL RELATIONSHIPS

"I came back from Nam and was never the same. That was forty years ago. I have never once seen my mother since my return. It was like I wanted her to just treat me as if I had died. In a lot of ways, I had. I dropped out, and just never figured out how to drop back in." ~ Vietnam vet

Do you want to either control your relationships or run from them?

Think about it. Every relationship we form in life is the result of our having taken some sort of a risk on something or someone. A huge percentage of our social learning is wrapped up around the topic of when it is—and when it isn't—a good idea to take a risk. In particular, from the moment of our birth, our social learning is designed to teach us ways of figuring out into whose care we can safely risk something as precious as our own wellbeing. "Will this person change me when I am wet or slap me?" the infant brain asks in each new situation. "Will this person comfort me when I fall and am hurt or leave me lying in a heap?" asks the toddler.

Every day, in thousands of ways both conscious and unconscious, our brains are busy playing a version of the old television game show "Let's Make A Deal." Is the best bet to choose Door #1, Door #2, or Door #3? The process of learning to distinguish between the good guys and the bad guys, figuring out which door they each hide behind, and acting appropriately upon that information is at the heart of the brain game when it comes to the ways in which human beings learn to cope with and manage risk.

Trauma is sort of like risk on steroids. It involves situations in which risks are extreme, where they could kill or injure us, in fact. And so our brains react by attempting to block off every possible avenue of risk in order to successfully cope with it. The trouble is that other people create some of the greatest risks that our brains have to cope with and sometimes block. This, not surprisingly, brings us to the topic of understanding how PTSD affects—and often interferes with—interpersonal relationships.

Here's a test you can take. Stand still and ask someone to walk slowly toward you. Stop the person when he or she reaches that uncomfortable spot commonly referred to as "in your face." How far away are they from you? Chances are they are within thirty-six inches away from you. What's magic about thirty-six inches? It's the average length of any human arm that has the capacity to reach out and grab you. It's like a yardstick that is deeply imprinted in your brain, and it is always there to unconsciously measure how close we should allow someone to get to us before we begin to feel uncomfortable or even unsafe.

> "I used to enjoy having sex, but now I don't want my boyfriend to even touch me. I'm afraid that if I give an inch, he'll take a mile and go farther than I want. I can't control the way he touches me, so I avoid it altogether. Frankly, petting the dog is the only safe touch I can count on." ~ Female Middle East vet

PTSD gets in the way of interpersonal relationships on a physical level. That's because the brain of a traumatized person is always trying to find ways of blocking the enemy's access. But let's face it: personal access is the name of the game when it comes to maintaining interpersonal relationships. If I were a PTSD sufferer, I could obviously feel safer if another person were always fifty feet or more away from me. But at that distance I would also never know the warmth of that person's embrace, the comfort of his touch, the fresh scent of his skin or hair, or the soft sound of this voice in meaningful conversation. The fact is, whoever gets close enough to love us also gets close enough to kill us. It's all part of the game of risk. So what's a traumatized brain to do?

DR. C:

I find it interesting that many vets are able to initiate close or romantic relationships only to find that the symptoms you talk about, Chaplain P, interfere once the relationships really get going. I think this is either because vets with PTSD are able to hide or partially control their symptoms early in relationships—something that becomes harder to do as the relationships progress—or because their partners are somehow attracted to the secretive and unusual behavior early on, thinking that with time and love they can change the PTSD sufferers.

PTSD also messes with our interpersonal relationships on a social and intellectual level. Socializing (also known as playing well with others) usually requires that we place ourselves in the presence of others in group settings. We've already talked about what a disaster that can be for some PTSD-affected individuals. Intellectually, it can keep us tied up in knots. How easy can it possibly be for us to get to know others, and to feel at ease in their presence, if our brains are working nonstop to assess the threat level posed by every person we meet? Just thinking about it is exhausting, never mind actually having to *live* that way.

But *live that way* is exactly what many people with PTSD have to do every single day. Trying to figure out how close is too close, when to pull up the drawbridge and take cover, and when to fling the doors of relationship wide open can be a hellish process. It is, in other words, an issue of boundaries.

In later chapters of this book, we will discuss human behavioral responses to PTSD in greater detail, including the two extreme profiles to which people tend to swing. For now, it is enough to say that people with PTSD have lost a sense of balance. That balance is known as *homeostasis,* and it's a lot like walking on the nice green median in the middle of the interstate highway. So long as you stay somewhere in the boundaries of that green zone, you're fine. Step out of it and you're sure to be outside your own boundaries and in someone's oncoming lane, ready to get hit. People with PTSD have problems learning where safe boundaries lie. They tend to jump other peoples' boundaries and get in their face, or else they create a boundary around themselves so impenetrable that it feels as though no one can get in.

CHAPLAIN P:

Most people don't understand that PTSD is rooted in actual biochemical changes that occur in our central nervous systems during es of life-threatening stress. The brain and central nervous system engage in a lightning fast, well-orchestrated dance in which they compensate in one direction or another in order to counteract a threat and save the body from injury or destruction. The three main ways in which we compensate in order to save ourselves are to (1) fight it out, (2) engage in a flight for our lives, or (3) freeze, i.e., we may become immobilized, hold very still, or retreat/withdraw.

Interpersonal relationships in which one party has PTSD reflect this. When feeling unconsciously threatened, a PTSD-affected vet may become aggressive and spoil a relationship by unintentionally making the other party fearful. This is his *fight* response getting in the way.

Alternatively, when the vet senses that someone is becoming emotionally committed, the closeness of the relationship may trigger his perimeter alert and signal the discomfort that he associates with approaching danger. He may react by *fleeing* an otherwise good and supportive relationship.

Yet another scenario plays out with a vet who *freezes*. He often copes with human relationships by playing dead emotionally. He acts like a terrified rabbit in the forest, which holds very still in hopes that a predator (i.e., another person) will pass him by without any notice.

In short, PTSD affects how we interact with people and also how we avoid them in our individual quests to win the brain game of "Risk Management and Survival." In the television show "Survivor," losing

I Always Sit with My Back to the Wall

the game of risk management is the result of teaming up with the wrong people. The worst that can happen in that situation is that they simply throw you off the island and back to Hollywood. Nobody dies. But in the game of posttraumatic survival, figuring out interpersonal relationships feels less like friendship and more like high-stakes poker. In the mind of the person with PTSD, whose very existence may have been threatened by past relationships with predatory people, making the right bet about who is safe and who is not is truly risky business.

4. RECOGNIZING PTSD IN SPIRITUAL RELATIONSHIPS

DR. C:

There is an issue in PTSD that people rarely speak about. Like the proverbial elephant in the living room, it can seriously impact peoples' lives, but they are often afraid to give voice to it. Even though I am a psychiatrist and not a theologian, I see it bubble up to the surface in many of my patients' evaluations—that is the issue of how trauma can destroy or damage one's relationship with God.

"How can God love me after what I did in combat?" "How can I believe in a God that allowed this to happen?" "How can I go to church when I don't like crowds, don't like to talk about my experiences, and everything the others want to talk about seems so . . . unimportant, trivial, silly?" "How can I listen to my pastor/priest/rabbi talk about how God loves and saves us when I don't feel that way at all?" "How can I listen to talk about forgiveness, when after what I did in combat, I'm no good?"

These are just some of the questions that vets ask themselves when they return from war and suddenly find themselves uncomfortable about returning to something that was formerly a significant aspect of their lives: the community of faith. The inability to believe any longer in something greater than themselves is one of the cruelest forms of disillusionment suffered by the traumatized veteran. The most striking and consistent aspect of the majority of soldiers with whom I worked was the degree to which their relationship with God had undergone a radical shift as a result of what they had seen and experienced in war. It is as though they could not reconcile the existence of a loving

God with the simultaneous existence of the damage, death, and destruction that mankind inflicts upon itself.

Have you fallen out with your congregation?

CHAPLAIN P:

In all the books I have read on the subject of trauma and PTSD, I've not seen any that really address what goes wrong in spiritual relationships and why they so often go south after warriors return home. As a trauma chaplain who serves recovering warriors, I feel that our reluctance to deal with this subject does a disservice to those who struggle with PTSD. So not surprisingly, you'll find that I won't shy away from speaking about the topic in this book. If there are things that need to be said about this subject, it only seems appropriate that a clergyperson, like me, probably ought to say them.

Maintaining our ties to a spiritual or faith community isn't just emotionally comforting; it is actually powerful spiritual, social, and biological medicine. Scientific studies have shown beyond question that maintaining a strong network of social connections is an important factor in maintaining resiliency in the aftermath of trauma. Now, when we talk about social connections, we're not referring to "social" as in a cocktail party or "high society." Rather, we're referring to the ties that help keep people bonded together and mutually supportive within the embrace of human society.

Some of the most important sources for these kinds of ties are spiritually based relationships. These include relationships that connect us to religious institutions and to those with whom we worship, as well as our connection to a primary clergyperson. These kinds of connections can last a lifetime and afford continuity through the many transitions of life, including birth, adolescence, courtship, marriage, divorce, illness, and death. Many who suffer from PTSD describe these longstanding spiritually based relationships as "lifesaving" and as indispensable in getting through the aftermath of war or other trauma. So one might assume that all people who start out with strong, spiritually based, social connections would be likely to maintain and derive benefit from them. But surprisingly, for many, spiritually based relationships are among the first social ties to become strained or even broken as an outgrowth of PTSD.

> *"My wife always wonders why I insist on sitting on the aisle, next to the exit, way in the back of the sanctuary, or why I always offer to take the children outside when they fidget—she doesn't 'get' that the aisle is the perfect place for me to sit in case I need to stage my escape . . ."*
> ~ *Iraq War veteran*

To understand this phenomenon, one must know something about how trauma affects the dynamic relationship between individuals and groups in society. One must also understand something about how religious congregations function. Most houses of worship seek to maintain an atmosphere that is intended to be joyous, uplifting, upbeat, and focused on life's blessings. People come to worship in situations where they sit in tight proximity, often facing forward in rows, without a view of what is behind them. They are content to "stay put" for an hour or even longer because "fidgeting" or uncontrolled moving around during a service would be regarded as inattentive or irreverent in many congregations. Members of a church, synagogue, or other worshipping community often engage in the physical touching and embracing of one another; indeed the exchange of embraces and wishes of "peace" are ritual parts of many worship services. In addition, they may ask about other people's personal problems or circumstances in ways that are intended to express genuine concern.

Now, picture in your mind a warrior who has returned from combat, affected by PTSD. Remember that trauma arises out of deeply terrifying experiences involving serious or even mortal danger. As we'll see in the next chapter, it alters one's perceptions about one's surroundings, causing the PTSD sufferer to view the world as a perpetually dangerous place in which almost anyone in his or her vicinity might turn out to be the enemy. For this reason, PTSD sufferers live in a state of either constant hypervigilance or one of withdrawal and retreat from other people. Either way, virtually everything about the typical worship setting I've just described is likely to feel challenging or even threatening for someone with PTSD.

An upbeat and joyous environment may seem very foreign to someone burdened by an overwhelming sense of terror. A vet who returns home feeling plagued by guilt because he survived (when his buddies did not) may not feel comfortable with a joyful atmosphere and may not even believe that he is "entitled" to feel joy at all. From a physical standpoint, the sounds and smells of burning incense, for example, may activate his startle response. The close personal contact and invasion of personal space, the restrictions on personal movement, the inability to know or survey what is going on behind him, and the potential for being on the receiving end of questions that may feel invasive, even if they are well-meaning, can all serve as barriers to the continued participation in corporate worship for a PTSD sufferer at the very time when he may need it most. Additionally, if the returning warrior feels that the other members of the congregation are "clueless" about the kind of horrific experiences that he or she may have suffered, then participation in worship may result in feelings of isolation instead of communal support.

Warriors who attempt to return to their relationship with a worshipping community often fail in the attempt because they feel intensely uncomfortable and don't know why. There are many reasons for this. Sometimes, church pastors are not well-schooled in the needs of returning veterans. If a vet and his spouse, for example, were to have a private visit in the pastor's office and explore the issue together, the problem might be resolved for the vet and, in the process, the pastor might gain valuable insight. Sometimes the preaching style of a pastor or the belief structure of a faith community may no longer feel supportive. In such cases, taking the opportunity to visit several new houses of worship may give a veteran a great feeling of having made a clean, fresh start.

Sometimes, when in religious services or fellowship gatherings, they feel as though they are standing far apart, as observers instead of participants. They may feel that, in comparison with the life and death struggles they have witnessed or been a part of, the everyday concerns of fellow church-goers are silly or meaningless. Unable to feel as though they fit, they simply stay away, becoming even more isolated and disconnected in the process.

Becoming involved in church outreach to the poor, the destitute, the imprisoned, or the hungry may help a vet to realize that suffering doesn't exist just in the combat theater. Indeed, it may exist around the block, and the people in his church may not be as naïve as he had previously believed.

It is truly unfortunate that in response to these problems, vets sometimes opt to run for the exits, instead of working to resolve what it is that makes them uncomfortable. Of course, if the actual theological content of a worship service feels condemning or disturbing to a vet, then it may be best for him to leave. But in many cases, the things which divide warriors from spiritual communities to which they have deep previous ties are social and physical. They are things such as "how do I sit still?" or "is it okay if I look over my shoulder?" or "is it okay if I feel the need to leave for a few minutes?" A simple talk with the pastor can usually solve these problems.

Other issues are subtle hints that the veteran feels spiritually isolated from his community. This is a problem that requires some pastoral counseling assistance. One veteran whom I counseled, who has been back from war for forty-three years and is still in acute distress, told me that, despite the fact he served on numerous committees of the church, fed the poor, visited the imprisoned, and made music for all the services, he still did not feel a part of things. He felt that he was being judged by his fellow churchgoers. In reality, it turned out that it was he who had been negatively judging himself for all those years. He had been assigning blame to himself for the unavoidable suffering of others during war, over which he had no control. By becoming a "professional church volunteer," he had been acting out a struggle to earn back favor in the eyes of God.

In counseling, I helped him to see that this favor did not need to be earned back because it had never been lost in the first place. I then helped him to reexamine his relationships with people in the church congregation from whom, he said, he felt isolated. It turned out that he had at least a dozen close friends in the congregation who made him feel loved and supported. The problem was not with the church or the people in it. The problem was the sense of shame that lay within himself. Once he realized that this was a burden he no longer needed to carry, he viewed his church community in an entirely new light and was able to truly receive and enjoy the blessings it afforded him.

In truth, most barriers to important spiritually connected relationships can usually be easily overcome, and the traumatized individual's situation can frequently be accommodated, as long as he is open about what his needs are. Unfortunately, however, many people find it too difficult to admit that they feel this kind of intense uneasiness; they feel vulnerable and fearful that they will be viewed as "crazy," or worse, "nonbelieving." Our goal is to disprove these assumptions and assure vets with PTSD that these feelings do not make a person "crazy." Nor do they make someone a person of "insufficient faith." They are simply a normal part of the illness that can be managed if approached with knowledge and sensitivity. You'll find more thoughts concerning seeking and obtaining spiritual support in Chapter Six.

DR. C AND CHAPLAIN P:

By now, you are probably getting the message, which is that damage to the important relationships in our lives is frequently the alarm bell that signals the presence of PTSD. What's more, where this kind of damage occurs to one type of relationship, damage to others frequently follows. If this sounds like the story of your life, then it's time for you to read on and become educated about the illness that may be having a profound effect upon your life.

CHAPTER TWO:

Educating YOURSELF ABOUT PTSD

CHAPLAIN P:

The fallen victims of wars—past and present—are all around us. They may stand upright and walk on two good legs, yet they may still experience hidden terrors that can knock them to their knees when they least expect it. They are deeply wounded men and women, emotional casualties who have suffered intensely painful injuries for which no Purple Heart has, to this day, ever been awarded.

Many of the veterans we have spoken with never even realized until as much as three decades later that the deep-seated psychological, emotional, and physiological changes that so greatly affected their lives were the result of service-connected Posttraumatic Stress Disorder. It is a name that did not even exist, for a condition that was never spoken of, at the time many veterans were in the service.

To most people, something does not become "real" until it has a name. So for many warriors who gave of themselves unselfishly, the hellish symptoms they suffered were not the result of a "real" illness. Instead, these vets blamed themselves, assuming that they were people of poor or flawed character whose behaviors were irrational. They became coated with that sticky ideological "lint" we call shame.

> *"I always felt ashamed, like I was unworthy. Finally, after forty-three years, I worked up the courage to take an honest look at myself. I was a person who fed the hungry, served the poor, visited prisoners and the lonely, and served my church in countless ways. I jumped in a foxhole under fire to save my buddy. Finally, I realized that the only one ashamed of me WAS ME and that other people weren't ashamed of me at all . . . it was just a lie I had told myself all those years. Now, after forty-three years, I am finally learning to think more highly of myself."* ~ Vietnam vet

Years have passed, the state of our knowledge about traumatic disorders has evolved, and still there are gallant men and women whose lives deteriorate into a state of terrible degradation due to PTSD. Now, as then, they continue to feel shame, engage in inappropriate self-blame, and fail or refuse to seek treatment for fear that they will be thought of as "crazy" or suffer a stigma that will stain their military careers forever. Since the era of Vietnam, we have moved four decades in time, yet it seems that we have advanced only a few inches in terms of helping our servicemen and women understand the disorder we call PTSD.

The first "E" in the R-E-C-O-V-E-R approach to PTSD stands for *educating* yourself, because if you don't seek to educate yourself, it is unlikely that anyone will do it for you. Knowledge is power, and knowing about the illness that impacts your life is essential to its management. If you have diabetes, the odds are that the first question you ask your doctor is the most important question of all: "What is this disease and what does it do to my body?"

No one would think worse of you for asking the question; in fact, most doctors would think you were in denial if you did not ask it. For some reason, however, it does not occur to patients that they should ask about the "mechanism of the illness," *even when that illness is psychological.*

The realm of the psychological is bathed in mystery. People fail to understand that psychological illnesses, just like physical illnesses, have causes and effects. They fail to understand this because they simply have never been told. The purpose of this book is to change that terrible state of affairs, to fill the informational void with knowledge, and to return a sense of empowerment to people suffering from PTSD.

In this chapter, you will hear from both of us about the causes and primary symptoms of PTSD. Dr. C provides explanations through the lens of his four decades as a psychiatric physician. I offer simplified explanations derived from my many years as a trauma therapist. No matter whose perspective suits you best, the most important thing is for you, as a reader, to understand that PTSD is a *real* medical illness with *real* medical causes and effects that are *not* just "all in your head."

THE DISORDER THAT'S NOT "JUST IN YOUR HEAD"

DR. C:

So, what is PTSD anyhow? Psychiatric disorders are described in a book published by the American Psychiatric Association: *Diagnostic and Statistical Manual of Mental Disorders, Fourth Edition (DSM-IV)* with the next revision (DSM-V) due out in 2013. Think of the *DSM-IV* as a sort of official dictionary or recipe book of mental health disorders. It is very important because it lists the symptoms that are required to exist before a person qualifies to receive a diagnosis for any particular psychological/psychiatric problem. According to the *DSM-IV*, Posttraumatic Stress Disorder (PTSD) falls in the group of disorders called Anxiety Disorders. The main PTSD symptoms listed in the *DSM-IV* are the result of anxiety-related changes that take root in the brain and central nervous system after someone has been involved in, or has witnessed, *a traumatic event.*

What, exactly, are traumatic events?

CHAPLAIN P:

A traumatic event isn't just any old garden variety scary occurrence. If it were, we'd all be getting PTSD just from watching horror movies or riding roller coasters. PTSD involves a different kind of fear, horror, or terror. When we experience something like a roller coaster ride, it's scary but fun—the kind of thing that we actually choose to do because it's a thrill. Deliberate thrill-seeking is not traumatic (unless, of course, it ends in an unexpected traumatic accident). By contrast, our brains respond in a very different way to the kind of event or occurrence that is not only truly terrifying, but that is believed by the person to be potentially lethal or dangerously threatening.

DR. C:

In fact, the *DSM-IV* actually defines a *traumatic event* as a very specific kind of occurrence. Clinically speaking, a trauma is defined as a situation in which,

"The person is exposed to a traumatic event in which both of the following are present:

(1) The person experienced, witnessed, or was confronted with an event or events that involved actual or perceived threat of death, or serious injury, or threat to physical integrity of self or others;

(2) The person's response involved intense fear, helplessness, or horror."

In the real-life veteran whom I see, PTSD is usually, but not necessarily, the result of traumatic experiences in combat—experiences in which the individual or others around him or her were injured or killed. But it is important to remember that traumatic events of any kind—auto accidents, rapes or assaults, natural disasters, or any number of traumas—can lead to PTSD. The *DSM-IV* makes no distinctions in the diagnosis of PTSD, and combat-related PTSD is not a separate disorder. However, most of my experience has been with veterans with combat-related PTSD, and there are hundreds of thousands of veterans diagnosed with this condition. Therefore, this book is primarily designed to help those men and women whose Posttraumatic Stress Disorder is a result of service-related stressors, usually those resulting from combat-related activities.

CHAPLAIN P:

As readers learn about the clinical definitions of trauma and PTSD, it's important to note two things. First, people aren't born with PTSD, and they don't "catch" it out of nowhere, like the common cold. They develop it either because they experienced something truly horrible, or because something truly horrible was done to them. This means that people with PTSD do not need to feel guilty or ashamed about having the disorder. By definition, it is not something that implies fault on the part of the sufferer. Actually, it is quite the opposite.

The second point I would emphasize is that the measure of whether an event is threatening is *whether the individual believes it to be so and not whether it is actually so*. For example, a teller who is held up in a bank robbery may experience it as a trauma, even if the gun that is held to her head is not loaded. So long as she perceives the gun to be loaded, and therefore believes that it is mortally threatening, it is traumatic to her. By way of additional example, in the early days of Taliban control in Afghanistan, stories circulated concerning the horrific and gruesome ways in which peaceable citizens—especially women—were publicly executed and mutilated in full view of their husbands, just to serve as "examples" to the rest of the population about the dangers of resisting the Taliban. Well, it didn't require that all men actually see their wives publicly executed; just the knowledge that such things had happened down the road in another village to other men and their wives and the threat that it could happen again was enough to instill stark terror and inflict trauma upon the population.

> *One soldier told me that just before he entered Afghan-*
> *istan, he saw pictures of captured soldiers being*
> *beheaded. He said from then on he lived in fear—not of*
> *being shot, but of being captured and tortured. He told*
> *me that although he was a cook and not a warrior, he*
> *lived in fear for the next three months.*

Unseen terrors can be some of the most deeply felt. Sometimes, what we simply know but cannot see is the most terrifying thing of all. I have spoken with warriors, for example, who heard the screams of their buddies being tortured or executed, and who suffered PTSD, even though they themselves survived imprisonment without physical injury.

Dr. C and I both work with people whose PTSD was caused by service-related stressors. In recent years, however, it's become clear that the variety of service-related stressors has increased greatly beyond our old stereotypes of what happens in combat. Military service is definitely not like a war movie.

Service-connected PTSD doesn't have its onset only after someone has gone through a firefight. The "combat zones" of current wars are many and varied. The emergency rooms of medical units are as terrifying as life outside the wire. Serving as a chaplain or as a medical caregiver to the injured can be as traumatizing as becoming injured oneself. Non-armed or non-combatant personnel in war zones suffer extreme terror in suicide bombings and terrorist attacks. With war comes the horror of rape and murder and mutilation. Service personnel who have never fired a weapon may nevertheless become extremely traumatized by working motor pools, where they must sort and match body parts found in exploded Humvees. And not to be forgotten are those who experience trauma as a result of the terror and excruciating pain that is unavoidably inflicted in the course of medical treatment for their service-connected injuries, especially burns.

Feeling that life has been thrown off balance

DR. C:

The human body is designed to seek and maintain a general state of balance. Scientists call this process of the constant search for balance *homeostasis,* meaning the biological drive to keep things in a state of normalcy, which is to say constancy. It strives to achieve balance between activity and rest, between inhaling and exhaling, between eating and digesting, between blood vessels expanding and contracting, between muscles building up and tearing down, between the taking of some substances in and excretion of other substances out, and so on. Our bodies are a lot like a pendulum or a rocking boat; when we go too far in either direction, there is an innate biological drive to swing back to the center where we are restored to balance.

Stressors are those things and forces in our environment that throw our bodily functions out of balance. Most of these stressors are minor; in fact, minor stressors are a natural part of daily life from the moment we are born. Nature knows how to deal with these. Our bodies come equipped with a natural coping mechanism called the stress response. It is a complex series of chemical processes through which the body constantly strives to get back to midline, or the balance point, after stressors have thrown us off center.

Stress disorder occurs when our bodies are thrown off center by stressors so severe that we can no longer biologically cope effectively; in other words, our bodies try to return to the balance point but cannot do so. When the body loses its ability to get back to the balance point because of a severe stressor, and when that severe stressor is a traumatic experience or event, we call the resulting condition Posttraumatic Stress Disorder. In other words, PTSD is the stress disorder (disruption of biological balance) that occurs post (after) trauma. The formula looks something like this:

Post (after)

+

Traumatic (experience of perceived lethal threat)

+

Stress (throwing body out of balance)

+

Disorder (body remains in threatened state, cannot regain balance)

=

Posttraumatic Stress Disorder

(Posttraumatic Stress Disorder: After an experience of a lethal threat to life or limb, the body is thrown so far off balance that it remains in a perceived threatened state and cannot regain its balance point.)

Now, the stress response actually starts out as a very positive thing. It is the collection of biological and chemical reactions in the body that counteract stressors and actually keeps us alive in the face of danger or potentially lethal threats. If things are happening too slowly, the stress response may cause us to speed up. If things are happening too fast, it may help our bodies to slow down. Once we get back to the balance point—the point where we regain our biological equilibrium—the body senses that our survival is no longer in danger, and the stress response subsides. We return—both biologically and psychologically—to a state of being calm and balanced.

There are two points, however, at which the stress response turns from a positive thing to a very negative one. These points occur when

> (1) Stressors are so severe and so overwhelming that the stress response must become engaged continually or repetitively in order for the body to stay alive or cope with external threats, and

> (2) This process of continual repetition of the stress response becomes an engrained habit. In other words, the stress response has stayed engaged "in overdrive" for so long that the body and brain don't know

how to downshift back to a calm state anymore. In a sense, the body gets "stuck" in a gear it can't get out of—an extreme state that we call "survival mode."

Getting "stuck" in survival mode

CHAPLAIN P:

The bottom line is that PTSD is a state of high anxiety in which the body has been exposed to such extreme stressors that it enters survival mode. Not only does it enter survival mode, but it also loses the ability to exit survival mode, even when the actual danger has long passed. The body continues to feel itself endangered even when it actually isn't. In response to this false sense of endangerment, it generates a full-scale stress reaction, over and over again, even when it is no longer appropriate or necessary to the person's survival. This constant process of "defaulting" to survival mode, even when survival is no longer endangered, is what causes the stress response to shift from ordered (functional and helpful) to disordered (dysfunctional and unhelpful).

> They teach us how to go to the combat area. And if they don't teach us all that we need to know, we get some pretty quick on-the-job training when we get there. It's like our inside alert switch gets flipped to the on position. The problem is that when we get home no one shows us how to move it to the off position! ~ Middle East vet

This is the reason that I often explain PTSD to my patients as "Posttraumatic Survival Disorder." PTSD starts as a good thing, e.g., the stress/survival response that nature gave us as a gift. The problem is that this is one gift that just keeps on giving. Not only that—it tends to run completely amok.

People who have never experienced PTSD or who have never cared for PTSD patients cannot begin to imagine how disabling it is to be "stuck" in survival mode. One of my patients describes it as "being trapped on the expressway of stark terror, going mach speed, without ever being able to find the off-ramp."

Others describe it as feeling as though they have been buried alive in a bunker they can never escape. It's bad enough when virtually your entire life feels like a continual struggle for survival. But when that continual fight for survival goes on indefinitely, and for no apparent reason, it leads to levels of emotional and physical exhaustion, frustration, and emotional fatigue that are inconceivable. It's like living in a zone that continues to take heavy fire in a never-ending war while everyone else around you is at peace. They look at you in amazement, wondering why you can't see that everything is okay. It's because, as far as *your* body is concerned, *everything isn't okay.*

In fact, some patients have such a strong perception of danger all around them that the only way they can mentally cope with the situation is to dissociate, or "check out" of their bodies. I have a patient who has severe posttraumatic reactions up to fifteen times a day. Each time he feels that his life is truly on the line. His own body feels as though it is too dangerous a place to stay in, sort of like a skid-row hotel that he has to check out of on a regular basis, in order to stay alive. He says to me, "My soul knows when it's not safe to stay in my body anymore; when that happens, I feel it pop out of my body. It flies around, well out of danger, until the coast is clear and it's safe to return."

Life, even with all its challenges, was meant to include peace, joy, and emotional abundance. When life is reduced to nothing but the feeling that one is in a never-ending struggle for survival, it saps the "life blood" out of people. This is the reason that PTSD becomes the cause of actual or attempted suicide for some people and should always be treated seriously.

EDUCATING YOURSELF ABOUT SYMPTOM CATEGORIES IN PTSD

DR. C:

Those who develop PTSD begin to experience symptoms that fall into three core areas. They are:

> (1) RE-EXPERIENCING of the traumatic experiences: Nightmares, flash-backs, sensory cues reminding us of the trauma, and reoccurring and unwanted thoughts of the trauma make the victim feel he is back in the situation experiencing the trauma again.

> (2) AVOIDANCE: The person avoids conversations, feelings, people, places, and events that bring back thoughts and feelings associated with the traumatic experience(s).

> (3) INCREASED AROUSAL: A heightened level of anxiety leads to sleep problems, irritability, suspiciousness, and increased startle response. So much energy is expended in the hyperaroused state that concentration is even decreased.

Initially, the response to a trauma may be a less severe and less permanent disorder known as *acute stress syndrome.* The individual experiences dissociative symptoms (such as numbing and diminished awareness of surroundings), re-experiencing, and avoidance to the extent that the person's normal functioning in important areas (such as work or family life) is impaired. According to the *DSM-IV,* the acute stress syndrome lasts two days to four weeks. After four weeks, the acute response may well become more prolonged. If it does not resolve, it can assume a more permanent form known as *acute stress disorder,* which is similar to PTSD in terms of its psychological and behavioral symptoms, but lacks the element of full-blown physiological reactivity.

In summary, then, PTSD represents an emotional or behavioral response to an overwhelming trauma, resulting in prolonged symptoms of re-experiencing, avoidance, increased arousal, and physiological responses. These symptoms may

(1) show up early and persist over time, or

(2) show up early and decrease or resolve over time, or

(3) begin months or even years after experiencing the original trauma.

Additional symptoms that accompany PTSD

When we speak about "symptoms" of PTSD such as (I) re-experience, (2) avoidance, and (3) arousal, we are referring to the primary symptoms of PTSD that are listed in the *DSM-IV,* which must be present for a diagnosis, but they are by no means the only problems or issues that are experienced by people with PTSD. There is a wide array of other problems that accompany the illness, which vary widely from person to person. Some of these problems include psycho-logical problems—such as depression, anxiety, phobias (both environmental and social), or substance abuse—or more physical symptoms—such as itching, hypertension, irregular or rapid heartbeat, physical fatigue, weight loss or gain, generalized inflammatory problems, and suppression of the immune system leading to more frequent illnesses. Many of the physical symptoms of PTSD are discussed in greater detail in Chapter Three.

THE CHANGING FACE OF TRAUMA

In recent years, we see that as the nature of warfare changed, the nature of trauma has also changed considerably. During WWII, for example, there were periods of battle at the front and periods of inactivity when no fighting was occurring. In Vietnam, there was often no front area of battle and no way to establish the location or existence of "enemy lines." Rather, the battle was going on everywhere, and all around the soldier. Unlike WWII, in which there was an established rear, there were no places in the jungle to which one could retreat and regroup behind one's own lines. Once the nature of war changed, and evolved into conflicts in which there was constant engagement and virtually no safe avenue of retreat, we began to see a much higher incidence of what is now known as *chronic, or recurring, trauma.*

In recent years, researchers have begun to see a difference between the traumatic effects of different types of events. In particular, they have begun to draw distinctions between those who suffer what is known as *single event trauma*, as opposed to those who suffer from *chronic (recurrent or multiple event) trauma*. Single-event trauma can certainly occur in combat. Seeing a buddy die, being injured yourself, encountering a suicide bomber or an improvised explosive device (IED), or accidentally killing women and children are certainly the kinds of single events that would be traumatic enough to lead to PTSD.

When I ask veterans to remind me of the one or two events that even today—decades later—cause them distress, they will often remember a battle or ambush during which many were killed. They frequently recall actually looking someone in the face as that person lay moaning, dying, or dead. It might have been one of their fellow soldiers, but even seeing an enemy soldier or civilian die in front of them could be traumatic to these veterans.

> *"I thought I was prepared after basic training to see people die. But I learned it was different when it really happened, and happened within feet of where you were." ~ Common vet comment*

Sometimes the military activity occurs far away, such as when aircraft are used to bomb a target. However, in both Vietnam and the Middle East, combat has more frequently been up close and personal, even involving hand-to-hand combat, seeing death in the eyes of the dying person and, with the advent of the IED (improvised explosive device), the severe mutilation of the injured.

I find that veterans of older conflicts are more likely to be sufferers of single-event trauma. This is especially true for men who are now in their 80s, who went off to Korea as fresh-faced young kids who had grown up in relatively wholesome, often rural, and small town environments, and with "traditional" family upbringings. These soldiers were much less likely to have had a traumatic experience previous to their entry into the military.

Once in the military, those who were injured in combat were much more likely to be taken out of service after a single traumatic event. That is because back in the day, the technology for medically treating warriors and restoring them quickly to active duty did not exist as it does today.

Additionally, in the days of the draft, manpower could be replenished more readily than in an all-volunteer force. So "a tour was a tour." You did your year and came home (unless, of course, you volunteered to "re-up" for another tour, which some certainly did). By and large, however, soldiers weren't subjected to the recurrent demands of doing multiple tours without ever feeling that they could "come home from the war" for good.

The current trend toward recurrent (multiple event) traumas

For veterans of Middle East conflicts, stressors also shifted from the single event to the recurrent type. For those involved in the Gulf War, it might have been the frequent threat of a chemical attack, requiring that the chemical protective gear be donned often. For those at the initiation of the Iraq war, it might have been facing the enemy without adequate protective vehicles or gear. For those who served later in the present war in Iraq, it may have been the constant traumas that resulted from the foot patrols during the "surge," as well as daily missions outside "the wire," in which American forces in vehicles patrolled roads that were mined with IEDs, causing recurrent, horrific casualties.

Added to these chronic and unrelenting stressors is the fact that terrorism has permanently changed the face and the "uniform" of war. The enemy who wears civilian clothing is no longer detectable. Anyone with a cell phone or other detonator may be a suicide bomber. Even areas like the Green Zone that were supposed to be safe haven't proved to be so. One veteran described to me,

> *"It was like being in a medieval castle—the enemy couldn't easily get in, but armament (mortars and RPGs now, arrows in medieval times) came over the walls." ~ Middle Eastern vet*

Another Iraq War vet told me, "We were running track in our short pants—doing physical training—when a mortar came over the walls and killed my best friend, not five feet from where I was standing." Prior to going to Iraq, this vet thought they would be safe on a sports track inside the Green Zone.

> And another Middle East vet said, "To me every day was like Russian Roulette, 'cause I never knew if today is the day some crazy with a suicide vest was gonna blow himself up and take some of us with him. I was trained to go into combat, but how do you prepare for this day after day threat from an enemy you can't even recognize as enemy, and doing it in an area that was supposed to be safe?"

So, even in combat-related PTSD, the stressor may not be a single event, but rather repeated events over time. What we know about repeated traumatic events is that they accumulate and kindle—in other words, they don't dissipate. Instead, they create a continuing build-up of traumatic stressors that eventually tip the emotional boat right over. In this way, recurrent traumas pre-dispose the warrior to develop PTSD more readily. In addition, chronic traumas do not necessarily have to be giant, cataclysmic events. The effect of exposure to even lower-intensity events, when repeated over time, is enough to create severe PTSD.

Life factors impacting levels of recurrent trauma in the military

CHAPLAIN P:

The extent of our scientific knowledge concerning the way in which people's life history, genetic makeup, and socio-economic background may make them more or less vulnerable to PTSD has expanded greatly in the past decade, not only in the context of combat-related PTSD, but also in terms of our understanding concerning the level of traumatic impact that results from the increasing levels of violence, sexual assault, and abuse and neglect that occur in a civilian context.

Deciding which is more dangerous—the combat zone or the drive-by zone—is sometimes a difficult call.

The notion that trauma is always a single, cataclysmic event is now considered to be grossly inaccurate, and this is having its effect upon military regulations. For example, when seeking VA disability, it is no longer required that a military claimant pinpoint the precise moment of a single trauma associated with his disability. This is due to the simple fact that there may have been literally hundreds or even thousands of such moments. Instead, the concept of recurrence has been expanded to include the ways in which trauma affects people across the broader continuum of their life history, both during military service and prior to it.

For example, we know that low socio-economic status can present special challenges for many people. Those living in poverty are more likely to experience environmental factors that are broadly referred to as *community-based violence*. This can include exposure to drive-by shootings, neighborhood drug trafficking, domestic violence, and violent crime. All of these factors can be sources of trauma for young people, even if their own families are not involved in these activities. Of the soldiers I worked with downrange, a significant number had experienced prior exposure to community or home-based violence.

Of course, if young people have also endured substance abuse, physical or sexual abuse, domestic violence, parental abandonment, or similar circumstances in their own homes, the problem is seriously compounded. Often, promising young men and women who have been previously trapped in these kinds of socio-economic circumstances turn to the military as a ticket out of these negative environments. In some cases, then, military recruits may already have experienced significant recurrent traumas, even before their enlistment. One soldier (whose story was characteristic of many) told me that he had been completely abandoned by his parents at the age of eight. He fell into the care of an uncle in a violent public housing unit. "I joined the Army and went to war because I wanted to go somewhere safer than my neighborhood," he told me.

We also know that there are many forms of trauma that can occur across all social and economic segments of our society. Accident; injury; crime; chaos resulting from a parent's untreated mental illness; and verbal, sexual, and physical abuse are no respecter of income, culture, or social status.

Finally, we know that the genetic makeup of individuals may affect their responses to traumatic events that occur in their lives prior to military service. Genetic makeup may greatly impact individuals' lives even though they have no control over it. Certain *genetic expressions* may cause an individual to be very stress-resistant, while others may result in significant increased vulnerability to traumatic stress in adult life.

Some people ask me how someone with a prior recurrent history of traumatic stressors can enter the military. In fact, many individuals with this type of history enter the armed services every day and serve admirably. You see, their prior experiences may have resulted in increased levels of trauma-related stress, but not in sufficient quantity to result in the onset of an actual traumatic stress disorder.

These individuals function well enough to pass the military psychological entrance screening. However, once they are inserted into a combat environment, their level of traumatic stress may escalate hugely. When this occurs, their prior stress responses may potentiate an increased level of susceptibility to these new stressors, making it more likely that PTSD will result. To put it simply, their emotional boats just tip over more quickly and easily.

Another reason that individuals with prior traumatic history are present in great numbers in the military is that psychological screening in advance of recruitment is a relatively recent innovation. Many people with PTSD or a history of traumatic stress were enlisted or commissioned without having to subject themselves to psychological testing unless or until their PTSD became actively symptomatic while on active duty.

A final explanation for this scenario lies in the screening procedures that the military uses. These screenings have flaws and can be easily evaded. So even if someone is being screened, it is possible that their illness will not be detected.

Increased family exposure to trauma

Once in the military, the opportunity for traumatic exposure is greater not only for service persons, but for their loved ones and families as well. The war is only a cell phone call or webcam session away. Many are the occasions when a soldier will be on the phone with a family member, who overhears incoming fire. Situations in which a loved one overhears an explosion that takes the life of a spouse in mid conversation have also been known to occur.

But even less dramatic events take their toll. Unlike warriors who served in "pre-cellular" conflicts, today's soldiers receive neither separation nor insulation from the stresses of home—they continue to manage dual stress levels from both home and the war zone. Levels of pre-existing stress are particularly high for members of the National Guard and the military Reserves who find themselves activated to duty with little or no notice and little opportunity to prepare themselves and their families psychologically, socially, and financially. After return from the war zone, active Guard and Reserve warriors receive no military pay, military benefits, or psychological treatment services, and they frequently find themselves unemployed in an economy where there are few if any jobs available. The stress of combat, imminent homelessness, and post-redeployment poverty form a dangerous posttraumatic "stew," in which warriors find themselves emotionally drowning. These warriors are more predisposed to the onset of PTSD, and yet are among the least likely to be noticed as the illness develops.

One of the factors that has statistically increased the rate of recurrent-event-connected trauma in the military is the increased level of females serving in all branches of the service. This is not because females are mentally or emotionally weaker than males. It is simply a result of the fact that females throughout society are much more likely to have experienced the trauma of sexual assault, an event that is estimated to occur to at least 1 out of every 2.5 women and that constitutes the most common trauma in our society. Because the pool of people from which our military is drawn now includes women, it automatically includes more sexual assault survivors. There are many ways in which a prior history of sexual assault may resurface in a traumatic fashion during military service. Some are more noticeable, such as when a female recruit has a flashback to a prior event of abuse in her lifetime because the voice of an aggressive drill sergeant cues her to the voice of a male attacker. Other incidents are much more subtle and harder to detect:

> *"They called a chemical alert. We had to get into full MOPP suits (hazmat gear worn to withstand a chemical attack) in 130 degree heat and stay in them for hours. The gas masks, especially were suffocating. I was sure I would die. I relive it every day. It was years before I recognized that it was the same suffocating feeling that would come over me when I was a small girl and was sexually molested by my father. ~ Female Middle East vet*

Recent research indicates that trauma rooted in early childhood (such as the traumas that many military members have experienced) has a host of special effects—not only emotional, but also behavioral, cognitive, social, and physical. It may also lead to the development of other co-occurring conditions, including major depression, attention deficit disorder with hyperactivity (ADHD), and dissociative disorder. Military members whom I have seen, who carry early childhood traumatic baggage, and who later develop PTSD due to combat stressors often struggle with these types of co-occurring issues as well.

Dr. Harry A. Croft, M.D. and Rev. Dr. Chrys L. Parker, J.D.

Psychological vs. physiological symptoms: are both "real"?

DR. C:

I began this chapter by describing PTSD as a psychological disorder. Sometimes people interpret this to mean "it's all in their heads." Why don't they "just get over it?" But that interpretation would be incorrect. The fact is that one cannot "just get over it." A psychological disorder is as real and perhaps as incapacitating as a physical disorder. The individual with PTSD can't simply *decide* not to have the thoughts, feelings, and behaviors he or she is experiencing. There are *biological* reasons why this is so. In Chapter Three, we will examine more about the structure and function of the brain and how these are connected to PTSD.

For now, however, it is enough to explain that the human brain is divided into three major regions. The thinking part of the brain that makes so-called cognitive decisions—such as a decision to just get over it—is not the part of the brain which has control over the posttraumatic stress reaction. And the part of the brain that does initiate the posttraumatic survival responses and that is at the heart of the problem is not initially under the conscious control of the individual.

In short, a person can *decide* all he or she wants, however, this will not make PTSD symptoms go away. All that this mindset will do is create an even greater sense of frustration and failure on the part of the individual, who becomes convinced that he or she has inadequate "will" or a bad attitude. It's critical, therefore, to understand that *treatment*—and not a so-called attitude adjustment—is needed to manage PTSD.

CHAPLAIN P:

As much as society and the military have increased awareness about PTSD behaviors, they have done little to increase levels of awareness about the biological roots of PTSD. As a result, the illness continues to be viewed as a purely behavioral problem. And since we assume that we can make intelligent decisions about our behavior, it is not surprising that the prevailing military view is that individuals can decide their way out of PTSD through a change in attitude, force of will, personal discipline, or a determination to get over it. Nothing in either Dr. C's clinical experience or my own supports this conclusion. It is at odds with all that we know about human biology.

The biological reactions that are at the root of PTSD are the most fundamental processes in the human body. They are the responses upon which our very survival depends. For this reason, they are biologically engineered to exert primary control over everything else that the individual thinks, does, says—or *decides*. As we'll see in later chapters, PTSD is actually a fundamentally biological illness. The behaviors it creates are secondary. In other words, they are after-effects of the primary biological stress response. But because the outside, or behavioral part of the illness, is what is visible to the eye, we mistakenly assume that it is the whole story. In fact, it is only the outside wrapping, like the jacket of a book. The more we continue to treat PTSD as a strictly behavioral problem, instead of as the real medical illness it is, involving biological, behavioral, psychological, and spiritual elements, the more people will die or suffer ruined lives as a consequence of it.

LEARNING THE SYMPTOMS: YOUR EDUCATIONAL FOUNDATION

DR. C:

In Chapter One, we spent a good deal of time talking about the ways in which PTSD appears in the situations of daily life. In the first section of this chapter, we've talked about the ways in which PTSD is experienced in society. Now, we will expand your education by helping you to learn more about the ways in which PTSD is manifested in the form of psychological and behavioral symptoms. Now, we know what you're thinking. It probably goes like this: "Oh no . . . clinical talk . . . not my area."

Well, hang in there with us. Your doctor is going to use clinical words right in your face. Do you want to sit there and not have a clue what he or she means? Of course not. We need to familiarize you with these words, because they may appear in medical records that will affect you for the rest of your life. You *need* to know what they mean. However, we also believe that one of the best ways of explaining the meaning of the clinical terms is to avoid using clinical language. Instead, we prefer to illustrate them through the stories that have been told to us by countless vets. As you go through the pages of this chapter, put a check mark in the margin each time one of them strikes a familiar chord.

SYMPTOM CATEGORY 1:

RE-EXPERIENCING THE EVENT(S)

The first category of PTSD symptoms is that of "re-experience." The first thing that every reader should know about "re-experience" is that it is NOT the same thing as "remembering." After all, there is hardly a person alive who doesn't have bad memories of at least something in life. So if re-experience were simply the same thing as remembering, what's the big deal? Well, it *isn't* like remembering, and if you have PTSD, you are undoubtedly aware that re-experience symptoms are, in fact, a *very big deal*. Here's why.

When you *remember* something, your conscious mind is connected to the present and to real time and place. You are able to construct a kind of timeline of your life in which events fall in logical order. You are able to distinguish what happened *then* from what is happening *now,* and because you can do this, you are consciously aware that even the very worst things that have happened to you that you can remember have happened at a prior time. Those things have come to an end and are no longer happening to you. In other words, your brain is consciously aware that you are out of danger.

Unfortunately, if you have PTSD with symptoms of re-experiencing, these processes may not operate as they normally would. To begin with, when you re-experience a trauma, your brain is not consciously aware of your surroundings, so you may be in your kitchen but truly perceive that you are in Vietnam, for example. Your brain is also not conscious of the order of events as they've happened in reality. Re-experience episodes emerge from an unconscious part of the brain that you do not control (we'll talk more about it in Chapter Three). This part of the brain doesn't contain the logical timeline of your life. So it can't distinguish between *then* and *now*.

It also stores events in extreme detail—every sight, smell, sound, and feeling (including extreme pain, panic, and terror) and can engage in the playback of those events. Once the playback has started, the brain is literally tricked. It perceives that "then" is really "now," in excruciating, terrifying, vivid detail.

A person with PTSD may re-experience everything about a trauma in the same way that he did the first time. So if you were shot, it feels exactly as if you are being shot again, in every detail. If you were burned by an IED blast, you may feel the horrific pain of it happening to you all over again, because your brain cannot tell the difference between what is past and what is present and still happening to you. Because the brain believes that the danger is continuing, it sends signals to the body that instruct it to react. As a result, people who re-experience trauma also react to it physically, in ways that family members or onlookers simply do not understand.

There are a number of ways in which PTSD sufferers re-experience their traumatic events. The common thread that unites them is that each of these types of symptoms has the ability to retrigger a posttraumatic stress reaction in the sufferer. Re-experiences include the following:

- Recurrent undesired recollections and thoughts

- Recurrent nightmares

- Flashbacks and/or feeling as if the traumatic events are recurring in the present

- Emotional and body reactions to cues (smells, sounds, sights, and internal physical feelings) that remind the vets of the events they actually experienced

- *Intense* distress at exposure to things or events that are in some way similar to the traumas that were actually experienced

Thoughts, recollections, and flashbacks

Vets often re-experience the traumatic events of their time in country in their thoughts, recollections, and dreams. Thus, the thoughts and images of their experiences are frequently present both day and night. They intrude into the streams of other thoughts the vets are having, often occurring without provocation and certainly without being wanted. They may be triggered by cues in the environment—a movie or TV story, a conversation, a sight, a sound, a smell, a place, or an event—or they can come out of the blue, without any apparent provocation. The vets might be actively involved in day-to-day activities—working, studying, conversing, driving, watching TV—and the next thing they know, they start thinking of experiences that took place back in the jungles of Vietnam or the deserts of the Middle East. One way of thinking about PTSD victims' memories for events they experienced in war is that they are *excessively detailed and vivid,* with the result that they continue to re-experience the trauma over and over again, just as they did the first time.

These thoughts may or may not include emotional responses, but they are generally bothersome and troubling. The vets worry and wonder, "What's happening to me? When will these thoughts go away—or will I ever be free of them?"

Many vets have even more alarming daytime recollections, called flash-backs. As we have previously explained, a thought is *remembering* an event. By contrast, a flashback is the overwhelming feeling that one is *actually reliving* an event (often with the sights, smells, or sounds of Vietnam or the Middle East), accompanied by an emotional response, and even by the same physical feelings (such as pain) that accompanied the original event. Vets often describe flash-backs as "nightmares happening while wide awake."

Although the frequency of flashbacks often decreases over the years, many vets still have recurrent daytime thoughts of war-time events, even without the experience of reliving those events. Often, these thoughts and emotions are brought about by exposure to sights, sounds, smells, environmental surround-ings, people, places, or dates that remind the vets of times or events in country.

Even the sight of a vacant field can provoke the thoughts and feelings. My office is on the fifth floor and is all glass on two sides. A very large vacant field full of trees and greenery is visible through one of the windows. Behind the lot in the distance are the mountains and hills of the beautiful Hill Country. When I ask most of my patients to look out that window and tell me what they see, they reflect on the beautiful hills in the distance. But the Vietnam veterans almost uniformly report seeing "the jungle" across the street—the same type of jungle they remember from Vietnam.

A Vietnamese or Middle Eastern restaurant or person or the anniversary date of a battle, ambush, or death can also provoke thoughts and feelings.

Seeing pointed hats (which the Vietnamese wore) or even Asian adults or children on the street often provokes problematic thoughts and feelings. The soldiers were taught that the Viet Cong (the enemy) wore black pajama-like clothes and "black pointy hats—you know, like witches' hats." They later learned that friendly South Vietnamese wore similar clothes, and some feared they had killed the "wrong person in the pointy hat," making them feel worse as they recalled. Thus the confusion over whom the enemy *really* was caused uncertainty, frustration, and resentment.

Often the sight of someone similar in physical appearance to the enemy triggers the re-experience. Thus, for the Vietnam veteran, it might be seeing a Vietnamese individual or for the Middle East vets seeing someone of Middle Eastern descent. It might be the beard on the man of Middle Eastern descent or the dress of the Middle Eastern-appearing woman. Children often bring back the sight of the kids playing, yelling, or crying that they saw in the combat zone.

It might even be the sight of American military personnel or the sight of wounded troops. San Antonio has large military facilities and a special treatment center for the wounded warriors. As they go for evaluation or treatment to these facilities, many retired military members with PTSD are exposed to the troops or the wounded individuals, and the sight of them provokes recollections of their own experiences in country, bringing about thoughts or emotional reactions.

Sounds

Sounds that often cause re-experiencing include the sound of a gun firing, a car backfiring, a helicopter flying overhead—or even simple "screaming or yelling." Many Middle East vets say the sound of chaos or even children playing or screaming causes re-experiencing of their own traumatic stressors. One vet whose military duty included picking up screaming, wounded Vietnamese babies couldn't stand it when he later went to work in a hospital nursery.

For some, the sound of thunder or rain falling (which was common during the monsoon season in the jungles of Vietnam) leads to re-experiencing. An Iraq War veteran told me that for him it was the sound of clothes or shoes in the dryer—the thumping of the clothes reminded him of the sound of the mortars hitting the ground, as did high-pitched sounds resembling incoming mortars. Emergency vehicle sirens can cause recollections of warning sirens or emergency vehicles in theater.

Smells

Smells such as freshly-mown grass, garbage, dead animals, burning meat, and even the "smell of rain" have all been described as causing recall. The odor of Oriental food or Middle Eastern food may provide a sensory cue. For some it is the nauseating smell of human waste, compounded by burning, reminding the vets of the smell of the burning of human waste in the barrels known as "honey pots" in the jungles of Vietnam. For many it is the smell of burning meat on the barbeque grill that brings back the recollection of burning flesh in the combat area they were in.

Many vets have told me that even the smell of body odor can cause recollections for them. Often days or weeks (or longer) passed between opportunities to take a bath or shower in Vietnam or the Middle East, and thus the smell of body odor causes a recollection of their own combat-related experiences.

Sensations

Sometimes internal feelings and physical sensations—like nausea, fear, dizziness, or the feeling of falling—bring back full-blown combat recollections. For one vet it was dizziness, and for another just the mere sense of "uncertainty and discomfort with my surroundings" that caused them to remember times of uncertainty in the combat area.

News/Current events

For many Vietnam vets, the events of Desert Storm or 9-11 or the present wars in the Middle East bring their re-experiencing back to the front of their minds. These events caused an unusual reaction in many. Some said, "I wanted to get back into the military when I heard about those events. I knew it was crazy, but it was my first thought when I heard the news."

The point is that it is not uncommon for vets with PTSD to be exposed to seemingly harmless events or sensory cues, and yet respond in a way that causes concern for them and their families. It is often their inappropriate or unexplained responses to this re-experiencing phenomenon that makes the vets (and those around them) feel they are "going crazy!" They usually explain their unusual responses in a way that "kinda makes sense" to them, but in reality neither they nor those around them really understand it.

Terrors during the night

Sleep does not bring freedom from their recollections of war. Many vets experience recurrent frightening, nightmarish-type dreams. When they first returned, the nightmares often occurred every night or even several times every night. The dreams were so frightening that veterans would either drink themselves to sleep or would avoid sleep altogether for fear of having the dreams. Many vets find themselves unable to sleep at night, but prefer to sleep during the day because they find they are bothered by fewer nightmares then.

As time goes on, the nightmares often become less frequent, occurring weekly or monthly, but are still as frightening and disturbing as ever. Sometimes it is the same dream, sometimes several different dreams. Almost always, however, the dreams are of death or threat or horrors related to combat or the inability of the vets to appropriately respond to the perceived threat.

Often the dreams involve running away, being vulnerable to capture, getting shot, or being unable to respond to a threat ("because I can't move or my weapon won't fire"). Frequently the vets awaken from the dreams sweating, confused, frightened, heart pounding, and overwhelmed.

Sometimes, they no longer remember the content of their nightmares, but they still wake up drenched in sweat and feeling scared and confused. Their spouses or bedmates tell them they yell or scream and often thrash about in their sleep. The bedmates might say the vets mumbled or yelled commands such as "down—fire—watch out—be quiet—oh, my God," or someone's name. Their thrashing or physical movements during sleep are quite vigorous, and some vets have told me they occasionally even fall off the bed.

Generally upon awakening from their sleep, whether or not they remember the dreams they were having, the vets will find they are drenched with sweat and have trouble catching their breath. Their hearts are racing and often they are confused or disoriented.

"Walking point" and "checking the perimeter"

Frequently on arising from the bad dreams, the vets will, without thinking, "get up and check the perimeter." They will check the hallways or the windows or the doors, checking the perimeter of their home just as they checked the perimeter of their area in the war zone. If their spouse asks them to explain this checking, they will say, "Oh, I heard a noise outside and went to see what it was." In reality, though, the vets really don't understand the checking—it occurs automatically and unconsciously. This "checking" is actually a symptom of hyper-vigilance (described later) but is so frequently associated with awakening from nightmares that it is also mentioned here.

Many vets find that when they awaken in such as state it can take hours to fall back to sleep—if they do so at all. Often after checking the house, they will go to their *special place.* For some it might be the garage or a special room they retire to. Many find that, at that point, they can no longer retire to bed, preferring instead to sleep in a reclining chair, where they feel they can "respond more quickly to any threat" if they need to. Because of the troublesome experiences during sleep, many spouses choose to sleep in another room or bed from the vets. Many tell me they have been kicked or hit by the thrashing of the vets during sleep.

> *"I once awakened in the middle of the night choking my wife. In the dream she was a Vietnam soldier, but in reality it was my wife. I was so horrified—I would never hurt my wife, but there I was choking her."* ~ *Vietnam vet*

For most vets with PTSD, the time to go to sleep is almost always accompanied by anxiety, fear, and dread because of the symptoms just mentioned. The inability to sleep leads to fatigue and inability to function at work or school. In some cases, it can progress to severe sleep deprivation, which can itself create serious psychological disturbances.

SYMPTOM CATEGORY 2:

AVOIDANCE, OR EFFORTS TO AVOID REMINDERS OF THE TRAUMA

This second cluster of PTSD symptoms is known as avoidance of stimuli (events, people, or activities) associated with the traumatic experiences. Avoidance may include any or all of the following symptoms:

- Efforts to avoid thoughts, feelings, and conversations associated with the traumatic stressors, as well as activities, places, or people that remind them of the traumatic events

- Feelings of emotional detachment

- A narrow range of emotions felt or expressed—usually limited to anger, depression, or numbness—a range of emotional affect that is restricted to primarily these emotional responses

- A sense of a foreshortened future—the belief that something bad is going to happen to them or their loved ones, something so bad that it will prematurely shorten their lives

- Trouble remembering details of the traumatic stressors

Not talking about it

Often vets avoid talking or even thinking about the war. Many of the vets I see have never talked to anyone—not their spouses, family members, friends, even other vets—about their combat-related experiences. Some may have spoken with another vet briefly, but the emotional response was so intense that they stopped and from that point avoided any further conversation. For them, even talking to other vets could provoke flashbacks, nightmares, or mood changes.

Vets are often required to talk to medical or other personnel at the VA, military facility, or civilian agencies, but many find that even clinical experience provokes thoughts and feelings that are so painful they avoid further visits, delaying or preventing needed treatment. Currently, an increasingly dominant trend has developed in which warriors mark false answers on their PTSD screening questionnaires. They hope that by denying any and all symptoms, they can avoid being subjected to further questioning about their traumatic experiences.

Not acknowledging experiences or medals

Even at home they may avoid anything that they associate with their stressors. Not only do they avoid talking to their spouses, but also they avoid talking to anyone in their families about their experiences. One vet told me:

> "My grandson had a project at his elementary school where they had to discuss someone who had fought in the military. He found out that I had been in Vietnam and had received the Purple Heart. He wanted me to talk to his little class about my HEROISM, but, Doc, I couldn't go. I couldn't even talk to a group of elementary kids—friends of my grandson, who was proud of his granddad. I didn't want to talk to them—or anyone—about that time in my life."

This former war hero was still avoiding any reencounter with this part of his past, almost four decades later. He had placed his medals and awards in a shoebox that he kept hidden in his closet—a box he hoped would not be opened during his lifetime. The implications of this are profound, ironic, and saddening. It was as though this vet had spent the better part of his life engaged in an effort to relegate this part of his existence to an early death. In his book, *Back from War*, Lt. Lee Alley, a recognized war hero, described his experience in a fashion similar to the vet just mentioned.

Not remembering

Although it often goes unrecognized as avoidance, one common avoidant symptom is the veteran's *inability to remember* things about the event. Many vets lament that they cannot remember the name of someone who served with them or who was killed in combat. Others can't remember a particular detail about a place, a battle, or an event that occurred. Their failure to recall those things distresses them, or as one Vietnam vet said, "It weighs heavily on my mind." What they don't understand is that the inability to recall those things is part of the avoidance symptom common in PTSD.

Avoidance includes more than just not talking about their experiences. Many vets avoid activities, places, or people that bring back recollections of their war experiences. They may stay away from Vietnamese or Middle Eastern people or restaurants serving that kind of food. They avoid VFW halls and even television shows or movies about war in general or about the war or region in which they fought.

Support is not enough to overcome avoidance

I always ask the Vietnam vets about participation in any of the vet organizations, such as the Veterans of Foreign Wars (VFW), American Legion, or Disabled American Veterans (DAV). These were common gathering places for WWII vets, but most of the Vietnam vets said they were uncomfortable in those places; although many joined, few went regularly. A number of Vietnam-era vets have explained to me that they went to one or more of the old-line veterans organizations when they first returned home. Sadly, many said they felt unwelcomed there by older vets at the time.

It must be remembered that in the years during and immediately after Vietnam, many WWII veterans, who would be very elderly or deceased today, were, back then, still in the prime of their middle years. They and their comrades from the Korean War were very active in these veterans organizations. However, numerous Vietnam veterans related to me that much prejudice toward them existed on the part of the veterans of older conflicts. Some actually reported being told by older veterans that they had "not fought in a real war, but only in a conflict, and one which they had lost, anyhow."

Fortunately, that attitude has now changed, and some Vietnam vets are now going to meetings of such vets groups. Many find the DAV to be particularly helpful in "giving tips on how to navigate the VA system." And, as we discuss later in the book, a new generation of veterans organizations has arisen. Unfortunately, however, the mere existence of supportive organizations does not alone suffice to combat the overwhelming urge to avoid any mention of traumatic events.

Markedly diminished interest

Vets with PTSD may suffer a form of avoidance known as *markedly diminished interest and participation in significant activities.* The significant activities they avoid often involve crowds—especially crowds of people unknown to them. Even more confusing to the vets and their families, however, they also avoid activities involving family or close friends—birthdays and weddings, school activities and children's games, holiday get-togethers, and family reunions. As mentioned in Chapter One, their refusal to attend special events in the lives of their families—even those involving their children—confuses and hurts family members. Relatives often misinterpret this lack of socialization. They think, "Dad or Grandpa doesn't care about me and what I'm involved in (my graduation, my coronation, my debut, bar mitzvah, etc.)."

The vets avoid them because of the uncomfortable feelings of anxiety or anger the events provoke, but family members think the vets are being obstinate or are just "loners." Even if the vets do go to the events, they usually isolate themselves. Many vets have told me, "I go because I have to go, but I'll leave as soon as I can. Often my wife and family have to find another ride home." If they do stay at the event, they often tell me, "It's like my body is present, but my mind is not there—I just zone out." If they don't leave, the discomfort becomes unbearable.

Emotional detachment

Veterans with PTSD often feel emotionally detached from others. This, too, is a form of stimulus avoidance. Rather than being aimed at the avoidance of a specific recollection, however, it is aimed at the general avoidance of life in general. Warriors constantly complain to Chaplain P and me that they can't experience true intimacy or closeness, even with those they love the most—spouses, kids, family members, or friends. One vet said that when he returned from Afghanistan, he didn't even tell his family he was coming home because he didn't want a welcome-home party or get-together. Another said his mom told him upon his return that he had "changed . . . was different . . . was a loner—a hermit."

Restricted range of affect

Yet another variety of PTSD-connected avoidance is something for which we have a fancy clinical name, *a restricted range of emotional affect*. "Affect" is a word that means one's ability to experience and express feelings. When a person's range of affect is restricted, it means one of two things. First, it means that they may experience a variety of feelings but can't experience any of them fully . . . like living life unable to get past emotional first gear. The second, and very common meaning, is that they can experience only some types of feelings and not others. In the case of returning warriors, this usually means that they can experience only a part of what human beings ought to be able to feel emotionally.

Both Chaplain P and I talk almost every day to vets who tell us they have a lot of trouble experiencing positive emotions—joy, satisfaction, closeness, intimacy, and love—but they readily experience negative emotions—anger, depression, isolation, and irritability. They don't laugh at good jokes like they did before the war, and they often have trouble feeling sadness, but they easily and often experience anger, irritability, depression, and emotional pain. Many feel guilty if they sense themselves beginning to feel positive emotions, and suppress them.

Others tell us that part of the reason they don't experience the range of feelings they once had is because they have lost interest in previously enjoyed activities that generated those feelings. So they no longer like being with spouse or family and don't feel the joy that came with that. Or they can't get into watching comedy on TV, so they no longer experience the laughter that came with that. Many drop out of church or synagogue, and no longer feel the sense of peace or inspiration that came with that, and so on. Some will say they have trouble experiencing feelings at all. They describe it as being "numb or distant or detached." In fact, many say that if it weren't for anger, they would feel little or nothing at all.

> *You know, before I went to Iraq, I was a normal kid. In high school, I had friends, liked to go out, and liked to dance or enjoy a party. But when I came back from the Middle East, I was different. I was a loner and didn't want to be around others unless I was drinking."*

This restricted range of emotions can interfere with intimacy with their spouses. Many vets reveal that their interest in sex is diminished or absent. After all, how can you enjoy sex if you can't feel? That's what it's all about—feeling, not just physically but also emotionally. But Chaplain P and I hear constantly from military wives who mistakenly assume that they aren't desirable any more.

We must constantly explain that the problem usually has nothing to do with that. It has to do with the fact that women, in particular, tend to experience sex as a combined physical and emotional experience. The two are a combined package that can't be separated, by and large. So even in situations where a returning warrior is willing to have sexual intercourse, it may seem vacant or empty or meaningless if his female partner senses that he is engaging only in the physical side of sex, without the emotional input. "It's like robot sex," one wife told me, as she wished for the old days of emotional closeness that used to accompany physical lovemaking.

Sense of foreshortened future

Another fairly common symptom of avoidance is technically called *a sense of a foreshortened future*. In everyday terms, it's like regularly having negative premonitions. Often it's a vague sense that "something bad is going to happen to me or my family" or that "I know my life is going to end too soon—I just don't know how or when." Recently, a vet recently returned from the Middle East had this to say to Chaplain P:

> *"In a split second, I knew I had stepped on a pressure plate IED. It was totally terrifying. I looked around me, wondering where the son of a bitch was who was waiting to detonate me to kingdom come. The blast never came. The bomb was a dud. I still live with it — why did 5000 other guys get blown, while I survived? What are the odds? I'll never be that lucky again. I've lived for a long time feeling sure that something really bad is just around the corner, as if my life is just waiting to implode." ~ Middle East vet*

The avoidant part of the phenomenon of foreshortened future may be felt indirectly or as an outgrowth of the things a vet no longer does in response to the feeling. For example, as a result of this sense of a foreshortened future, many vets avoid driving in certain situations or going to specific places. Although many say they know it is "crazy" to have these negative premonitions, they feel powerless to make them go away. Often the sense of a foreshortened future involves thoughts or feelings about what might happen to their family members. The vets tell me, "I don't care what happens to me, but I worry about what's going to happen to my wife or children."

Another form of avoidance may present as a dropping out of memory for details of a traumatic event. In contrast to the person who has post-traumatic recall in excruciating detail, many people find that they cannot remember the details of their traumatic event. This often leads to a feeling of confusion between what is reality and what is not. "Did this really happen? Surely, if it happened, wouldn't I remember?" many vets say. They do not realize that this type of avoidance is the result of a natural process of *triage*, through which the brain seeks to avoid mental overload. Areas of the midbrain will focus intently on the most critical, survival-based issues and push extraneous or unnecessary detail to the side. The fine details may not actually be overlooked or forgotten but, rather, may be archived in an area of the brain that is below the level of conscious awareness.

Denying new information

Finally, avoidance sometimes comes packaged in the simple refusal to accept new incoming information. It's as if the veteran doesn't want any more "intel." Most Vietnam vets avoid the news on TV about the Iraq/Afghanistan war now being fought. It's too painful "to think about what I know is happening to those kids over there," it brings back too many flashback experiences, or "it makes me too upset and angry." If the news happens to come on the TV unexpectedly, the vets commonly say they leave the room to avoid it. An exception to this seems to occur with vets who have buddies still in Iraq and Afghanistan, and whose welfare is still a serious concern.

Even many Middle East vets avoid the war coverage because of the emotional effect it has on them. Most are "proud of the job our guys are doing over there" but are frustrated by how the war is being covered in the media. ("They always show the negative things, but never the positive things our troops are accomplishing over there.") For many Middle East vets the frustration is because "we are still over there, and I don't see the point."

Some of the Vietnam vets, although proud of the job being done in the present war, have a sense of frustration about the way the present Middle East vets are being recognized by the American people. They recall the negative way they were treated by civilians, while noting (sometimes with envy) the positive response of the public toward the Middle East vets. Many Vietnam vets have confided to me that "I feel guilty about being envious of those guys—after all, they deserve the respect and admiration of the public—it's just that *we never got the same recognition!*"

On the other hand, some vets feel comfort in watching events they can relate to. In those instances, several vets told me they "stay glued to the TV" even though the news upset them.

SYMPTOM CATEGORY 3:

DO YOU EXPERIENCE EXCESS OR HEIGHTENED SENSORY AROUSAL?

The third and final cluster of PTSD symptoms is called *increased arousal* and may involve one or more of the following:

- Difficulty going to sleep, staying asleep, or getting restful sleep (Note this is different than nightmares, which are in the cluster of re-experiencing.)

- Irritability or outbursts of anger

- Exaggerated startle response

- Hypervigilance (e.g., always "watching your back" or a loved one's or buddy's back)

- Difficulty with concentration

When you read Chapter Three, you will gain a good working understanding of how the human stress response works. Increased arousal plays an important role in this process at both ends, so to speak. This is because arousal propels the stress response into action (at the front end) and is also a continuing result, or byproduct, of the stress response (at the back end).

In this section on symptoms of arousal, it will be sufficient for the reader to understand that one of two branches of the central nervous system—the sympathetic nervous system—is the part that controls a person's responses to extreme stress. After one or more incidents of stress that are traumatic (in other words, perceived as life-threatening), this system may become supercharged. By that, we mean that it stays turned on even when it doesn't need to be, even long after the threat has passed. In military terms, this part of your brain is like a soldier who continues to walk point long after the war is over and the shooting has stopped.

Sleep disorder and arousal

You are probably saying to yourself, "Didn't he just talk about sleep disorder already?" Well, yes, in part, but not in full. Earlier, we discussed the way in which night terror events occur during sleep. Now, we will address sleep disorder as a symptom of PTSD in its own right. You see, sometimes, one symptom of PTSD is connected to another. Sleep disorder (or the chronic inability either to get to sleep, stay asleep, or get restful sleep) is one of those three-in-one special conditions. It is (1) a result of other symptoms, (2) a cause of still other symptoms, and (3) a symptom on its own. For example, nightmares (another symptom) cause sleep interruption or sleep phobia (fear of going to sleep—the result). Sleep interruption or deprivation can cause depression, daytime fatigue, or even hallucinations. And finally, the inability to sleep is a PTSD symptom all on its own, related to elevated levels of certain neurochemicals.

One thing connects to another, and on and on. Most of the vets complain that without medications (or alcohol/drugs), they rarely sleep the whole night through. As mentioned previously, many experience repeated nightmares and frequent frightening awakenings. As a result, they often fear or dread even going to sleep—a condition known as sleep phobia. They sometimes avoid sleeping at night, attempting instead to sleep during the daytime hours. If they do sleep at night, they tend to keep a light on in the room because they feel safer than they do in the dark. Many choose to sleep sitting up in a recliner chair because they imagine they can "come to" more easily if there is a "threat" while they're sleeping. Sleep is usually described as "fitful" and almost never results in feeling rested upon arising.

Rarely do the vets get anywhere close to eight hours of restful sleep, and I have talked to many for whom three to five hours of sleep (usually disturbed by waking up several times) is the norm. Vets with PTSD may toss and turn for hours before they are finally able to drift into sleep. They often awaken frequently during the night and find it difficult to go back to sleep. Many mumble, talk, or yell during sleep. Often the mumbling can't be understood, but sometimes the vets might yell a name or orders or "Watch out—get out of the way!" Many kick or thrash about in their sleep, often resulting in their partner choosing to sleep in another room.

Long-term implications of sleep deprivation due to arousal

Losing sleep over a prolonged period of days, weeks, or years has enormous health consequences, which reinforce the reality that PTSD is a real medical illness, with real medical consequences. Short-term consequences include impaired function and concentration, as well as fatigue. These can really impair performance on the job and even result in the inability to maintain employment if not corrected. Long-term sleep deprivation can give rise to severe psychiatric symptoms, including altered mental status and hallucinations, as well as stress symptoms such as inflammatory responses, elevations in blood sugar, and hypertensive symptoms.

A common result of prolonged sleep deprivation in vets is depression. This is because the neurochemicals manufactured in the body, which are our natural antidepressants (including serotonin), are made only during a particular phase of sleep. If your hyperaroused state causes you to awaken often, you are not likely reaching the point in your sleep cycle where this occurs, and your natural supply will drop, causing the onset of depressive-appearing symptoms.

Although nightmares, per se, are part of the *re-experiencing* cluster of PTSD symptoms, the impairment of effective sleep is thought to be part of the *increased arousal* cluster. Though they are often related and always bothersome, they are believed to be caused by two different biological phenomena. It is possible to have trouble getting enough restful sleep even without ever having nightmares, although they usually go together. It is now believed that treatment for re-occurring nightmares, on the one hand, and treatment for the lack of restful sleep, on the other, may be different.

Irritability and anger ("going postal")

Irritability and outbursts of anger are some of the most common symptoms of increased arousal. The anger is frequently unpredictable and difficult to control. It may seem to come from nowhere and often causes severe and repeated problems with relationships, jobs, and even the law. These vets explain that they were somehow changed by their experiences in combat, and, although they may try to control the anger, often they feel helpless to do so, or they find the amount of emotional energy required to do so overwhelming.

Anger and irritability, often totally unexpected and without apparent provocation, have led to divorces for many. Even if spouses put up with their irritability and anger, the relationships usually suffer as a result. The irritability and anger of PTSD-suffering vets may be especially difficult for children to handle. Often children blame themselves for angering their parents. Frequently, children rebel as they grow up, and often the anger (as well as detachment and lack of intimacy) results in the grown children wanting to have nothing to do with the vets.

Anger and irritability also affect performance in the workplace. In fact, many vets are unable to work effectively at their jobs because of their anger. As mentioned in Chapter One, many Vietnam vets got jobs at the post office. The problem with anger in those working for the postal service is legendary.

Fortunately, in the past it was difficult to fire workers at the post office, and many of the supervisors had anger issues as well. Thus, many Vietnam vets working at the post office kept their jobs (often for many years) but admit to me, "If I had worked anywhere besides the post office, I would have been canned a long time ago."

Most vets with workplace anger issues have been counseled, and many have been through repeated anger management courses, which usually don't work well unless the underlying PTSD disorder is addressed. Many try desperately to control their anger. They may learn techniques like waiting, counting, breathing deeply, talking to themselves, or others.

Sometimes they can control it at work, but most find it harder to do so at home. Even in those instances where vets control the anger on the job, the work environment can be difficult, and the home environment—well, *tough,* for family members and vets alike. Most vets are perturbed and perplexed by their anger, but feel, for the most part, helpless to do much about it.

As they think back, most vets say they noticed the anger after returning from the combat deployment. For some their "fuse is too short," that is, they react too quickly. For others their "explosions are too big," that is, they overreact to even minor provocation. Often it is that "people don't listen, or take things serious enough, or don't follow the rules, or don't show proper respect." For all however, their anger is usually a problem.

For some Vietnam vets, the anger has persisted for years, and has been directed at events that occurred decades ago. Such was the case for one vet I evaluated who told me:

> *"Doc, I am so angry at something that happened over 30 years ago,"* said the large, muscular, Hispanic vet. *"In 1977, do you know what happened? That was the year the President of the US pardoned all those who ran off to Canada to avoid the draft."* The anger in his face was apparent, but quickly changed to sadness. Tears filled his eyes and rolled down his cheeks as he continued, *"And you know what? The public treated those returning draft dodgers like* HEROES. *We were treated with hatred, and they were worshipped!!!"*

Cognitive (thinking) impairment

Impaired concentration, another symptom that falls under arousal difficulties, can range from simple things—like forgetting a name, phone number, or directions—to serious problems—like forgetting to pick up the children from school. Of course, there are many possible causes of lack of concentration, but for vets with PTSD, this symptom can be due to preoccupation (often unconscious) with thoughts from deployment. After a while, the vets may no longer be aware of this preoccupation and only know that they cannot seem to focus, think, concentrate, or remember.

Recent theories concerning impaired concentration and memory involve problems with the hippocampus (the part of the brain controlling ongoing memory functioning) being damaged by the original stressors. The confusing part about this memory problem is that the vets have "too good a memory" for re-experiencing the stressor-related events and yet great difficulty in remembering what they are supposed to do next. This apparent disconnect of past memory and present memory often confuses the vets' families. They believe the vets must be "not paying attention to what I just asked him to do" since his memory is "too good for the traumatic events that happened a long time ago."

Startle response

A symptom of arousal well known to vets involved in combat is an exaggerated startle response. They jump at such things as loud noises, unexpected sounds, or even a casual touch. Vets commonly report that gunshots, the backfiring of cars, and the sound of fireworks around the Fourth of July cause this inappropriate startle response. Other startle-provoking sounds include the unexpected sounds of people yelling or a loud siren or bell. These sounds often cause the vets to "jump" or even at times to "hit the ground."

Some of the veterans who work at the post office say that some of their fellow workers used to drop something to make a loud noise "just to see me jump." The fellow workers thought it was funny to watch what they considered weird behavior (vets falling to the ground or crawling under a table), failing to understand the behavior is part of the PTSD symptom complex. Over the years, this *hit the ground* startle response may be replaced by a less severe response to unexpected events, but the vets still flinch or respond in an exaggerated way to unexpected sensory experiences.

In addition, often people coming up from behind the veteran who has PTSD will cause a heightened startle response. Many of the vets have told me, "My wife and kids and grandkids know not to startle me, not to come up and touch me when I don't expect it. They know better than to shake me to wake me up—I could come out swinging if I'm startled like that." As many of the Vietnam vets age, they don't hear as well, making them even more vulnerable to becoming startled by those unexpectedly coming up from behind them.

> *"You know, Doc, one time my little grandson—he couldn't have been more than three or four—came up from behind me and put his hands over my eyes, you know, like little kids do. I wasn't expecting it, and I'm so ashamed, but, Doc, without thinking at all about it, I took my arm and flung him across the room into the wall. I could have killed him. Thank G-d I didn't hurt him. He, of course, didn't understand, and I'll never forget the look of terror in his eyes as he looked back at me after hitting his head on that wall. I was just startled, and reacted without thinking. I've never forgiven myself for that."* ~ Vietnam veteran

"Watching your back": hypervigilance

Another of the arousal symptoms, *hypervigilance,* keeps the vets constantly vigilant and "on guard." It certainly made sense in the jungles of Vietnam or the deserts of Iraq or Afghanistan, but this continuing hypervigilance becomes a problem when it is no longer useful or even desired. The symptoms of hypervigilance make it very hard for the Vietnam vets to ever fully relax, except, perhaps if they are chemically altered—either intoxicated or stoned. Their emotional motors are always running. They are always "keyed up and on edge."

Those in the combat arena, especially those in Operation Iraqi Freedom and Operation Enduring Freedom, have been taught to be keenly observant, to look for anything that might be out of place—a broken-down car, a piece of trash, or a rock on the side of the road might be loaded with explosives. In large crowds of people, a suicide bomber may be hiding and unseen until it is too late. It makes sense for the soldier in combat to be vigilant, maybe even hypervigilant. However, it makes little sense in the middle of a city in America.

As a result of this vigilance, many vets have a difficult time in Target or Wal-Mart, at a parade or a celebration, a crowded mall—or anywhere a large group of people are gathered. An Iraqi vet told me:

95

> *"Doc, I'm one of the luckiest guys around. I was driving down the freeway the other day, and on the side of the road was this old broken down jalopy. I guess it was there the whole time, but I didn't see it. I was driving, had the air on, and the radio blaring. All of a sudden I saw this car, and without thinking or looking in the rearview mirror, I hit the wheel and swerved two lanes over to avoid that car, which in Iraq might have been loaded with explosives. The reason I'm so lucky is that if there had been cars coming in those two lanes next to me, I would have been dead."* ~ *Middle East vet*

This type of response as a result of extreme hypervigilance is repeated often by those suffering from PTSD. They are suspicious of those around them, especially those they don't know. As for being in crowds—as one Vietnam vet said, "Forget about that." The clearest example of this phenomenon is illustrated in the example I gave in the Introduction to this book and that is also shown in the box on the next page.

> *I ask, "If you go to a restaurant with many open tables and the hostess says, 'Sit at whichever table you choose,' where do you generally sit?"*
>
> *Most people without PTSD will have a favorite table— it might be a booth, a table in the middle or on the right or left; however, for most it doesn't matter that much where they sit.*
>
> *But without hesitation, vets with PTSD almost always say, "I sit in the back of the room, at a corner table with my back to the wall so I can see everything that's happening."*
>
> *In actuality they sit with their back to the wall so that no one comes up behind them unexpectedly. They never give their back to anyone. This one answer is so typical that it is almost diagnostic of PTSD, hence the title of this book.*

Many vets with PTSD tell me that in addition to avoiding crowds, they have also become "security nuts." They check and recheck the doors and windows and locks of their houses. They respond to any unexpected sounds, especially at night. Upon awakening to the slightest noise, they frequently will "walk the perimeter" around their house night after night, even though they have never found anything that was really menacing! They often sleep with a weapon (unless their families or physicians take it away from them). They often purchase elaborate security systems. One Middle East vet said, "Doc, I live in a virtual prison—iron gates all around the perimeter, bars on the windows, extra locks on the doors, and a security system that won't quit. Yet I still don't feel safe." The lack of confidence in the security around them is the result of the vets' PTSD.

CHAPLAIN P:

The stories told to me by the many veterans I have worked with are amazingly similar to the ones that Dr. C has related so very well. Among the warriors I have seen are not only the armed combatants, but also unarmed non-combatants, such as Army photographers and military chaplains who have repeatedly gone downrange, and who have returned with PTSD just as severe as those involved in combat. These men and women demonstrate consummate bravery through their willingness to remain embedded with their troops—often traveling outside the wire with them—despite the fact that they are obligated to remain unarmed and are therefore exposed to high levels of physical danger. They are in the same combat zones, experience the same degree of shelling, and are exposed to the same horrific sights, sounds, and smells as the men and women they care for.

I have sat for many hours and listened to them ventilate their pain through the telling of their stories. They perform many acts of unselfish dedication, not only in providing desperately needed spiritual and emotional care, but in doing gruesome tasks like gathering body parts and headless corpses in the aftermath of battle. Or they may have had to document war fatalities in grisly detail. In addition to all that they themselves suffer, some non-combatants bear the additional responsibility of keeping it together so that they can continue to be the caregivers for others. But almost no one is there to care for them.

> *"I came back from the Gulf more than 20 years ago. But I still have the same nightmare, about some poor sailor who came too close to an aircraft prop on a carrier deck and got decapitated. I was sent to take the forensic photos, and I still see them in my mind as if it were yesterday. I thought that to get PTSD, you had to get shot or something. They never told me that something like this could cause it."* ~ *Gulf War Army photographer*

I make special mention of this because, in the midst of the many stories of combat and battle, we may forget that there are millions of stories left untold by those who were not engaged in combat, and yet were terribly traumatized by their service experiences. Few people seem interested in their stories which, in my opinion, speak of unsung valor and commitment to service as great as that demonstrated by any combat warrior.

Because this book is especially focused on the experiences of warriors and their families, it is also important to remember that families who are left behind when a loved one goes to war are themselves extremely vulnerable to developing either posttraumatic stress syndrome or full-blown PTSD. The levels of anxiety that they experience are very acute, and their helplessness to control the situations in which they find themselves is often equally great. However, as we'll examine in later chapters, their situations, as well as their traumas, often go unnoticed. And their symptoms tend to be of a much more silent, withdrawn, and internalized sort.

Explanatory Note to Readers: The list and variety of PTSD symptoms can be confusing. Vets often ask, "Do I have to have ALL of these before I am considered to have PTSD?" The answer is "no." Whether someone meets the diagnostic standards for the disorder isn't just a matter of the number of symptoms he or she has, but is also the particular way in which the symptoms are distributed among the three categories we have mentioned (e.g., symptoms of re-experience, avoidance, and heightened sensory arousal). So you may have PTSD even if you don't suffer from every symptom I have described. You might then ask, "What about the person who has lots of symptoms, but not in all the *right* categories? Does this mean they he or she isn't affected by traumatic stress?" The answer to that question is also "no." Even if the assortment of symptoms from which you suffer doesn't meet the criteria for a diagnosis of PTSD, you may be suffering from another traumatic stress-related dysfunction or disorder, such as Acute Stress Syndrome or others. These can become progressively worse and have serious implications for your health and well-being; they should receive attention, care, and proper treatment. In addition, since the exact symptoms necessary for the medical diagnosis of PTSD may change with the new edition of DSM V, we refer you to mybacktothewall.com for the precise and up-to-date symptoms of PTSD.

Chaplain P giving a graphic demonstration
of the energy surge often experienced during traumatic events

CHAPTER THREE:

Connecting Biology to Your Psychology

"The man in civilian clothes approached me after my lecture. With moist eyes and a drawn face, he identified himself to me by handing me his calling card. Scanning the card, my eyes took immediate note of the high rank at which the man had retired, the doctoral degree and professional licenses behind the name, and most of all, the high position he had held in the mental health treatment field. This man, charged with the responsibility of directing the mental health treatment of others, had never begun to heal himself. 'I was a caregiver, but there was no one to whom I could turn to for my own care,' he said. 'So I just shut my mouth and said nothing and suffered with it. Until today, I never understood what was going on with me. If only I had known before . . . how different my life and that of my entire family would have been. But I'm grateful to at least know I'm not crazy . . .'"

CHAPLAIN P:

The faces of the veterans and soldiers whom I have trained are all different; the combat patches are all different; the insignia they wear are of every rank. After the lecture, there are always three or four who approach the lectern for a private word. Even though they are strangers, there is something about their faces that always speaks volumes to me of their traumatic past. I am happy to make time for them.

Surprisingly, the words they say to me are almost always identical. The sentence always begins with the words: "If only I had known . . ." They are almost always uttered with the feeling of initial remorse that comes over a person who has suddenly realized how much of his or her suffering was unnecessary or might have been prevented through a better understanding of his or her own illness. But soon after the remorse usually comes an audible sigh of relief, and often a relieved smile. It is the laying down of a burden by one who, at last, knows he really *isn't* crazy . . . he just has a *real* medical illness.

UNDERSTANDING PTSD AS A BIOLOGICAL PROBLEM

DR. C AND CHAPLAIN P:

For many years, PTSD was not discussed in our society. Now, by contrast, PTSD is discussed so often that it has become the subject of common stereotypes, some of which are incorrect. Typically, those stereotypes characterize PTSD as a strictly behavioral problem, rather than a medical illness with *both* a psychological and a biological root. For over two-and-a-half decades, the attitude taken by many in the military has been (1) that PTSD-related behaviors are caused by distorted thought patterns, (2) that these thought patterns are "irrational," and (3) that these behaviors are under the conscious control of the vet and can be changed or reset, like a button, if vets exercise sufficient will to simply change their ways of thinking.

Often, this notion of PTSD was emphasized in programs of soldier education that were thought to be "progressive" means through which traumatic stress could be prevented, by showing warriors slide shows about maintaining a "strong mindset" or by supposedly inoculating them in advance of combat by displaying pictures of dead or wounded bodies, or even trips through local morgues so that soldiers could get used to death and somehow not acquire PTSD.

These approaches, unfortunately, were based on oversimplified and inaccurate views of the disorder and failed to meet their objectives. Despite the fact that they went through such preventative programs, more soldiers than ever developed PTSD. Those who did were made to feel that they had either lost their mental faculties or had somehow morally failed to control their behavior. It was a terribly stigmatizing way of addressing the problem, and one that to this day continues to drive people away from treatment for PTSD.

Change has been needed, and slow in coming. Since the initiation of the wars in Afghanistan and Iraq, both society and the military have gradually moved toward removal of the stigma of PTSD, which had for so long placed warriors in fear for their military careers and which served to obstruct treatment instead of support it. Unfortunately, despite these well-intentioned efforts, not much has changed. Rather than be told by a military mental health provider that they need to "change" their PTSD-connected thoughts and behaviors, most soldiers simply opt to give false answers on the many so-called clipboard PTSD screening checklists that they are administered.

The underlying approaches to treatment continue to be based upon the notion that PTSD-connected problems are primarily an issue of the soldier's *behavior,* rather than the central nervous system stress responses that actually form the root of the illness.

This book seeks to shed a new light on PTSD, which is likely to communicate a message that differs from those which the reader may have previously heard. Our message is simply this:

- PTSD is a psycho-neuro-endocrine disorder. This means that PTSD is, at the same time, both a psychological and biological condition that has behavioral, emotional, and medical consequences.

- The stress reactions caused by PTSD are rooted not merely in the perceptions of the mind, but also in biological processes in the brain, the central nervous system, and the endocrine (or hormone) system, which are involuntary, automatically initiated, and not generally under the individuals' conscious control.

- The development of PTSD is not a moral failing. It affects individuals of all backgrounds, degrees of education, socio-economic levels, and military rank.

- Although the observable symptoms of PTSD are psychological and behavioral, its underlying causes are *physiological.* Therefore, as with any medical illness, anyone who suffers from PTSD should feel entitled to seek treatment for it, without shame or embarrassment.

This chapter is designed to provide you and your loved ones with a simplified explanation of the biological connections between PTSD and the kinds of thoughts, feelings, behaviors, and physical symptoms suffered by people who have it. It will also help you to understand that PTSD, like other physical illnesses, can have both immediate and long-term physical effects. Many of these are rarely discussed and can be very serious if not properly treated. We hope that this information will help to better the lives of many individuals, by removing shame, expanding knowledge, and encouraging them to seek treatment.

WHY MEDICAL ASPECTS OF PTSD ARE OVERLOOKED

DR. C:

My more than forty years of medical practice, including more than thirty years as a research psychiatrist, have left me with a deep and abiding commitment to the concept of treating the whole individual. And treatment of the whole individual requires the recognition of the whole illness. PTSD is no exception to this principle.

Much of Western medicine has become increasingly mechanistic in its approach. By that, I mean that it tends to view the body as a machine, which is "fixed" with drugs, procedures, or surgery. But the human organism is more complex than just the things we can see or splint or suture. Bodily processes, thinking processes, and emotional states of being all travel in a never-ending circular relationship in which each part influences the others in ways that cannot be separated.

Unfortunately, the ways in which modern physicians and healthcare providers are educated, licensed to practice, and paid for their services encourage segregation and specialization, often at the expense of cooperation and collaboration. Western modes of medical practice often operate to artificially separate those things which in real human beings *are not separable.*

According to Western models, we have doctors to deal with physical illnesses, which are supposedly visible or measurable. And we have doctors to deal with emotional illnesses, which are supposedly invisible and less susceptible to direct measurement. Both kinds of sickness are understood to be absolutely real. But the practitioners who deal with each kind of problem often do not communicate with one another, because neither is usually trained to deal with the other's territory. Too often, practitioners of physical and behavioral medicine act as though they each, respectively, have control over a different medical kingdom. We must do a better job of recognizing that human beings are greater than the sum of the parts into which we try to artificially divide them for purposes of medical convenience.

Most psychologists and many psychiatrists are well trained to deal with the emotional pain of the individual but spend very little time considering the physiological (or biological) dimensions of emotional problems. And on the other side of the coin, most general medicine doctors are focused only on the physical. With only a few minutes to spend with a patient, they have neither the time nor the training to listen to the patient talk about emotional or psychological factors that may actually underlie their problem.

PTSD is in a unique class of disorders, because it is psychological and neurobiological at the same time. But the dual nature of the illness became misunderstood from the start. Unfortunately, the psychological aspects of the illness were the first to be identified, long before any extensive research was done into its underlying physical causes. So early on, PTSD became regarded in medicine as a purely psychological disorder.

As a result, the people who became the spokespersons about PTSD were most often the psychologists and psychotherapists and some psychologically oriented psychiatrists. Because the medical aspects of PTSD had not been widely understood or advertised, it was common for doctors to continue operating upon the presumption that PTSD should fall strictly within the province of psychologically oriented psychiatry and mental health. The physical—chemical and neurological—aspects of the illness became overlooked.

Over time, these attitudes within the medical profession fueled negative public perceptions of PTSD. They reinforced the idea that the illness was something that existed "in your head" and not in the body as well. In Western culture, psychological illnesses are often misperceived as either imaginary or as failings or weaknesses in the person, whereas only physical illnesses are perceived as "real."

Fortunately, these misperceived notions are slowly changing. It has only been within the last fifteen years that the discipline known as psycho-neuro-endocrinology has developed. The researchers in this field combine principles of psychiatry and psychology with those of neurology, neurochemistry, and endo-crinology (the study of the hormonal and immune system).

In my opinion, if psycho-neuro-endocrinology had existed when PTSD first became identified as a disorder, then its biological causes might have become more properly clarified many years ago. If this had been the case, PTSD sufferers might have been recognized as a group of individuals suffering from a bona fide medical illness and would probably have been met with greater understanding than they presently are. Instead, many vets assumed that they didn't have a "real" (e.g., bio-physical) illness. They thought that what they were experi-encing was imaginary or "all in their heads" or the result of personal weakness or cowardice. Understandably, they did not want to come forward and reveal their condition for fear that they would be shamed or rejected by society, their community, and the military.

CHAPLAIN P:

Today, thankfully, our knowledge is much broader. We can, and must, acknowledge that PTSD is in a class of disorders that are connected to neuro-chemical changes and imbalances in the body, as well as to perceptions in the mind. To help spread this important knowledge, this chapter is designed to provide a medically accurate but very simplified explanation of the biological processes involved in PTSD, written in a way that everyone can understand. We believe the key to relieving your-self of the false belief that PTSD is "all in your head" is helping you to realize that, in fact, PTSD is largely "in your brain."

IF PTSD IS A PHYSICAL PROBLEM, WHERE IS IT LOCATED IN THE BODY?

DR. C:

PTSD is not like a physical wound site that occupies a distinct space on or in the body. Instead, it is a process of reactions and responses that originate in the brain, are communicated through chemical messengers (neurotransmitters and stress hormones) throughout the central nervous system, and eventually come to involve virtually all parts of the body. The part of the brain that is most closely associated with stress responses involved in PTSD is known as the limbic system. Located deep in the midsection of the brain, the limbic system is an ancient area that houses the survival mechanisms that became well developed in human beings long before civilized society came into existence. It contains three principal structures that regulate emotion, behavior, long-term memory, and smell. We'll talk more about these structures and the jobs they perform later in this chapter.

While the neocortex (at the top of your brain) is busy handling complex intellectual and reasoning activities, the limbic system takes care of a much more basic and essential function: the job of protecting our bodies and our survival in times of acute stress, danger, or threat. In addition, the limbic system regulates the way that our bodies try to swing back to normal, in other words, to a state of balance, after our coping mechanisms have been overwhelmed.

The limbic system: home to the stress and alarm response

The limbic system, deep in the midbrain, contains a horn-shaped structure called the hippocampus, which is a center for our long-term recollection about things we've experienced as we go through life. It's one of several memory systems in the human body, but it has special importance where survival is concerned. That is because it specializes in housing our *long-term* memory about events to which we attach special importance. Some of the most important of these memories are associated with threats to our survival.

Different memory systems in the brain handle different "assignments." For example, some memory systems specialize in the handling of short-term memories, like your ability to remember the kind of "to-do list" that most people mentally compile in their heads at the beginning of each day. These types of memories fade away quickly, in order to make room for new information, such as the next day's list. By contrast, the hippocampus is reluctant to give up any part of its "stash" of information. It tenaciously holds onto its storehouse of important, survival-connected information almost indefinitely. So when you experience something of special significance in combat, during some aspect of your military service, or in some other aspect of your life, the memory gets stored *in the hippocampus*. And it is stored with an amazing amount of detail and emotions associated with it. In time some of the detail decreases, but the emotions that go along with the memories sometimes increase.

Also, contained in the limbic system, and connected to the hippocampus, are the amygdalae. These are two, small, almond-shaped lobes, one at either end of the hippocampus, on both the left and right sides of the brain. The amygdalae may be small, but they exert a great big impact on your life. For starters, they act as interpreters or analysts of information that is stored and recalled in the hippocampus, as well as things we see, hear, smell, touch, or taste that might be threatening in our immediate environment. They are especially alert to analyzing experiences that have emotional importance to us, such as events or stimuli that are terrifying, frightening, noxious, or disgusting.

Not surprisingly then, the amygdalae also play a critical role in our sense of smell. Smell is not only important to us for emotional reasons (we all know the distinctive smell of our mothers from birth, and later, of our children, loved ones, and sexual partners), but it is also one of the most essential senses through which we detect danger. Even in our language, we refer to recognizing a dangerous situation because "it just didn't smell right" to us.

Think of how many times you avoid eating or drinking something that might be rotten, spoiled, or poisonous to your system just because your sense of smell alerted you to the fact that something about it wasn't right. Well, thank your limbic system for saving you from food poisoning—that is your amygdalae at work. Similarly, people who survive serious traumas almost always have intense memories of the smells associated with those dangers or threatening experiences. Vets can always tell you the special smells that trigger them the most. The smell of rain, dirt, human waste, burning trash, blood, and death are often mentioned by vets, but there are many smells that trigger memories. That too is because your amygdalae are especially sensitive to such smells and act on them virtually instantaneously. But smell is not the only thing the amygdalae clue in on—sights, movements, feelings on the skin, and other senses are used to discover things around us that are potentially dangerous to us.

The amygdalae are also responsible for setting into motion the processes creating anxiety. When things don't smell right—or when they smell (sound or look) like danger—we experience the state known as anxiety. The amygdalae create the anxiety based on sensory input *before* the neocortex (the thinking brain) has a chance to analyze whether the threat is real or not. In an emergency situation, we have to react quickly to get out of danger. Even if later it becomes clear that the sensory information was not what we thought it to be (i.e., the movement we thought we saw was not the enemy, but a branch moving in the wind), our bodies have responded quickly enough to hopefully prevent us from experiencing helplessness in the face of danger. The body makes a habit of relying upon this information and errs on the side of being "safe," rather than "sorry." Safety is more important than accuracy.

PTSD is a disorder of anxiety, in which we become overly anxious about our survival. So your amygdalae are like a dual-edged sword. They are connected to saving your life—an undoubtedly helpful thing—but also can make your life miserable by creating the anxiety and alarm that help create PTSD.

Our last stop on this very simplified tour of the limbic system includes the hypothalamus. The hypothalamus is an amazing and mysterious organ with many vital functions. Its location places it at the center of a major intersection in the brain, where it stands sort of like an omnipotent traffic cop in the middle of a complicated expressway interchange, directing brain signaling in two different directions. It is the connecting mechanism, which funnels signals *upward* to the thinking and reasoning parts of the brain. Equally important, it also serves as a sort of master control center for signals that flow *downward* in our central nervous system, and which regulate some really important things, including digestion, cardiovascular function, breathing, temperature regulation, sexual responses, and last but not least, defensive mechanisms.

The hypothalamus acts as a control center for the endocrine (hormone) system. Like a chief emergency dispatcher in a crisis, it sends out directions to glands throughout the body, telling them about which hormones are most needed—where, when, and in what amounts. These hormones determine how your bodily parts and organs respond to the crisis.

So, if you are a veteran who survived a traumatic event, it is largely because your hypothalamus was able to act on information supplied to it from the hippocampus and amygdalae. Your hypothalamus directed your hormonal system to send chemicals to various parts of your body so those parts could function in whatever way was best adapted to ensure your survival. In this way, the hypothalamus has special effects upon our behavior when we are endangered. So for example, when you "hit the deck" whenever you hear a Huey fly up from behind a tree line, you are acting on chemical signals sent by the hypothalamus.

Other parts in the brain are also involved in survival-based stress responses and PTSD, but their functions are too complex to include in this book. It is enough to say that certain areas, for example, keep track of the amount of stress and chaos that is occurring outside your body and help to ensure that this is accurately detected inside your body. Still other structures are responsible for acting like filters, which, in a time of crisis, tune out information that isn't absolutely critical to the survival experience.

The coordinated dance through which these portions of the brain communicate and cooperate in an effort to save the human being is one of the most complex and miraculous occurrences in nature. For most of us these processes are very beneficial. And if you are a veteran reading this book, your brain's responses are what kept you alive, so that you could have the experience of doing so.

"UPSTAIRS/DOWNSTAIRS: YOUR BRAIN AS AN OFFICE BUILDING©"[1]

CHAPLAIN P:

Now that Dr. C has given you the physician's medical description of the parts of the brain that are involved in trauma, I'll take a turn

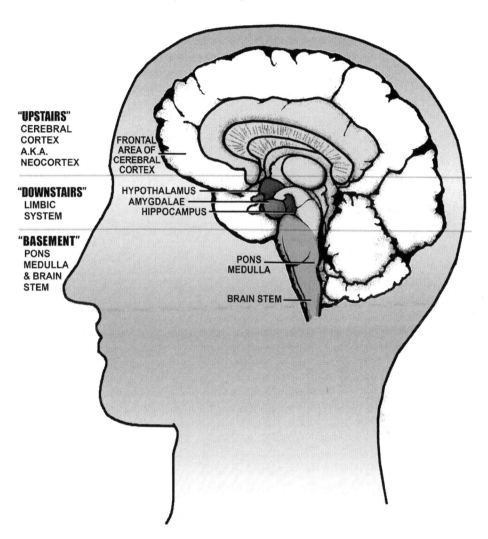

"UPSTAIRS"
CEREBRAL
CORTEX
A.K.A.
NEOCORTEX

FRONTAL
AREA OF
CEREBRAL
CORTEX

"DOWNSTAIRS"
LIMBIC
SYSTEM

HYPOTHALAMUS
AMYGDALAE
HIPPOCAMPUS

"BASEMENT"
PONS
MEDULLA
& BRAIN
STEM

PONS
MEDULLA

BRAIN STEM

at this complex topic from my standpoint as a therapist. I try to give people a simple and concrete approach to understanding the stress response, in a way that makes sense and that they can remember and even explain to their families. I created a model for thinking about PTSD that I call *Upstairs/Downstairs*. It compares your brain to a corporation located in an office building. If you can remember what goes on in an office building, you will easily be able to understand what happens in the brain during a stress response. For purposes of this example, let's tour a fictional company, The Acme Insurance Company, and its offices located in downtown Chicago. (Remember that the same model can apply, using the Headquarters building of a military command in place of an insurance building. Every veteran knows where the command suite is versus the offices where the subordinates and the "underlings" are . . . I use the "Headquarters" analogy when teaching soldiers and officers.)

1. UPSTAIRS (a.k.a. the Neocortex): The most intellectual, rational, and sophisticated thinker in the company is its leader, the CEO. Like the upstairs part of your brain, the CEO runs the company, makes the important decisions, and pretty much drives the train most of the time. The CEO's biggest problem, however, is that he gets bogged down in complex issues, and this means he can be slow to make a decision about what to do. His other problem is that he often doesn't have all the information needed because some of the most important files are stored in the records department, located downstairs and below the level of conscious awareness. As smart as he undoubtedly is, the CEO makes decisions too slowly in times of crisis and often finds himself without the needed information to make rapid-fire, life saving decisions.

2. DOWNSTAIRS (a.k.a. the Limbic System): To deal with problems that the CEO is too slow to handle, the company has hired a special crisis management team, whose offices are downstairs in the building. The company's crisis team takes over responsibility from the CEO when the chips are down and when lightning-fast decisions affecting life and death need to be made. The members of the team are:

(a) The Records Manager (a.k.a. the Hippocampus): He's the keeper of the company archives, which are stored on a non-erasable hard drive that contains the records of virtually everything that is important to the company's survival, especially information about old threats the company has already run across. He stores these records so that they are immediately available to refer to if danger should present itself again. In fact, the Records Manager can search for and locate old information about a threat or a crisis in only a few thousandths of a second. The whole task is completed before the CEO even knows it ever occurred. This is one reason that you may react to something before you have a chance to think about it. Once the Records Manager has information about a threat, he will pass it on to the company's Risk Manager for analysis.

(b) The Risk Manager (a.k.a. the Amygdalae): Based on the extensive information that's been passed on to her about past experiences, the Risk Manager instantly analyzes the crisis and evaluates whether it poses a serious danger or a lethal threat. The Risk Manager pays a lot of attention to what has happened before. If something presented a threat in the past, it will most likely be considered to be a threat in the present. If so, the Risk Manager sounds the alarm to alert the Crisis Dispatcher.

(c) The Crisis Dispatcher (a.k.a. the Hypothalamus): He is like the company SWAT team leader. His job is to take the information that the Records Manager and Risk Manager provide and use it to almost instantly create a response plan that will avoid danger or overcome threats. The Dispatcher operates at lightning speed and handles crises by deciding what chemicals need to be used in the team's response to different crises. He ensures that the right chemical supplies are delivered to all parts of the company within just a few seconds, guaranteeing a swift reaction to the crisis. This, of course, happens so rapidly that the CEO doesn't even have the time to interfere with, or slow down, the process. The chemicals used by the Crisis Dispatcher are like those that stream through your body in a time of crisis, enabling all your body parts and systems to respond appropriately.

3. BASEMENT (a.k.a. Pons Medulla and Brainstem): In the brain, the basement is occupied by the pons medulla and the brainstem. Surrounded by the thickest part of the braincase, just above the spinal cord, these structures occupy the protective "bunker" of the brain. Nature has placed them there for good reason, because their functions are so vital to the survival of the "building" that is the body. Things like water, building temperature, hydraulic pressure, and plumbing are constantly monitored here, so that others in the company don't waste precious seconds thinking about them. Maintenance Man may be the most primitive guy in the company, but what he does is so basic to everyone else's ability to function that he is widely admired and appreciated. (I like to think of him as being like the janitor in my old elementary school—kept the place running through thick and thin, not very sophisticated, but very important. After all, what the principal did or didn't do wasn't of much consequence if the physical plant wasn't running.)

In your brain, problems are handled in ways very similar to the way they are handled in the Acme Insurance Company:

(1) Information about old problems is quickly accessed;

(2) the brain's old solutions are stored and often repeated and applied to new problems, for better or worse;

(3) functions are delegated to the parts of the brain that can respond the fastest during a crisis; and

(4) the internal response to crisis occurs so quickly that it happens without your conscious awareness. In other words, you literally react without thinking.

WHEN STRESS RESPONSE BECOMES STRESS DISORDER

As you can see from our respective explanations of the stress/alarm response, nature has equipped us with some remarkable mechanisms to help ensure our survival. These responses are far more complex than can be detailed in this book. It is enough, however, for the warriors and family members who are reading this book to understand that these responses are to a large extent *physically dictated* in the brain and central nervous system. They are related to our most basic, hardwired biological needs to survive and are *not* simply imaginary alterations in behavior.

The alarm response that we've described is known medically as the *hypothalamic-pituitary-adrenocortical axis (HPA axis)*. It's the biological response pattern that saves your life and ordinarily serves a very positive, helpful, and adaptive purpose. The HPA axis doesn't just function in times of trauma. It is on duty continually throughout life. It houses the alarm system that sets off mechanisms through which your body copes with countless stressors in your environment. And after your body gets thrown off balance by stress or trauma, this system works to return your biological systems to a balance point called homeostasis. Your body seeks to maintain a certain *set point* that is normal for you, much like the idle at which a car engine is set. It does this through a complex set of interactions between many body systems such as

- Your cardiovascular system (heart rate and blood pressure);

- Your respiratory system (breathing and oxygenation of blood);

- Your endocrine system, including the adrenal glands sitting atop your kidneys (hormones that control many things, including your glucose and protein production, fluid balances, sexual response, sleep and waking cycles, cellular repair, and weight regulation); and

- Your immune system (which controls inflammation and response to infection).

"So how is it," people ask me, "that something intended to *save* your life winds up making life miserable for people with PTSD?" It's a very good question! How is it that a process that starts out being so *adaptive* can actually become *maladaptive*? The answer lies in our brain's capacity for three things: *reflex, habituation, and generalization.*

REFLEX: One reason the brain can handle lots of complex processes at once is because it knows how to multitask. It doesn't have to learn everything from scratch every time. While some parts of the brain are busy dealing with new information that you have to consciously think about, other parts of the brain are equipped to handle ongoing business without any conscious thought at all. We call these responses *reflexive*, and they are controlled by the *autonomic nervous system*. Think *autonomous*, something that acts on its own without direction.

The HPA axis, or stress response, described in this chapter is controlled by the autonomic nervous system. In a life-threatening crisis, this is a great advantage. Your body knows how to react to danger without the need to consciously think about it. The downside of the situation, however, is that once the danger is passed, you may be in situations where you want and need to exert control over your reactions and can't do so. That is because, in addition to autonomic control, the brain learns to habituate, or react by habit.

HABITUATION: The brain learns its lessons well, and it stores experiences for future reference. Once the brain learns about a particular threat and has orchestrated a successful response to that threat, it flags that information and keeps it handy, thereby cutting down on its response time in the event the threat should present itself again—i.e., the response plan is already mapped ahead of time. As a result, the default response occurs more and more rapidly.

Now, think of what happens when you learn how to drive between your home and your office, and you always want to get there faster.

What do you do? You learn a shortcut. The brain does the same thing. Once the brain has been exposed to *several* traumatic incidents that are alike, or alternatively, to a single incident that is "retriggered" *several times*, a shortcut is learned. The amygdalae (the Risk Managers) may react and sound the stress alarm independently, without waiting for the hippocampus to check things out again in the records department. This means that every time a stressor is encountered, there is an increasing likelihood that the brain will respond just the way it did before. Sometimes this is lifesaving, as when a soldier learns to avoid incoming fire over and over again. But sometimes, it is not helpful. Habituation may cause the brain to react to new problems with old solutions that aren't appropriate anymore. That is because, when confronted with external stressors, the brain learns to *generalize*.

GENERALIZATION: In situations where survival is at stake, the brain reacts to stressors without examining *the context*, or circumstances, in which they occur. Reactions to things that *originally occur in a threatening context* may *continue to occur in a non-threatening context*. For example, if your survival has been threatened by gunfire, your brain quickly learns to associate the crack of an incoming round with anything that makes a similar sound. The sound is called an *external cue*, commonly referred to as a *trigger*. The brain may remember a trigger but not take surrounding circumstances, or context, into account.

So, for example, the brain will generalize the threat of gunfire to all things that make a similar, sharp crack. But "sharp cracks" might also include fireworks on the Fourth of July, the cracking of hardwood floors, the slamming of a door, the sound of someone cracking walnuts, or even something as harmless as a breaking tree branch. Pretty soon, vets may realize they are reacting to every cracking noise that comes their way, whether it is threatening or not. That is because the stress response to the trigger occurs by force of habit and has been generalized to many other things or situations, including those that are not harmful at all. And because the response is reflexive, the vet often lacks conscious control and, quite literally, reacts without thinking, whether danger is present or not.

Thinking about the biology of PTSD requires that we resist the temptation to impose judgments on stress responses that categorize them as "right" or "wrong." Remember that "right" and "wrong" are *cognitive and moral concepts*—the kind of complex ideas that live upstairs in the CEO's office. Remember that the folks downstairs are not concerned with social rules. They are only concerned with keeping you alive.

So, a better way of thinking about PTSD from a biological standpoint is to examine whether your responses are *adaptive* or *maladaptive*. Adaptive responses serve their purpose both effectively and appropriately, e.g., they go far enough, but not too far. Maladaptive responses, on the other hand, aren't appropriate. They go too far. So for example, if the only time you respond to triggering stimuli (e.g., sights, sounds, feelings, smells) is when you are *actually* in danger, then your responses are *adaptive*. These reactions are appropriate and are exactly what the military trains warriors to do. If they did not react in this way, many would be dead. On the other hand, you need to become aware if you are either

(1) reacting to triggers as if you are in mortal danger, even in situations that are not actually dangerous at all, or

(2) constantly mistaking harmless stimuli in your environment for dangerous ones.

When either of these two kinds of reactions occurs and you begin to overreact, your responses are no longer appropriate to the context, or circumstances. This is what makes them maladaptive.

PTSD is kind of like having a home burglar alarm system that constantly goes off, sounding alarms that are false but that still cause the police to come running. The overactive alarm system is triggered by the amygdalae, which may sound false alarms because it perceives danger that is no longer really there. The brain's development of a continuous, habituated pattern of responses to danger that *was originally perceived during a past event, but which no longer actually exists in the present* is the basis of what we call Posttraumatic Stress Disorder, or PTSD.

FIGHT, FLIGHT, AND FREEZE: IDENTIFYING YOUR BODY'S LIFE-SAVING RESPONSES TO TERROR AND THREAT

So far, we've talked about the ways in which different lobes of the brain react, almost instantaneously, to create a coordinated response by the body to terror, fright, and threat to survival. But what are these responses? In general, scientists have emphasized two major reflexive behaviors that occur in response to trauma. We have come to know these as *fight* and *flight*. My work in PTSD has been especially focused on the identification and analysis of a third reflexive response, known as the *freeze* response.

Each of these three response patterns has a very important job to do. Despite the importance of each of them, however, the three primal responses have all become somewhat stereotyped and clouded by misunderstandings. Some of these lead to unnecessary shame or self-blame. In this section, we hope to clarify some of these misconceptions and provide information that will help you, the trauma survivor, understand more about the responses that your own body may have employed to keep you alive.

Fight responses are often thought of as always involving soldiers or people who are engaged in some sort of aggression or combat, leading to the idea that a person who has a fight response is inherently aggressive or antisocial. But that is not strictly the case. Fight reactions can, of course, involve some kind of physical battle, but they also include many other kinds of behaviors, situations, and types of people. For example, fighting is not limited to hand-to-hand or close contact encounters. One can fight at a distance, by firing a weapon or throwing an object or building an obstacle to the enemy.

Some fight responses are reactions to a threatening situation rather than a threatening person. An example is the behavior of people buried under earthquake rubble. In such situations, people might fight through the use of their voices by screaming or yelling, by climbing over/under/through obstacles, or by digging their way out of buildings. Fight responses don't necessarily imply that a person is socially aggressive or a persistent troublemaker, under normal circumstances. Some of the greatest war fighters I know are "special ops" warriors who may be, under normal circumstances, very gentle and well-controlled individuals.

In fact, aggression may not even be part of the picture of a fight response. For example, for firefighters, medics, and first responders, lifting heavy objects with a sudden burst of superhuman strength when coming to the aid of another person can be a form of fight response. To minimize misunderstanding about this response, I do not use the word *aggression*. Instead, I prefer to explain fight responses as behaviors that are (1) physically active and that (2) involve the recruitment of large muscle groups, thereby (3) allowing the body to respond in a way that *outwardly engages* a source of danger or threat.

Flight responses are equally misunderstood, and sometimes get a bad rap. Just as fight responses are mistakenly thought to always be aggressive, flight responses are often incorrectly perceived as involving cowardice, such as when one flees the scene of an accident. But that is simply not the case. A flight response is simply a behavior that is (1) a reactive response (2) that involves the recruitment of large muscle groups, but does so in a way intended to (3) evade or avoid an enemy or threat.

It may involve staging a strategic retreat or running away from an oncoming threat in order to escape it. It can also include behaviors that don't involve running at all, like ducking an incoming round, sidestepping an obstacle, or taking cover. Many of these flight responses don't involve leaving the scene, such as when one remains involved in close combat, but moves to avoid taking fire. In many cases, fight and flight responses can, and often do, occur together. Soldiers alternate between fight and flight every few seconds when they are in combat.

Freeze responses may be the most misunderstood of all. The word *freeze* is really a misnomer. Many people think of freezing as involving shock and fear, like a deer caught in the headlights of an oncoming car. Others think of it as being connected to cowardice or incompetence, as when one doesn't know how to handle an emergency. Neither is necessarily true at all. First, freeze responses are just as purposeful as fight or flight. The only difference is that instead of involving movement, freeze reactions are static (stationary) rather than active. In other words, freeze responses help to save your life in situations where moving around might get you killed.

The word *static* in this context doesn't necessarily mean that one is motionless like a statue, although in some situations that is true. It also includes situations in which *staying quiet or still, minimizing or refraining from physical movement, is the most protective behavioral response. It also usually means that in order to refrain from moving, one must stay in the midst of the trauma instead of escaping it.* This is certainly not cowardice, but its exact opposite.

There are many times when refraining from movement is the right thing to do to save your life or someone else's. For example, women with young children who are trapped in a traumatic situation will most often freeze; in other words, they will immobilize and stay in the midst of the trauma in order to avoid abandoning a vulnerable child.

In combat, there are countless situations in which warriors must immobilize because moving might give away their position. For example, Army snipers are highly trained so that freezing and holding still becomes second nature to them in order to hide from the enemy. If warriors are ambushed, they may likewise need to immobilize and hide. Freezing is also the primary response of young children, who hide and hold still when in the presence of an adult enemy. Those who work with abused children who must hide from abusive parents know that this is the case.

Freezing is a lifesaving response for people whose brains tell them that fighting or fleeing will be futile because they are outgunned, outweighed, or overpowered, and that remaining still and conserving their energy for a later time, when the odds are in their favor, is the better part of valor. Women who experience rape or other forms of sexual assault must often adopt a freeze response, because they are outsized, outweighed, and overpowered by their attackers. An attempt to overcome the perpetrator by brute force is usually futile and can create more physical trauma and injury than it avoids.

I have spoken to a number of soldiers who have a somewhat unique experience of the freeze response. Because of their repeated experiences with explosive ordnance, including IEDs, they may freeze in response to the non-event, e.g., the bomb blast that *doesn't* happen. In most instances, these soldiers have stepped on a pressure plate IED or other ordnance that just happened to be either a decoy or for some other reason failed to detonate. This experience can be intensely terrifying. The silence that they actually experience (in contrast to the explosion that they expect) becomes deafening in its own way. These soldiers may actually become highly reactive to situations in which things are *not* happening. They feel as though they are walking on eggshells, waiting for the other shoe to drop. Because they sense that they have somehow "cheated death," they perceive the fact that they are alive as being against all odds. As a result, they believe their luck cannot possibly hold out and live life in terror, on the edge of an imaginary precipice that they believe they are doomed to fall over as soon as their luck runs out.

Another little-recognized group of trauma survivors who must freeze are medical patients who experience fearful and traumatic treatment that requires that they be placed in restraints or are otherwise *medically forbidden to move* because it would disturb their wounds, skin grafts, sutures, IV lines, etc. Finally, freezing must be adopted by those who are *physically, psychologically, or relationally entrapped,* such as prisoners, abduction victims, or victims of chronic domestic battering and abuse. These are people who know that any movement on their part might result in severe retaliation, injury, or death.

Thus, to freeze *does not mean* that one fails to respond. On the contrary, freezing is an entirely legitimate response in many situations.

It is simply static, rather than active. It is designed to protect the body in circumstances when movement might expose it to further danger. It is also nature's way of slowing the body's metabolism down, as a way of conserving energy and resources in a situation where food or water may be in short supply or cut off. Finally, freezing is an effective way of immobilizing someone who needs to stay put for the benefit of someone else. Not surprisingly, people who are professional caregivers for others, such as doctors, nurses, medics, and chaplains, often adopt a type of freeze response because it is the most *adaptive* response for them. It helps ensure that they will stick around to take care of others who depend on them for care, rather than take flight.

Examining your body's choice of responses

Understanding why you behave the way you do *today* may make more sense if you examine how circumstances forced you to behave *in the past*. If, years ago, you were in close combat situations in which you were required to take both offensive and evasive action many times in order to stay alive, you are likely to have depended heavily upon fight-or-flight responses. Do you see these kinds of responses recurring in your present life? In relationships with loved ones, do you go on the offensive? Do you "shoot first and ask questions later?" Do you lob verbal "grenades" at others and then stage a retreat to the bedroom or garage to avoid return fire? Do you throw the first punch so you won't get caught off guard in an argument, pack your bags and leave, or go ballistic and take off in the car or on your motorcycle when something irritates you? If so, you may still be relying on fight-or-flight responses.

By contrast, there are many people—including very courageous human beings—who have relied on freeze responses to survive in times of war or extreme crisis. They may still default to these behaviors in the present day. These are people whose survival depended upon *what they did not do*. In fact, their survival may have hinged upon their doing absolutely nothing. That is a lesson that can stick in the brain and get recycled thousands of times.

A powerful example of the importance of freezing is found in a story I was told by the daughter of a World War II war hero. Her father was very detached and unfeeling, and his family never understood why he was so unexpressive. They assumed it was because he was unloving, but this was not actually the case. A little investigation revealed that when the father was a young man, he was part of a platoon that was overrun by the Germans, who first shot and then bayoneted all the Americans to ensure they were dead. The woman's father managed to stay alive by playing dead so convincingly that he remained totally motionless even when he was bayoneted. His lifelong pattern of playing dead emotionally was a throwback to the defensive responses of his youth, when he froze and remained motionless in order to stay alive.

For some people, military service is not their first experience of the freeze response. The response may have originated in early life or childhood, particularly when they were much smaller, entrapped, or helpless because of age or gender. Even though years have passed and their bodies have become much larger, their brains still identify with, and resort to, the survival patterns established many years before. Some female soldiers who have been sexually assaulted or abused by a domineering father have told me that they experience a freeze response when an aggressive military drill instructor (DI) gets in their face. Yet they rarely draw the connection between how they reacted to their fathers and how they react to the DI.

Do you see yourself coping with life today through inaction rather than action? Do family members complain that you won't take steps to help yourself or that you are not proactive or that when problems occur, you do nothing and simply avoid them? Do you feel yourself freeze up when you are under stress, as though you have stage fright in the theater of life? Do you suddenly clam up and lose your ability to advocate for yourself? Do you freeze and stay put out of a sense of duty to others? It's possible that your past life includes situations in which you have had to freeze in order to survive or get by and that you are still doing so today.

If you keep a diary of your responses *now*, and compare them against responses that you adopted *then* in order to survive earlier traumas, you are likely to see a pattern. Patterns of response learned during early life traumas, when our brains and nervous systems are most impressionable, are often seen to repeat themselves in later life.

Taking a careful and thoughtful look at what you've been through and how you've survived it can yield many helpful clues. Knowing in advance which responses you are likely to default to in present day situations can help you be more conscious and predictive of your actions and reactions and can help your loved ones adapt more effectively to your behaviors.

Relating physical symptoms to behavioral patterns in PTSD

In addition to the *behavioral* response patterns of fight, flight, and freeze, there are actual *physical* symptoms of PTSD that tend to accompany each dominant pattern. Many years ago, I began examining whether connections existed between (1) the type of traumatic events that a person has experienced, (2) the PTSD-type behaviors they display, and (3) the physical symptoms that they experience. In the course of doing observation and follow-up with several hundred patients, I observed some interesting patterns emerging.

First, I observed that "fight/flight" behaviors appeared to be associated with *high rates* of energy expenditure in the body (sometimes referred to as an *up-regulated stress response*). This kind of response is tailor-made to encourage movement of large muscle groups that are used in fighting or escaping. So it was not surprising to me that the people who displayed up-regulated physical symptoms were also the people who tended to be more physically active and aggressive, not only in the original event, but whenever they would get retriggered or re-experience an event.

Second, I observed that "freeze" behaviors appeared to be associated with a *low rate* of energy expenditure (sometimes referred to as a *down-regulated stress response*). These were the patients who looked different than the stereotypical image of a PTSD sufferer. They would often present with low vital signs and other physical symptoms associated with the slowing down of the body's "energy engine," or metabolism. They would also often report secondary symptoms such as increasing levels of sugar and fat, water retention, and inflammatory responses. They were often lethargic and fatigued. Although these symptoms were highly unpleasant, they appeared to be very *adaptive*. In other words, they made sense from the standpoint of a human body that was striving to "slow down its engine" and conserve its energy supplies in order to adapt to or cope with a situation from which the body could neither fight nor flee.

Now, down-regulated stress responses have been identified by medical science for many years. So I wondered: why had they not been connected to PTSD? The down-regulated patients I worked with met all of the criteria Dr. C has explained; all of them qualified for, and actually received, a diagnosis of PTSD due to their *psychological* symptoms. But physically, they just didn't present like the hyperactive and aggressive warriors I had always heard about. I was interested in learning whether there was any particular type of traumatic experience or history that seemed to go along with these people, most of whom were women or people who had been abused as children. I knew, of course, that traumatic responses are the result of many complex social, environmental, and genetic influences. To my surprise, however, I found that *in general*, the people whose biological presentation was down-regulated were those whose traumatic histories involved being in some way trapped or restrained (this might be physical, psychological, relational, or even occupational) or who needed to remain immobilized to protect themselves or others.

"In general" is an important phrase to keep in mind; most of the patients whom I followed adhered generally to one pattern or another. But they didn't always necessarily adhere to a pattern in every single respect, and there are some patients who are exceptions and appear to combine both patterns. But two general patterns continued to emerge. To help explain what each looked like, I created two fictional characters who serve as models of each general type. I call one "Locked and Loaded" and the other "Hunkered in the Bunker."

Because so many of the warriors I have worked with clearly saw their own situations reflected in these characters, some soldiers actually worked with me to craft an image of each general pattern, which they themselves saw reflected in their own life experiences. Chaplain (CPT) Stephen Dicks, a talented cartoonist, undertook to bring these characters to life, and his drawings are the result. Let's take a quick look.

"Locked and Loaded"

Locked and Loaded (L&L) can be a person of either gender, but is mostly likely to be a teenaged or adult male who responds to threats by expending energy outward. L&L recruits large muscle groups that are needed for the behaviors that ensure his survival, including fighting or running or both. He tends to be Locked and Loaded for more rapid, explosive response. Here is what you are most likely to see, generally, in the L&L who suffers from PTSD.

First, he has enough metabolic energy to power his muscle masses in fighting or fleeing. He usually experiences a rapid pounding heartbeat and increased cardiac output during stress, or perhaps even chronically. He leans more to the aggressive side and may be hypervigilant and ready to get the jump on external threats. Even after returning from combat, he may alienate his family by treating his home as an armed encampment. For example, he may continue to walk point in the middle of the night, or he may be ready to respond with deadly force in response to even the slightest noise, which may turn out to be a terrified wife. His endocrine system sends high levels of norepinephrine and dopamine into his bloodstream during stress. When he's not in combat anymore, he may miss this hormonal exhilaration and may try to seek it while engaging in risky activities, such as skydiving or extreme sports, extramarital affairs, or pornography, as these boost his dopamine levels.

Some L&L warriors are actually anxious to return to the combat theater so that they can regain this feeling of being intensely alive. It's common for an L&L to have a real problem with maintaining relationships, including marriages, due to irritability, aggressiveness, and an over-controlling nature. He may verbally or physically get in the face or personal space of other people in public. Or he may embarrass his children, family members, or himself with his exaggerated startle responses, such as when he "hits the deck" in a public place at the sound of a firecracker, helicopter, or other noise associated with combat.

A light-hearted demonstration of
"Locked and Loaded;"
soldier training,
Victory Base Camp, Iraq

"Locked and Loaded." 2010 Stephen L. Dicks. Printed with permission of the artist.

"Hunkered in the Bunker"

Hunkered in the Bunker (HIB) tends to slow down his engine now and save/store energy for the future. He adapts by surviving trauma over the long haul, which is very important in situations in which the battle can't be won or the traumatic stress overcome in the present moment. Whether male or female, HIB is most likely to be someone who was physically, situationally, or relationally entrapped in chronic, recurrent trauma as a child or adult. His facial expressions may appear flat, and he may be emotionally numb and avoidant to what's going on. HIB is often a pleaser, either because it's his nature, or because his job doesn't allow for whining or complaining. He gets people to go away by acting as if nothing is wrong, or nothing is a problem, even when it is.

Even if he is not presently entrapped in a physical sense, the HIB may be in a job situation that is overwhelming and that he cannot offload. Even if it's a job he loves, it may still feel like entrapment. Or *she* (many HIB's are women) may be entrapped in a relationship or abusive situation that cannot readily be escaped. Since he doesn't ventilate stress through outward physical actions like fighting or running, the HIB's stress becomes internalized like a pressure cooker. And since his response to traumatic situations is less physically active, his body becomes a storehouse for the sugars, fats, and water that serve like a personal energy pantry for the future. Sometimes, because he lacks a physical avenue of retreat, the HIB's only available escape is to check out mentally or emotionally. He is more likely to be withdrawn, reclusive, or avoidant.

"Hunkered In The Bunker" 2010, Stephen L. Dicks. Printed with permission of the artist.

Which, if either, of these are <u>you</u>? Or are you somewhere in between?

Both the Locked and Loaded and Hunkered in the Bunker patterns are *descriptive;* neither is intended to be *diagnostic.* Diagnosis is the function of your doctor or health provider. The chances are, however, that many readers of this book may see themselves reflected in one or the other of these general trends. So what should you do, if this is the case? I'll let Dr. C address that.

DR. C:

First, you should seek treatment. Physical symptoms of PTSD can be treated, and when they are, the psychological symptoms often improve significantly. Second, you absolutely should make your physical signs known to your doctor. (See Chapter Four for a list of signs and symptoms that a physician would want to be aware of.) Explain that you want to be evaluated as a whole patient—not just on the basis of your psychological symptoms, but your physical ones as well. After all, your physical stress responses are one very important cause of your PTSD, so it's vital that they be taken into consideration. This is especially true if your doctor proposes to give you medication. It's very important that the medication that you are given to address a *psychological* symptom be appropriate and not contra-indicated for your *physical* symptoms as well.

. . . And there's more to the story . . .

In addition, as a result of the mind and body changes coming from PTSD, there are a variety of additional conditions that may occur. These may include ongoing physical symptoms such as headaches, stomach and other gastrointestinal symptoms (nausea, indigestion, diarrhea), problems with the urological systems (frequent urination), sexual systems (decreased sex drive and desire, erectile dysfunction), neurological systems (dizziness), and many related symptoms. These may be caused by the same physiological responses that cause the PTSD symptoms we talked about, or they may be caused by changes in the mind and body as a result of suffering from PTSD for a prolonged time. All these symptoms may have real physiological causes related in some way to the PTSD.

ARE YOUR DOTS CONNECTING?

DR. C AND CHAPLAIN P:

This chapter has been devoted to providing you with basic information you need to understand that PTSD is a medical illness and to help you more easily recognize the ways in which it may affect you (or your loved one)—physically, emotionally, and behaviorally. We hope that a healthy conversation is beginning to take place between your biology and your psychology. For even more information on the biology of PTSD, we suggest you visit the My Back to the Wall website at www.mybacktothewall.com.

In the next chapter, we'll examine the questions: "So now what do I do with this information? Where do I go with it? How can I use it to help myself get better?" The answers to those questions have to do with *organizing a care plan* for the management of your PTSD. That's the "O" in R-E-C-O-V-E-R, the next phase of this book.

As a result of the fact that you have gotten this far in the book, you have acquired more information about PTSD, its symptoms, its diagnosis, and its biology than many mental health and medical professionals have received in the course of their training programs. We hope that you will take time to digest this information and reread information that may have been difficult to understand the first go round. We know that it is a lot of information to absorb, and you are to be congratulated for getting this far. So it may be time now to put the book down, head to the gym or track, or watch a good movie. When you are ready to learn about organizing a plan for improving your life, we'll be waiting for you.

Demonstrating "Hunkered in the Bunker;"
soldier training, Victory Base Camp, Iraq

CHAPTER FOUR:

Organizing A COMPREHENSIVE CARE PLAN FOR PTSD

"It's been 43 years since I went to Vietnam. In all the years since, I can't remember a single day that I wasn't filled with fear. Finally, I just figured that feeling fearful was just the way life was supposed to be." ~ Vietnam vet

BAD JUST ISN'T GOOD ENOUGH

DR. C:

Several months before the publication of this book, I made a decision to be interviewed on an early morning television show, during which I invited vets to call me if they wanted to get together in a very small group and just talk. Nothing more—just talk about their PTSD. I waited to see what would happen. To my surprise, several responded. During the next ten weeks, they met for ten hours over pizza and diet Coke and talked with Chaplain P about what it was like to return from the war, yet without feeling that they had ever really come home.

We learned a great deal from these good men and many other men (and women) like them. We learned that fear, terror, depression, flashbacks, anxiety, anger, and rage had been their daily companions. We learned that finding mental health care had been difficult for most and impossible for many. We learned that no one had ever explained to them that PTSD was a real medical illness or educated them about the specific process through which the disorder creates the symptoms they were suffering. And we learned that no one had ever educated them about these things in a way that reassured them they were not "crazy." In short, they did not understand the illness any better than they did the day they stepped off the plane on their journey back from combat.

We also confirmed our understanding that for many combat veterans, PTSD is not just about combat itself. Many military personnel who had undertaken treatment without success expressed the feeling that their issues were greatly impacted by their combat experience but had connections to other aspects of their lives (such as spirituality) and were therefore never understood. They attributed this, in part, to the fact that for many years, military and VA caregivers have only cared to inquire about whether a vet has (1) seen dead bodies or (2) fired one's weapon or received fire by the enemy. It was, and to an extent still is, presumed that in the absence of these, vets really shouldn't have anything to be traumatized about.

But for a very large proportion of the patients that both Chaplain P and I work with, traumas are not necessarily related to dead bodies or firefights. They are as likely to revolve around what has *not happened* as they are likely to be connected to what *has* happened. They frequently involve traumatic relationships, not just traumatic occurrences. They are present in the lives of military personnel serving every type of duty, and not just those who bear arms and go outside the wire or perimeter. They may not involve a single major event at all, but rather, a series of chronic or recurrent situations which may have continued over many years, or over an entire lifetime. Until recently, those who could not pinpoint the moment they were traumatized felt misunderstood and disenfranchised by the military or VA mental health treatment system. It is a hopeful sign that, just recently, the VA has changed its stance on this issue, at least to some extent.

Among those vets who were taking medication provided to them by the VA or some other source, few of them knew what the pills were intended to do or how to know whether or not they were getting any better. Although both the availability and variety of PTSD treatments have advanced considerably within the clinical community over the past forty years, the vets who have presented to me and to Chaplain P rarely report that they have experienced significant improvement in their symptoms. Despite the fact that both the Army and the VA have stepped up their treatment efforts considerably, these vets' past experiences with treatment had, for the most part, left them feeling helpless, suspicious, and reluctant to try again. Since they didn't know how their pills were supposed to affect them, they couldn't measure their experiences. So if they were taking a medicine that didn't work for them, they really had no way of knowing that. They simply assumed that however they felt was the way they were supposed to feel, even if that was lousy. They had, at some point, decided to do what most vets have always done—just "suck it up."

The fact that these vets were continuing to suffer through lives heavily burdened by PTSD, with little or no guidance about the wide variety of treatment options that could be explored, left me filled with sadness. I thought not only about them, but about all the family members whose lives had been needlessly affected. I became convinced of the importance of writing a chapter to help vets and families approach the seemingly overwhelming task of getting proper care and treatment so they wouldn't have to continue believing that feeling bad was ever "good enough."

"EMBRACING THE SUCK"

CHAPLAIN P:

My experience with vets who were struggling with PTSD has mirrored Dr. C's experience exactly. In clinical and pastoral practice, I learned from them what I could never have learned in a formal educational setting. I learned, in intimate detail, how pervasively PTSD had affected their lives. I learned that some had received no help at all before seeing me (which was often many years after their combat experiences), while others had previously seen as many as ten therapists and had experienced little improvement.

I learned that they were not likely to receive highly individualized approaches to their problems under existing systems, because this kind of care requires personal interface and attention and is therefore more time-consuming than governmental systems of care are usually able to offer. As a result, instead of receiving targeted care, many vets continued to receive "standardized therapies" that were basically mass-administered, in which the clinical provider was usually very insulated from the unique problems of each vet or soldier.

To the vets, it felt as if their concerns were too time-consuming; if a caregiver stopped to render personalized aid, it would hold up the line. This added to their loss of self-esteem and self-worth. I learned that billions of dollars were being thrown by the military and the VA at the problem, but that few seemed to recognize that dollars alone do not heal the human psyche. In short, I learned a lot about *what does not work.*

While my life was being changed by my personal, pastoral, and clinical relationships with hundreds of warriors, I was also preparing for deployment downrange at the invitation of the Central Command of the U. S. Forces–Iraq. While there, my partner Dr. (CH) Glenn Sammis and I were to undertake a mission in support of the Army Chaplaincy, through the standing up of the Spiritual Fitness Initiative, a pilot program that we had created to address trauma and PTSD in warriors using approaches that were spiritually framed and wellness focused, rather than pathology based. I read, watched, and otherwise absorbed everything I could about the circumstances of our soldiers in the Middle East since our troops entered Afghanistan after the terrorist attacks on 9-11. Among the books that I devoured on the subject was Benjamin Tupper's powerful war memoir, *Welcome to Afghanistan: Send More Ammo.* It impacted me greatly.

If I were to name one thing that Tupper described that became seared in my brain as a symbol for the experience of the troops, it was the soldiers' common use of the phrase "embrace the suck." This, he explained, had first become the informal motto of the courageous embedded training teams (ETTs) who served in Afghanistan. Day after day, these warriors would go out on their mission two by two into hazardous terrain teeming with enemy insurgents. Foregoing the protections that a larger force would have provided them, they carried out their mission to place themselves in harm's way in order to teach Afghani national fighters the art and science of hunting down and destroying the Taliban.

"The suck," as it came to be called, referred to any and all manner of pain, discomfort, and degradation to which these soldiers were subjected. As Tupper explained, soldiers had a choice. Each and every day, they could either succumb to the suck and become incapacitated or else embrace the suck and accomplish the mission. I saw immediately that embracing the suck involved simply resigning oneself to whatever was. This served the needs of the military mission, but over time it

worked to badly deteriorate the emotional, social, and spiritual foundations of soldiers.

And since these foundations are fundamental to long-term operational effectiveness, embracing the suck eventually operated to damage
that, as well. It did not make soldiers stronger; it only made them more
likely to become mental casualties of war.

As time went on, "the suck" took on a broader meaning for me, as
I applied it not only to active duty personnel, but also in the context of
the lives of the returned and retired soldiers with whom I was working.
It was, I decided, the best possible name for the indescribable stuff that
made its way into soldiers' lives, took the emotional life out of them,
and left them feeling hollow and, for the most part, empty of anything
but anger. It was what separated them from the more abundant life
they could be experiencing but weren't. I understood that embracing
the suck meant that warriors detached and resigned themselves to their
condition without attempting to change it, often because militarily
speaking, they were simply not at liberty to do so. But this affected the
way they lived for years after combat tours had ended. By embracing
the suck, they learned patterns of passive-aggression and learned helplessness. And they learned that just about the only good feeling was an
angry feeling.

While this situation might not seem dysfunctional in combat, it is
proving to have very damaging effects upon vets who have returned to
life from the war. Having learned to embrace the suck during combat,
countless vets have gone on to accept it as a condition of their daily lives
thereafter. Tupper wrote that he felt that his life was coming apart at
the seams and that he sought treatment for his PTSD, but few of his
combat buddies followed his example. Instead, they entered a state of
denial and helpless resignation. The fact that so many good men and
women who had sacrificed so much for their fellow Americans were
going through life thinking they had no option except to resign themselves to chronic PTSD made me frustrated, angry, and determined to
change things in any way I could.

Like Dr. C, I hope this chapter can serve as a guide in helping warriors seek and receive the care they deserve. For some, navigating that process must seem about as hazardous as going outside the wire. It shouldn't have to be that way. I encourage vets and their families to read this chapter and not only learn something about treatment, but become inspired to *seek it* and do what they can to manage their PTSD in partnership with their providers. With some sound advice and a modest investment in their own care, I believe that veterans can quit embracing the suck, and start embracing life.

STEP ONE: DECIDING TO SEEK TREATMENT

DR. C:

Treatment is not one thing, but many. It can include medication, psychotherapy, or counseling, and also one of the many adjunct (i.e., additional) therapies that have proven benefits to body and mind. Treatment may be provided not just by one person, but also by several. Individuals with PTSD may receive part of their treatment from a psychiatrist or other medical doctor; another part from one of many types of psychologists, counselors, or other therapists who engage in PTSD treatment; and still another part from someone who is highly specialized in a particular area such as nutrition, exercise, or (very importantly) spirituality.

Treatment is not one method, but many. There are methods that emphasize talking, those that emphasize taking pills, those that emphasize restructuring the way you think about the world around you so that you can react to it in new and healthier ways, and those that provide ways to improve bodily functioning to make you physically healthier. There are also methods we call *multi-modal* or *interdisciplinary,* which may include elements of several or all the above.

One thing that treatment for PTSD normally does *not* routinely involve is hospitalization, unless some other illness—such as alcoholism or drug addiction or active suicidal behavior—mandates it. So don't equate treatment for PTSD with rehab or inpatient care, for example. For the overwhelming majority of people, treatment may involve seeing your counselor or a group that you find helpful for an hour a week, and your doctor once or twice a month and less frequently later on, all on an outpatient basis. For many people, finding the right types of therapy, conducted by the right providers at the right time of their lives can actually be an enjoyable experience. Leaving your counselor's office with the feeling that you are putting a part of your burden down each time can be downright liberating.

Every vet suffering from PTSD who reads this book and who is not already receiving treatment will, at some point, need to make a decision whether or not to do so. I am going to emphasize, very frankly and straightforwardly, the reasons I believe that seeking treatment is essential.

Reason #1: You have a bona fide medical illness, so treat it. If your child had a broken leg, you would treat it. If your spouse had cancer or clinical depression, you would treat it. There is no reason or justification to behave differently toward yourself. Having read Chapters Two and Three, you now know that you have a physical disorder that is rooted in the brain and central nervous system, which causes chemical changes in the body, which in turn cause altered emotions and behaviors. You were not born with it, and you, undoubtedly, didn't ask for it, but you are responsible for managing it. If you don't, you will not only place yourself at risk, but also potentially impact both the emotional and the physical health of your family. Do they deserve that?

Reason #2: You do not need to be ashamed that you have PTSD. Current statistics indicate that nearly 25% of soldiers in the current conflicts develop PTSD. You are not alone. In addition, well-intentioned training you received in preparation for combat through programs such as "Operation Battlemind" (used in the military from 2007 through 2009) may actually have enhanced the chances that you experience some of the symptoms we have previously discussed.

Battlemind, for example, would have trained you to take care of your battle buddies. As a part of this, you probably learned to become vigilant about everything going on around you: sights, sounds, things out of place, movements, and smells. You may have learned to consciously record every detail of what you experienced for purposes of future operational debriefings. You may have been trained to suppress your anger in order to stay in control during combat, or alternatively, to channel anger or aggression as an aid to accomplishing your mission. In short, you may have learned to turn on your Battlemind switch, and you may, understandably, have found it difficult to turn OFF when you were no longer in combat.

Reason #3: This disorder will not get better with time. PTSD is an illness that does not go away the more you ignore it. In my work with thousands of vets who did not seek help, it has become absolutely clear that the disorder gets worse over time. This applies to both the psycho-emotional symptoms and the physical symptoms. When you return home to a situation where the behaviors you learned and practiced in combat no longer make sense to the people around you and don't make it easier for you to cope with stress, then those behaviors will eventually begin to interfere with the day-to-day conduct of your life—make no mistake about it. It also will *not* get better if you deny the illness and place the blame on other things or other people. Blaming others for circumstances that are, in all likelihood, the product of your PTSD will not improve things and will simply increase the level of misery for all concerned.

Reason #4: PTSD can extend to, or be accompanied by, other conditions. Symptoms or conditions that can occur along with PTSD are called *co-occurring conditions.* These may include depression, anxiety, panic, guilt, fatigue, bereavement, risk-taking behaviors, eating disorders, and obsessive compulsive disorders. One of the main co-occurring conditions is substance abuse, whether from alcohol or drugs. None of these conditions should go without proper treatment and attention. Doing so could cause serious risk to your health or your life.

Reason #5: The one thing that has improved is new types of treatment. No one is more sympathetic than I am to the past problems that vets have encountered with treatment. But do not hold the inept attempts of prior generations of caregivers against those good clinicians who are serving now. PTSD treatment isn't much different than care for other medical conditions—because all people are different, some time and patience are required to determine which methods will work for you. Keep an open mind and continue to seek improvement. Simply failing to get help altogether is dangerous and is no longer an acceptable option. One of the first places that you can invest that time and patience is in doing some basic self-care and self-monitoring, which Chaplain P explains below. Trust me when I say that the few moments a day you spend doing this will potentially reap significant benefits. The bottom line is that, when it comes to PTSD treatment, many new methods exist, and a good number of them are provided by both the military/VA and private sources of care, *if you know what to search for and where to find it.* This book can help arm you with the information you need to get the best out of the care available to you and prepare yourself to do this in the most effective way.

Some additional reasons to seek treatment

CHAPLAIN P:

I agree completely with every one of the reasons given by Dr. C and will add some of my own:

Additional Reason #1: There are serious downstream medical risks. Studies have shown that men and women with PTSD are significantly more vulnerable to a host of medical conditions, some of which can be life-threatening. These include increased risks of heart attack, sleep apnea, stroke, metabolic syndrome and diabetes, cardiovascular disease, infection, gastrointestinal disorders, and suppression of the immune system. This occurs, in part, because some of the biochemical changes that PTSD can cause (such as inflammatory response, reduced immunity, elevated heart rate, elevated fats and sugars, and hypertension) are also connected to serious illness and disease processes.

Additional Reason #2: PTSD is often a cause of death or serious injury. Hundreds of veterans of Operation Iraqi Freedom and Operation Enduring Freedom have died in violent incidents, assaults, and vehicular crashes. Still others have committed assaults or homicides against others that were prompted by their PTSD. Finally, a distressingly high number have committed "self-murder"—suicide. The alterations in perception and behavior that accompany PTSD are known risks that contribute to these types of incidents.

Additional Reason #3: Untreated parental emotional illness affects children. Every day, I treat children who have themselves developed secondary PTSD because of the intense anxiety and fear they have experienced as a result of one or both parents' behaviors. These kids not only wind up having to struggle with terror, nightmares, flashbacks, hypervigilance, hyperarousal, or withdrawal just like their parents do, but they also become very prone to drug abuse and criminal conduct. Remember that *you*—not your children—signed up and took the oath. So don't make spouses and children suffer for your unwillingness to get help for your own problems.

143

DR. C:

So now we've each said our piece. As you can see, Chaplain P and I both feel strongly that avoiding treatment just does not work to anyone's benefit. At the same time, we understand how difficult it can be to know where to begin. So let's assume that you've wisely decided to recognize that something is wrong and to get help. You're ready to go on to the next step. Unless yours is an emergency situation, I strongly urge you to devote at least as much time preparing to enter treatment as you would preparing to buy a new car or a washer-dryer combination. Particularly if you attempted treatment before and were not satisfied with either the "system" or the results, it's important that you try again, but in a better informed and more knowledgeable way. The best way to start is simply by doing your homework. And you can start this process by assessing yourself.

STEP TWO: ENGAGE IN "SELF-INVENTORY"

CHAPLAIN P:

There is no method of treatment that can be expected to yield good results if your clinical caregiver doesn't have honest and accurate information about the your past social, emotional, and medical history, as well as a good fix on what problems, symptoms, and feelings you are currently experiencing. This raises two important considerations you need to be aware of and assume some degree of responsibility for, if you want to get good care and maintain appropriate control over your life:

- First, as we've pointed out, the problem you are grappling with may not be readily obvious or may lay buried in the past. So it's very important that you pursue active self-awareness. Patient history is like a mineral deposit. You have to mine it, if you intend to find and offer your caregiver the nuggets of information that can spell the difference between standing still and making real progress. For example, I cannot begin to tell you the number of patients who came to me for mental health care armed with a host of complaints, but who never bothered to tell me that they had been sexually assaulted. Usually, they would say, "I didn't think it mattered." Well, trust me— *it matters.* Examine your life carefully for things like past incidents of physical/emotional/verbal abuse, neglect, assault, domestic or criminal violence, vehicular accident, restraint during medical treatment, or incidents such as a natural disaster or the traumatic loss of a loved one.

- Second, your caregiver may have a very limited amount of time in which to assess you. It's a common complaint, but it's also an unavoidable fact in many situations. For lack of sufficient time, particularly in military and VA-connected settings, caregivers often do not gather adequate patient history. Or, due to current protocols of care, they may be excessively focused on looking for battle-related issues and miss outside or surrounding life issues that are actually most critical to the individual. You will save your caregiver valuable time by being well-prepared with your own history, compiled in advance of your visit. The more time your caregiver doesn't have to spend digging for what is significant in your life, the more time he or she can devote to your care and treatment.

An important change in the military and VA-connected mental health system has to do with the way in which conditions are assessed. The personalized clinical interview and assessment process that used to take place between a patient and a counselor, with whom the veteran would visit consistently and come to trust, has become much less common as the demands for diagnostic and treatment services have skyrocketed. The soldier may not see the same counselor at each visit. Continuity and personal knowledge are often lost. As a result, **soldiers repeatedly tell us their government therapists often fail, or are not able, to find the essential issue that lies at the center of their problem. And there is risk associated with any process in which a therapist is attempting to provide treatment without knowing what problem the treatment is required to address or**

remedy. We do not believe that this is a result of government therapists being uncaring or unconcerned. We DO believe that this situation is connected to lack of input, as well as the obligation that is placed on government therapists to use methods of assessment that are not necessarily well-adapted to finding the root problem.

It is our observation that some warriors have unknowingly contributed to this situation. If there is one thing that has given rise to universal resentment and avoidance among warriors, it is their dislike for the infamous "clipboard PTSD assessments" that Middle East vets have had to undergo repeatedly throughout their service. The introduction of these standardized assessments was intended to maximize the number of patients a caregiver could see by minimizing the amount of time spent with each patient. Although based upon a desire for a standardized "test" to assess the presence and severity of PTSD, as well as to be able to measure response to treatment methods, these "clipboard assessments" have taken on another function. In this new role, the clipboard approach to assessment has been utilized widely because it was believed that it would save time, personnel, and cost.

In application, it has done none of these things. After many years of waging an unsuccessful war on PTSD, the reality is that over the long run, fewer hours of more personalized, human care are more appreciated and more effective than multiple uses of a clipboard in the assessment, diagnosis, and treatment of PTSD.

As a clinician, I understand well and sympathize with the need for standardized assessments across a large population of warriors. More than the assessments themselves, it appears that their *method of administration* is what has turned soldiers off in a hurry and sent them racing for the exits. They have resented the extremely impersonal quality of this kind of care, which often requires weeks to receive an appointment, and thereafter, hours, or even days, waiting or returning to the clinic to be seen for that appointment. This process is usually followed by the inevitable encounter with the clipboard, which feels to soldiers as if they are taking the standardized tests taken in grade school, only the subject matter is excruciatingly painful from an emotional perspective.

Having to answer questions about such painful subjects is not easy, especially when they are posed by a blank sheet of paper attached to a clipboard instead of by a caring human being interested in the answers and genuinely concerned for the individual's welfare. In addition, when clipboard assessments follow on the heels of multiple operational debriefings, their use has made warriors feel interrogated and out of control.

Many of the forms are difficult to read, understand, and fill out, especially for warriors suffering from the negative effects that trauma often has on reading, thinking, concentration, memory, and language skills. These preprinted assessments do not allow soldiers to make statements about themselves that they feel are personally accurate; rather, they measure the extent to which soldiers fit into a predetermined series of "boxes." Finally, soldiers continue to fear that their careers will suffer if they answer "yes" to anything on the survey, even though it is, in theory, illegal to penalize soldiers for acknowledging they have PTSD symptoms.

It is an unfortunate fact that the military's growing usage of so-called clipboard assessments caused its mental health system to depend upon paper instruments or written or electronic (computer) interface, when the very thing that soldiers need most is an hour of another human being's sincere and undivided attention and willingness to listen without being overly judgmental. In response to this impersonal approach, the majority of soldiers soon began to circumvent the assessment system by giving false answers to the questions asked. Typically, soldiers will still mark "no" to every question or else rank every symptom on the PTSD questionnaire at level "zero" and hand the clipboard back.

The result of this system is that the clinical caregiver is forced to rely on false data. Soldiers, on other hand, may avoid an unpleasant process, but do not get the help they need. Of the active-duty soldiers who commit suicide, virtually all have been given clipboard PTSD assessments at a point in time close to their deaths. Yet, few of their assessments resulted in their being given follow-up referrals for mental health treatment that might have saved their lives. We suspect that this points to a fundamental flaw in the military mental health assessment system.

So, soldiers have, quite simply, learned to circumvent the assessment instrument, and because caregivers know this is going on, it is possible that clinical providers have learned to ignore clipboard results as presumably false. Since accurate diagnosis depends upon accurate assessment, this problem in the military assessment system virtually guarantees problems in treatment from the start.

To help warriors navigate around these obstacles and also to help their clinical caregivers provide proper care, we have several recommendations. The first is to engage in thoughtful self-assessment on a continuing basis. We suggest this, not as a replacement for medical or mental health treatment, but as a way of empowering oneself to seek the right type of treatment, for the right issue, at the right time. You are not qualified to replace your doctor. Ironically, however, you are the person most qualified to inform your doctor about the factors in your life that will affect your treatment.

"Patient, inventory thyself"

There is an old Latin maxim that says "Physician, heal thyself." It means that a physician who engages in the treatment of others should be willing to, first and foremost, take a look at his own health problems and take constructive action toward recovery. I think the same thing should be said of patients. In fact, I tell all the patients I work with that they have a responsibility to be their own "co-physician." This does not mean that the patients should attempt to exercise the functions which only a doctor has the knowledge, training, and expertise to perform. Rather, I mean this in the sense that they should exercise **ownership** of their healthcare and be the first to step up to the plate in acknowledging their problems honestly and in seeking treatment. If they do not, there is little that any doctor can do to help them.

In both my personal opinion and my clinical experience, the first and most important person who needs to have a solid grasp of what is going on is YOU. Without that awareness, you cannot maintain ownership of your own care. And if you do not exercise ownership of your own situation, impersonal institutions and governmental systems will move in to assume control where you have failed to exercise it on your own behalf. This is the very thing that leaves vets feeling helpless and intensely frustrated. But it is largely avoidable.

I believe strongly in approaches that empower the patient to (1) identify his problem, (2) understand his treatment, and (3) assume part of the responsibility for the way treatment is conducted by engaging in self-help. Each of these is examined in this chapter. In this section, we'll start with assessment, which is the clinical name for the process by which we gather the information needed to identify a problem. Accurate and adequate assessment is the basis on which your doctor builds a proper diagnosis, and there are several reasons why your proactive participation in this phase of care is important.

1. Yours is a critically important role, because only you can play it. Identifying the heart, the essence, or the nugget of one's traumatic issues requires an assessment based upon patient history. You are the only one who holds the history. No one can have a more personalized conversation about the events of your life than the one you can have with yourself. So it's vital that you, the patient, find a means of engaging in self-assessment. This section offers several methods for doing this, which will be discussed below.

2. Empower yourself: Make assessment a two-way process. Although a doctor or licensed therapist is the only one qualified to *diagnose* you, your doctor is not the only one who can help *assess* you. Assessment is, by definition, a cooperative activity in which the patient should be involved, but often isn't. That is because the assessment process depends upon information that can only be provided by the patient.

Self-inventory is not a replacement for your doctor's medical assessment but an essential component of it. It is simply a process for making an inventory and summary of your thoughts, feelings, behaviors, reactions, and past history. *You* have the right and the obligation to inventory yourself psychologically, emotionally, spiritually, and physically. This is not only so that you will get a good feel for what your situation is, but also so you yourself can become the expert on your own life, instead of expecting your doctor or caregiver to invent things about you that may prove to be inaccurate. Remember that if you leave critical blanks in your history, someone is bound to fill in those blanks. Don't create the risk that they will do this by inventing inaccurate information just to fill in blanks that you leave behind.

3. Determine if you are an appropriate candidate for self-inventory. The following format for self-inventory for the purpose of history and symptom gathering is not appropriate for certain individuals. Do not spend the time needed for self-inventory if you fall into any of the following categories:

> (a) If you are having thoughts of suicide or harming yourself or others. If so, you must proceed immediately to your nearest emergency room.

> (b) If you are abusing alcohol, drugs of any kind, or other substances. Substance abuse indicates that a person is either caught in the grip of addiction or can no longer cope without using a substance as an escape from his suffering. Such a person needs immediate and specialized medical care and should report to the nearest emergency room.

> (c) If you cannot be honest with yourself in recording your own information. If you cannot be honest with yourself, you will not be honest with your doctor or clinical provider, which undermines the process to begin with.

If you do not fall into the above categories, then move on to the next step.

4. Experience the advantages that self-inventory offers. The most frequent complaint I hear from soldiers is that they don't want to be questioned. But engaging in self-inventory has a very different feel to it. Even if you are using the same form that the military or VA uses, it feels different when you are in private, in control, and when you are the one asking the questions of yourself. Inventorying yourself makes you less fearful of the process and also familiarizes you with the kind of questions that doctors are usually required to ask you in order to make a diagnosis and to provide you with treatment.

As impersonal as it seems, those questions and forms exist for a reason. Doctors are not allowed to simply assume or make an educated guess that you have a condition. They have to get information from your own lips or from your own written answers that confirm this. They also are required to document that your symptoms meet certain criteria before they can take steps to treat you.

Eventually, you must be formally assessed by someone who is clinically trained and legally authorized to do so. But you will be better prepared to see a provider, and feel calmer about doing so, if you have carefully inventoried yourself first. I can virtually guarantee you will become the favorite patient and command the respect of your caregiver if you have put some time and thought into pulling together a history and an inventory of yourself and your experiences

5. Take your time: Set aside adequate time for self-inventory. Most doctor appointments must be made several weeks in advance, so I suggest that this waiting time be set aside as your self-assessment period—assuming, that is, that you are not deployed and in a combat zone, in which case you will need to seek clinical help sooner. Unless you are in the midst of either a psychiatric emergency or combat, I believe that it is a good idea to spend about fifteen minutes a day for a full month on self-inventory. If this sounds like a lot, consider that the average person spends at least that much time watching TV commercials in a single hour. What's more important to you? Saving 15 minutes a day or *getting treatment based on accuracy, which may prevent misdiagnosis, drug errors, and treatment errors?* You be the judge.

Why spend this effort over time? It's really very simple. One of the main problems that soldiers experience is that their caregivers do not devote enough time to assessment and yet are very quick to prescribe very powerful psychiatric medication, with potentially serious side effects, after a visit of only a few minutes. Very quick clinical visits have built-in dangers. Every person with PTSD experiences ups and downs in the way their symptoms present. Simply getting a snapshot view of how you feel at one moment in time is not enough. You may feel very differently a week later.

Therefore, the best kind of overall patient assessment is approached as an unfolding process rather than a one-shot event. With so many veterans needing attention, mental health providers do not have the time or leisure to let this process unfold. But you do. You can take advantage of a system that I created for warriors and which is done in the comfortable and non-intimidating atmosphere of your own home. If you follow its guidelines, the system will allow you to see and record how things in your life unfold gradually, over a month, instead of limiting yourself to what the military or medical system tries to do in a few minutes. By doing this, you will probably be very surprised by what you learn. You also will be more likely to obtain a better result in treatment.

You can actually conduct a PTSD self-inventory by following the protocol found in Appendix A of this book.

STEP THREE: USING INFORMATION GAINED THROUGH SELF-INVENTORY IN LAYING FOUNDATIONS FOR YOUR PTSD CARE PLAN

After following the protocol for self-inventory found in Appendix A, you'll have one of the most valuable records any doctor, psychologist, or therapist could wish to receive from a patient. And it will help you to determine which doctors to head for and in what order.

To begin with, examining your self-gathered record (including the results of the screenings filled out by you and your significant other) will help you see whether your symptoms are predominantly PSYCHOLOGICAL (related to disturbances in the way you feel emotionally), COGNITIVE (related to disturbances or impairments in the way you are able to think), or PHYSIOLOGICAL (related to the way your body is responding internally to stress, as detailed in Chapter Three), or whether they equally impact all three domains.

Here is our suggestion for taking a well-ordered approach to the use of the information that you yourself have gained and for laying a foundation and developing an organized plan for your care. It will help ensure that your doctor has the means of gaining the information needed, and on which he or she can base helpful and appropriate recommendations. (Remember: This process is not intended for people experiencing substance abuse or a psychiatric emergency or for anyone who is suicidal. If that's you, then you need to go to the nearest emergency room).

1. Look first at your physical symptoms. What does your record reflect about your vital signs? If your heart rate and/or your blood pressure are elevated consistently, or if your record shows sharp spikes in heart rate and/or blood pressure that appear to coincide with times that you experienced posttraumatic triggers, then I suggest you FIRST consult your primary care physician. Remember that PTSD is, at its root, a physical condition. It is very important that primary medical problems such as chronic tachycardia (increased heart rate) and hypertension (elevated blood pressure) be promptly treated. This is most commonly done with antihypertensive (blood pressure) medications.

You should remember that psychiatry is considered a medical subspecialty. The general rule in medical practice is to narrow diagnosis and treatment down, by starting with the general and working down to that which is increasingly specialized and/or specific. This is why medical treatment begins, in most cases, with a primary provider who is, in turn, responsible for making referrals to more specialized care providers, if they are appropriate.

How and why would this apply to treatment for PTSD? There are several reasons for taking a primary medical approach to these symptoms. The first reason is that rapid heart rate and high blood pressure may also cause or intensify posttraumatic anxiety. When these primary medical conditions are rectified or controlled, the psychological symptoms of PTSD frequently decrease, or may even go into remission.

Second, the antihypertensive medications propranolol (Inderal®) and clonidine (Catapres) also happen to be some of the most inexpensive AND effective medications for PTSD. This is because they do not merely treat surface symptoms; rather, these medications actually serve to interrupt the activation of the HPA Axis (hypothalamic-pituitary-adrenocortical axis), which is the medical term for the stress response that triggers PTSD.

Propranolol (Inderal) is a very effective antianxiety agent and is most effective for people experiencing the Locked and Loaded profile. Clonidine is a very effective drug that acts selectively to lower blood pressure only when needed. As a result, it will not act to cause an excessive drop in the blood pressure of trauma survivors whose blood pressures are often low to begin with. It is therefore often helpful for those who are Hunkered in the Bunker.

A third antihypertensive medication, Minipress® (prazosin), has special effectiveness for those suffering from serious PTSD-related nightmares. All three medications will help to encourage sleep for the first few weeks. Importantly, none of these medicines will induce mania in individuals suffering from bipolar disorder, like antidepressant medication can.

Simply by reducing anxiety, normalizing blood pressure, and fostering improved sleep, many PTSD symptoms often improve. This type of primary medical intervention may also help the patient engage in psychotherapy with less fear of being retriggered. For these reasons, primary medical care is a good place to start, even if mental health care is eventually sought as well.

CAUTION: Receiving preliminary help from your primary physician should be limited to the physical symptoms of sleep disorder, rapid heart rate, and elevated blood pressure. It is generally *not* recommended that you seek antidepressant medication from your primary doctor (though there may be exceptions if your primary physician is knowledgeable and proficient in dealing with PTSD), as these are psychiatric medications that should not be dispensed without proper psychiatric evaluation.

2. Examine what your record reflects about your thinking. Are you frustrated about a lack of concentration, difficulty reading, and difficulty focusing? Although they often masquerade as depression, these problems are a frequent after-effect of trauma and relate to disruptions or dysregulations in neuro-transmission, the process through which signals are sent through the nervous system.

The first and most important treatment for these conditions is to improve sleep. Requesting the help of your primary care doctor in devising appropriate short-term strategies to improve sleep may go a long way toward improving these cognitive symptoms. A second and very helpful strategy is to take certain *essential fatty acids* as nutritional supplements. These essential compounds are the raw materials of your neural gray matter and neural wiring. Nature uses these acids to sustain natural processes of repair that occur in your brain and central nervous system as you sleep, with supportive effects on concentration and mental focus. For more information about these excellent nutritional resources, see materials in Chapter Seven.

3. Examine what your self-inventory reflects about your psychological symptoms. If these are causing you significant distress (such as paranoid thoughts, chronic fear, or hypervigilance) or are impacting your behavior toward others (such as creating aggressiveness, a hair-trigger temper, or the feeling that you will die prematurely or that you cannot ever go "off guard"), then mental health care is likely an important element of your care plan. It may be helpful for you to put your doctor's orders into effect and get your blood pressure and heart rate regulated first, in order to see how this impacts your other symptoms. If your cardiovascular problems do not subside, then it is very wise to seek psychiatric help.

Your vital signs are important external indicators of your stress hormone levels. Your numbers will play a critical role in helping your doctor—especially your primary care provider—decide if you are actually displaying full-blown symptoms of PTSD, or whether your symptoms, such as rapid heart rate and hypertension, are physical, and ought to be addressed with basic, nonpsychiatric antihypertensive medication such as propranolol or clonidine.

If your emotional symptoms are not overwhelming to you, and you are not having thoughts of suicide or harm to yourself or others, it may be appropriate for you to have an examination by your primary care physician or other primary provider. It's very important that you bring your record of vital signs along with you to this visit. It's also important to explain to your doctor (or other provider) that you would like him or her to take a primary medical approach to your problem, such as looking at what can be done to manage your physical symptoms.

If your record of emotional symptoms, such as triggers, indicates that you are experiencing significant problems, then your primary physician can help you determine whether to seek mental health treatment. Your primary physician may also decide to continue treating your primary physical symptoms, such as rapid heart rate and elevated blood pressure; he may then refer you to a psychiatrist for additional, specialized help and medication for psychological symptoms, if needed.

The value of a self-inventory is that it can help your doctor be aware of all the kinds of symptoms you experience—*both physical and psychological*. In this way, you will not become so focused on your psycho-emotional symptoms that you overlook the very physical symptoms that may be driving your stress responses in the first place.

If, after a discussion with your primary provider, mental health intervention appears to be the right course for you, then the information provided in the following sections of this book by Dr. C will provide you with valuable information.

STEP FOUR: SELECTING FROM VARIOUS TYPES OF CLINICAL CAREGIVERS

DR. C:

To help you decide to whom you should turn for help, it's important to know what types of clinical caregivers are available and what each can do for you. Different types of providers are described below, along with suggestions about when specific providers may be appropriate for you. Keep in mind that you can receive referrals and recommendations about different providers from your military or VA mental health center. Also, mental health care providers can offer recommendations about other providers in fields other than their own. For example, counselors may be able to recommend psychiatrists who they feel are particularly skilled and vice-versa.

General hints and recommendations

(1) Check out your benefits since they may determine the type of providers covered on your payment plan. At the VA, your primary care provider may be the entry point into the system.

(2) It's important to go to a provider with whom you feel a sense of confidence, ease, or rapport. If you feel so uncomfortable around a provider that you are tense and anxious, you'll wind up sharing very little or avoiding treatment appointments, and this will defeat the entire process.

(3) If you feel uncomfortable, try to honestly evaluate why. Is the provider nonresponsive? Preoccupied? Non-empathic to your concerns? Devoid of emotion or depressed? Does the provider seem to be a healthy and well-adjusted person in his own right? Occasionally, you may encounter a therapist who wants to spend time talking about his or her own experiences rather than yours. If you feel your provider is doing his or her own therapy on your time, it's perfectly acceptable to change. Consider that your own anxiety may also be a

contributing factor, and talk honestly to the provider about this issue; it may be correctable.

(4) If you are fortunate to find a provider in whom you have trust and with whom you feel a sense of comfort and rapport, be assertive about requesting to always see that provider, where possible.

(5) Ask your providers about backups or on-call assistance in case you find yourself in a critical emergency when they are out of town or on vacation.

Types of mental health providers

Psychiatrists are specially trained medical doctors who treat mental and emotional illnesses (like PTSD). Psychiatrists evaluate individuals for the purpose of diagnosing PTSD and can prescribe medication to treat it. In general, psychiatrists today are most likely to treat mental and emotional problems primarily with medications. (If you are seeking disability due to PTSD, you will usually have to be evaluated by a psychiatrist or clinical psychologist for this purpose).

After the initial evaluation, psychiatrists usually have short appointments, known as *med checks*, in which they monitor the patient's status and the effect of medication. They do not normally have time to provide much individual therapy, although there are exceptions. Therefore, a comprehensive care plan will often divide treatment responsibilities between a psychiatrist who provides medication management and some other type of professional who can take the time needed to provide psychotherapy or counseling.

You will need a psychiatrist if you . . .

(1) have high levels of anxiety, flashbacks, rage, or anger that is hard to control, or

(2) have the impulse to engage in risky behaviors, or

(3) are experiencing severe mood swings or depression, alterations in your thinking patterns, or significant physical symptoms that have not been adequately addressed by your primary physician, or

(4) have other psychiatric problems or disorders occurring along with your PTSD (like bipolar disorder, substance abuse disorders, phobias– or other "co-occurring disorders").

These may require management with medication. You will also need a psychiatrist if you are applying for VA disability or if you have a co-occurring illness such as substance abuse or bipolar disorder.

Primary Care Physicians (PCPs) are general practice physicians who usually have a longer term, and perhaps a closer, personal relationship with their patients. Their limitations include the shortness of most visits and, usually, their lack of formal training in diagnosing and treating illnesses like PTSD. Their strength is that they are more immediately accessible to the patient and may have a lot to offer the patient in dealing with three primary physical symptoms of PTSD: (l) sleep disorder, (2) rapid heart rate, and (3) hypertension. They may also catch a co-occurring problem if it is medical (e.g., thyroid disease, diabetes, heart disease). So even if you ultimately require psychiatric care, an initial consultation with your primary provider for these basic medical problems is a good place to start.

Some PCPs actually practice what is known as primary psychiatry. They may have extended training and experience in dealing with the more common types of mental and emotional issues that come up in the midst of general family medical care. Other primary care physicians may not be adept at dealing with mental or emotional problems, may not feel that these are as important or as real as physical illnesses, or may just not be willing to treat illnesses like PTSD. Some mental and emotional illnesses may masquerade as something else, creating a risk of misdiagnosis by a primary doctor. For example, primary physicians are prone to misdiagnosing complex PTSD as simple depression or other types of anxiety disorder. Misdiagnosis may lead to serious errors in medication. Notable exceptions to this are primary care physicians and physician assistants who practice in Troop Medical Clinics and at VA facilities. These practitioners are, as a whole, more capable of accurately recognizing and treating PTSD because they see and deal with it every day.

One way in which primary care physicians can be very helpful is in treating the physical symptoms of PTSD over the short term. Some of the most effective treatments for PTSD symptoms are standard nonpsychiatric drugs, with which primary care physicians are very familiar. The behavioral and mental symptoms of PTSD often significantly improve once the underlying physical symptoms are dealt with.

It's very helpful to go to your primary care doctor for a general physical exam, especially if your self-assessment (discussed above) reflects that you are experiencing insomnia, water retention, chronic infection or inflammation, rapid heartbeat, or hypertension as a symptom of PTSD. To rule out other causes (e.g., diabetes, thyroid disease, heart problems, sleep apnea, kidney, gastroen-terological, or neurological disease) for these symptoms, a visit to your primary (VA or civilian) physician or Troop Medical Clinic may be an excellent place to start in the management of your symptoms. The risk of misdiagnosis or failure to prescribe the most appropriate medications for a mental disorder by a PCP can be well managed if you simply agree to consult your PCP for primary medical problems and generally do not use your PCP as a source of any psycho-active medication, including antidepressants. You can then complement their primary treatment with PTSD-specific therapies by a mental health provider, whom you can authorize to stay in contact with your physician.

Physician Assistants (PA) are licensed health professionals who have completed a training program that includes courses similar to those required for physicians. However, PA programs are shorter in duration than medical school, and physician assistants do not have to complete internships or residencies. Under the supervision of a physician, PAs can provide about 80% of the services the physician can provide. They work in the same areas of medicine and share the responsibility for patient care with the supervising physician. In most states, PAs can write prescriptions. Although PAs work in all areas of medicine, about half of them are in primary care. PA's are one of the backbones of the military healthcare system and are generally very familiar with PTSD. Whether you seek care in a military or civilian venue, your primary care physician may delegate exams, tests, and treatment of your primary medical conditions to a physician assistant, who may be able to spend more time with you.

Psychiatric Nurse Practitioners are specifically trained to diagnose and treat mental health conditions such as PTSD. More easily accessible and less expensive than psychiatrists, psychiatric nurse practitioners have prescriptive authority and can provide medication in the same way that psychiatrists can. They usually practice in conjunction with hospitals or clinics.

You may want to consult a psych nurse practitioner as a baseline provider who can help route you to more specialized or higher levels of care if they are needed. Also, if you become stable on medications, you may want to ask your clinic if your med checks can be conducted by a nurse practitioner, whose appointments may be more readily available.

Psychologists are doctoral-degreed mental health providers who are usually licensed by the state. They do not ordinarily have authority to prescribe medication. Some psychologists specialize in either research or testing and do not provide the type of individual therapy needed by PTSD sufferers. Other psychologists specialize in clinical treatment of emotional illnesses and do offer therapy. Psychologists often choose to become specialists in a particular method or modality of treatment. The method (modality) in which the psychologist specializes may, or may not, be particularly useful for PTSD. How to determine this is discussed in more detail later in this chapter.

A psychologist specializing in clinical care may be a good resource for psychotherapy or counseling; however, you should be very up front about asking the psychologist how much experience he or she has in treating severe trauma. Many psychologists are not trained in trauma generally, and especially not in battlefield-connected trauma. Again, exceptions are military and VA-connected psychologists, some of whom have significant expertise in this area, while others do not. Some psychologists are excellent resources for limited sessions of particular techniques in which they specialize, such as cognitive behavioral therapy (CBT), neurofeedback, or Rapid Eye Movement Desensitization and Reprocessing therapy (EMDR).

Licensed Professional Counselors (LPCs) and **Licensed Clinical Social Workers (LCSWs)** are often referred to as psychotherapists or counselors. They are mental health providers who are degreed at the master's or doctoral level, state licensed, usually trained in a variety of methods of therapy, and typically accept different types of insurance in compensation for their services. LPCs and LCSWs are a good choice for many people as an adjunct to the services of a psychiatrist. While the psychiatrist provides medication, the LPC, the LCSW, the psychologist, or other qualified therapist provides the individual psychotherapy that is important to healing from PTSD.

LPC and LCSW counselors are the most widely accessed form of mental health provider. Before engaging in treatment, it is important to establish whether they have experience in the treatment of severe trauma. Ask them what methods they prefer to use.

Licensed Marriage and Family Therapists (LMFTs) do not typically specialize in the treatment of trauma. However, because PTSD is a family affair that affects the dynamics of all the relationships within a family, they are a source to which people can turn for help in resolving marital or family conflicts related to a family member's PTSD. Including your family members in your treatment in some manner is almost always advisable and helpful. Family counseling can be essential in avoiding the breakdown of family relationships.

Marriage and Family Life Consultants (MFLCs), who are LMFTs contracted by the military, can be an excellent resource over the short term. Their services are free, available on the military installation, and often extremely helpful in helping people to identify that a problem exists and to ventilate feelings. A limitation of MFLCs is that (depending on the individual) they may have little experience or in-depth knowledge about the realities of combat and may be unacquainted with life inside the military culture, in general.

Family Life Chaplains are members of the military Chaplaincy Corps. They are extremely well-trained to the master's level and specialize in areas of counseling that impact soldiers' and families' lives, as well as the way in which spiritual issues intersect with emotional problems and distress. As active duty, or active Guard/Reserve service members, most of whom have themselves deployed to the combat zone, they are intimately familiar with the problems created by service-connected trauma and are usually very sensitive to the way prior life traumas also affect the individual. Family Life Chaplains do not diagnose or treat mental illness. However, they are adept at recognizing PTSD when it presents and can discuss with soldiers their resources for treatment within the military system.

They cannot, however, make a referral of a soldier to treatment without the soldier's written consent. This is because consultations with a Family Life Chaplain are held in the strictest pastoral confidence. As a result, many soldiers feel comfortable with an FLC because they know that what they say to the Chaplain will not be included in their military record, nor can it be shared with other types of military caregivers without the express written permission of the soldier.

A critically important skill of Family Life Chaplains is their ability to discern and address spiritual issues in trauma. Spiritual issues are present in a very large proportion of individuals who suffer from service-connected PTSD. Family Life Chaplains' services are available without charge to active duty personnel and their families, including activated Guard and Reserve forces. They are seen on base or on post and are contacted through the installation chaplaincy.

Pastoral Counselors and Psychotherapists are very important, and frequently overlooked, professional resources. Formally trained and credentialed, pastoral counselors are not the same thing as either parish pastors or Christian counselors, although there are some individuals who might be both simultaneously. The services of true professional pastoral counselors are not confined to any particular religious denomination or even any particular world religion. They serve all faiths and traditions without distinction, upon the theory that all are variations upon one unifying theme, which is the connection between man and God.

Pastoral counselors are very extensively educated and trained—usually to the master's level or beyond—in both the mental health care and theology/spiritual care fields. Most pastoral counselors are ordained clergy who also have acquired the same type of training as an LPC, LCSW, or LMFT and are qualified to conduct ongoing psychotherapy. Look for a pastoral counselor who holds one of several levels of accreditation in the American Association of Pastoral Counselors, whose online website (www.aapc.org) will provide you with a great deal of information concerning this process.

Pastoral counseling is a licensed discipline in some states and not in others. In some states, pastoral counselors even accept secular insurance. Pastoral counseling is accepted and reimbursed by the military through the One Source system. It is a discipline of counseling that is especially helpful in identifying underlying, interconnected issues of spiritual trauma or crisis. These issues are sometimes well-hidden and are often missed by secular counselors who do not have the specialized training to deal with them.

Pastoral counselors, like other types of counselors, differ in their level of training to deal with trauma. As always, it is wise to be open and ask about their level of expertise in this area. Also, ask if they accept insurance. Some do and others do not. A well-trained pastoral counselor who is experienced in trauma can often serve as the primary therapist for a trauma survivor or the pastoral counselor, alternatively, can serve in cross-consultation with the psychiatrist. If the pastoral counselor is clergy, his consultations will be subject to pastoral confidentiality, and the soldier's written consent is required for any sharing of information between the pastoral counselor and another mental health provider.

You should attempt to find qualified pastoral counseling if you

- are experiencing rage or anger at God that you cannot resolve, or

- experience intense feelings of worthlessness or shame in God's eyes, or

- feel intense spiritual guilt over things that happened or that you may have done in combat, or

- feel that you are condemned, or not forgiven for transgressions that occur in life.

STEP FIVE: EXPLORING PROFESSIONAL TREATMENTS AND THERAPIES FOR PTSD

DR. C AND CHAPLAIN P:

You have probably made a great deal of progress through the R-E-C-O-V-E-R system simply by reading this book. So let's review where you are in the process.

By now, you may RECOGNIZE that something is wrong (Chapter One).

You've EDUCATED yourself about PTSD (Chapter Two).

And you've begun to understand the critical CONNECTIONS that exist between your biology and your psychology (Chapter Three).

Now that you understand more about the problem, you have decided to ORGANIZE a plan for your own care (Chapter Four). You have completed the following steps to accomplish this:

- you have determined whether you need to present to your nearest emergency room;

- you have engaged in an honest process of self-assessment;

- you have initiated your care plan by first consulting with your primary physician; and

- you have determined which type of mental health provider or pastoral counselor may be best suited to your needs.

Now, having accomplished these steps, you have concluded that you need professional mental health treatment. What types of treatments can your provider offer to you?

Available formats for PTSD treatment and therapy

Treatment and therapy for combat-connected PTSD are offered in a wide variety of formats, which include

- traditional psychiatric treatment of PTSD as a single diagnosed illness;

- so-called dual-diagnosis treatment, which refers to the treatment of co-occurring medical/psychiatric conditions (such as PTSD and substance abuse or depression, for example);

- individual and group psychotherapy and counseling;

- traditional medical treatment of the symptoms of PTSD; and

- adjunctive (complementary/alternative) therapies.

Our decision to maintain a website (www.mybacktothewall.com) about PTSD in conjunction with this book has been intentional. We expect that the preceding list will expand in the years to come and do not want you to rely only on what you read in the pages of this book today, as it is liable to become outdated in two or three years. Therefore, we will offer you a general outline of where treatment has evolved to date, but encourage you to continue checking our website for new and updated information.

Obtaining mental health evaluation

The treatment process must begin with a *full and accurate diagnosis* of the veteran's emotional condition. Although a primary care physician can legally make the diagnosis, and many PCPs do so, there are risks associated with this. Many mental disorders have common symptoms, and distinguishing between them can be tricky. If a mistake is made in diagnosis, it may filter down to produce a mistake in medication, with serious results. On the other hand, if the primary physician is *not* placed in the position of making a psychiatric diagnosis of a soldier, then his/her diagnosis will be confined to primary medical problems, which create no stigma for the soldier if they appear in the military record. For this reason, it is wise to keep the primary physician in this non-psychiatric zone if you are an active duty service member.

So now that you have concluded that you require evaluation by someone other than your primary physician, to whom should you look? First, seek out a mental health professional who is legally licensed to formulate a diagnosis, preferably one trained in the diagnosis of PTSD and other possible co-occurring (also called co-morbid) disorders. Because PTSD permeates through so many layers of our society, there are several types of mental health professionals who can formulate a diagnosis, including psychiatrists, licensed psychologists, licensed professional counselors, and licensed clinical social workers. Currently, all of these levels of mental health care are available in the civilian world. However, at the time this book is being written, licensed professional counselors are not available within the active duty Army mental health system, which relies primarily upon licensed clinical social workers and psychologists. LPC counselors, however, do serve as the backbone of the counseling force at the VA.

Active duty soldiers seeking mental health support and diagnosis may start in several places. They may wish to start by having a consultation with their unit Chaplain or with a Family Life Chaplain and see how much progress they make in resolving some of their issues before moving forward in the treatment process. They may call Military One Source, which provides offline mental health service—a choice for many soldiers.

They may also go outside the military system to obtain private care. If they pay for such care with their military insurance (TRICARE), their mental health records will become part of their military records.

They may also voluntarily present to the on-installation mental health service for the military branch. They may report to their nearest emergency room, including the ER of a military hospital, if they are experiencing a psychiatric emergency, are having thoughts of suicide, or are considering harm to self or others.

Veterans who have separated from the service can go to the emergency room of their nearest VA hospital for a psychiatric emergency. *In a psychiatric emergency, however, the hospital of choice is the nearest facility, without regard to whether it is civilian or VA.* For situations that aren't emergencies, the best place for an evaluation and diagnosis to take place (other than a private provider) would be at a Vet Center or the Veterans Administration.

Veterans may access free licensed services for diagnosis, as well as counseling for themselves and family members, at any of the approximately 200 Vet Centers throughout the United States. Vet Centers do not offer psychiatric services, so medical treatment and medication management must still be sought elsewhere, such as the VA clinic. The VA outpatient clinic is usually adjacent to a VA hospital, although some VA hospitals are large enough to have several outpatient clinics scattered throughout a given area.

One of the first things that veterans must do when presenting to the VA clinic for mental health care is to determine the purpose for their visit and whether they will pursue (1) *a treatment track* or (2) *a disability track*. If it is possible they will require both, they must determine the order in which to pursue assistance and must be proactive if they want to receive it.

The first order of business should be to consult with a Veteran's Benefits Counselor at the VA. In some VA hospitals and clinics, all of the counselors are VA employees. In some states, however, a state Vet Counselor may also be present. Although located in an office within the VA institution, the state Vet Counselor is an independent voice. These counselors are well-educated in the laws governing VA benefits, are oriented to getting vets the greatest benefits to which they are entitled, and are not employees of the VA. If you can access such a counselor in your state, it is recommended that you do so.

Once you have gotten yourself to a benefits counselor, you can discuss distinctions between treatment and disability. The difference between these two tracks, and the impact which they have on your treatment and benefits, is often unknown and unexplained to the veteran. It is helpful if you see a VA benefits counselor pre-armed with background information. So pay careful attention to the information below:

a. Treatment Track: Your first question is whether or not you are entitled to receive evaluation and treatment through VA. Different standards of qualification apply, depending upon when and where you served; whether you have another existing, qualified, and documented disability; and whether you qualify for special assistance based on low income. If it appears that you qualify to receive mental health evaluation and diagnostic services from the VA, you must go to that clinic.

Be aware that if caregivers at the VA clinic provide you with treatment services, and even if it is apparent to them that you suffer from a mental health disability, it is not their responsibility to refer you to the "disability side of the house" for the purpose of seeking compensation for that disability. You must do so on your own.

Why is this important? Well, many vets who receive mental health treatment have the mistaken belief that this treatment will serve to document the existence of a disability. It will not. They may also mistakenly believe that entering the treatment process will trigger the disability compensation process into action. It will not. In fact, veterans waive the right to receive disability compensation for all the time that they spend waiting for this to happen.

b. Disability Track: To obtain disability, you must file a claim with the disability section of the VA. It may not initially have access to your treatment record, which remains in the "treatment side of the house." Therefore, your treatment evaluation will not serve as the foundation of your disability claim. You must file an application for disability benefits and request a psychiatric evaluation. When you are sent to the evaluator (who will be a psychiatrist or psychologist of the VA's choice, not yours), you will be reevaluated and diagnosed, even if you already have an existing diagnosis. This physician is only there to evaluate you for purposes of disability and is not there to treat you for your PTSD. Do not, therefore, expect to receive a follow-up appointment with the psychiatrist who evaluates you for disability.

If you want *treatment* for your mental health condition, you must take the initiative of requesting it through the "treatment side" of the VA. You may then find yourself assigned to go to a preliminary class in PTSD and something referred to as Anger Management 101 before beginning treatment with an individual provider. Treatment through the VA may include psychiatry, medication management, psychotherapy, and counseling. Many vets also choose to supplement their VA services with those available through the Vet Centers or by private mental health professionals.

Obtaining mental health diagnosis

After an evaluation occurs, or concurrent with it, an accurate *diagnosis* must be made before treatment can begin. To receive appropriate treatment, you as a potential patient must tell your treating professional all of your symptoms. Often the accurate diagnosis of PTSD is hindered because the patient describes only one or two of his symptoms—such as insomnia, anger issues, stomach pains, racing heart, headaches, or panic feelings around groups of people or in certain situations. If only one or two of these symptoms are revealed (especially if the mental health professional doesn't know about the vet's prior life or combat experiences), the patient may receive treatment for those symptoms only (e.g., sleeping medications, tranquilizers, or suggestions for anger management therapy) instead of treatment that is more appropriate for the PTSD condition.

For example, if you suffer from PTSD and mention only that you are experiencing "fatigue," "emotional withdrawal," and a loss of interest in life, you might well be misdiagnosed as depressive, if you do not also tell your doctor about your nightmares, flashbacks, hypervigilance, hyperarousal, persistent anxiety, and physiological stress reactions.

The bottom line? Appropriate treatment begins with an accurate diagnosis. If patients are not forthcoming about the many thoughts, feelings, behaviors, and physical reactions they are experiencing, the entire diagnosis may be missed altogether.

Patient education

DR. C:

After the diagnosis (or multiple diagnoses if there are co-existing conditions like substance abuse, depression, or other anxiety disorders), you must be proactive about requesting education from your doctor or caregiver about the condition. Your doctor may have insufficient time or materials to offer you, so in addition, you will want to *educate yourself* about the conditions that have been diagnosed and the treatment options for each.

Education includes learning all you can about the various treatments available, who provides them, and what they entail. This book is an excellent place to receive self-education about PTSD. For information about other conditions, check with your local Mental Health Association, your public library, your governmental Mental Health/Mental Retardation office, and, of course, with resources that will be linked from our website (www.mybacktothewall.com).

To be most effective, treatment should be a collaborative effort between the patient and the treating professional. Treatment is not something the professional does to the sufferer—rather, effective treatment should be a process that the veteran believes and actively participates in. This requires that the veteran be willing to take an active role in co-managing his care alongside the treating professional. It also requires that the treating professional, in turn, provide the veteran with the kind of specific information the vet needs to play a proactive role in his or her own care.

Treatment of co-occurring conditions

Most research suggests that it is critical to treat not only the PTSD, but also to simultaneously address all other psychiatric disorders (such as depression, bipolar disorder, other mood and anxiety disorders, substance use disorders, and others) that affect the patient. It might seem reasonable to think that the PTSD might cause the other disorders, and therefore if the PTSD is treated, the other disorder(s) will improve or disappear. And the opposite might seem reasonable as well: if the other disorders are improved, the PTSD will also improve.

Though this type of thinking might seem reasonable, research has shown that it is not true. In fact, the opposite is true. If both of the disorders are not dealt with, neither will improve completely, or the relapse of either or both disorders is more likely. In addition, the medications which are most useful to treat one disorder may have a negative effect on another disorder (e.g., antidepressants may help with treatment of depression but might have a negative effect on bipolar disorder). Therefore, proper treatment is not a matter of picking-and-choosing. To obtain safe treatment and good results, *all* the presenting conditions and *all* the medications used must be considered together as part of a unified plan of care.

So if you have PTSD and a substance abuse problem or depression, anxiety, or another psychiatric disorder, you must receive treatment for both for best results. If you are seeking treatment from a professional, make certain that you reveal all of your symptoms, especially if you think you might have a co-existing disorder.

Psychotherapy

Psychotherapy is *talking therapy with or without behavioral therapy* and comes in several different forms. For example, psychotherapy can be aimed at understanding and relieving problem behaviors such as anger or isolation. It can be focused on helping the veterans understand their condition more fully and deal with it more effectively. It can help the veterans understand and reframe patterns in their thinking that may have become confused and distorted because of the persistent terror to which they have been subjected. Or it can be aimed at relieving their symptoms, such as unwanted recollections and nightmares, insomnia, hypervigilance, or other troublesome symptoms. Therapy can be performed individually (with one therapist working with one patient) or in a group setting (with one therapist working with several patients in a group). In a variety of scientific studies, psychotherapy has been shown to be, by and large, the most effective treatment for those suffering from PTSD. There are, however, several types of psychotherapy available. The choice of which method you use is an individual decision and will be based on a number of factors that we will present in this section.

Before talking about the methods themselves, let me mention two very important concerns that keep many vets from engaging in any type of psychotherapy. The first is that engaging in psychotherapy will focus the veteran's attention on the trauma and may stimulate neurological processing about the event. For this reason, it is not unusual for therapy to provoke and perhaps even worsen symptoms of PTSD such as nightmares, flashbacks, and unwanted thoughts, at least for a time. The second concern is that therapists who are not themselves combat veterans cannot understand or help veterans with combat-related PTSD.

You have already learned from this book that consciously avoiding thoughts or memories of the past combat issues does not prevent PTSD-related symptoms from continuing. There is no lasting safety to be found through the avoidance of treatment any more than there is with avoiding treatment of any medical illness. While it is true that reminders of the past traumas can temporarily "kick up emotional dust" in the short run, research has shown that receiving competent treatment with the aid of an experienced therapist who specializes in trauma is the best way to silence these symptoms in the long run. The key here is to deal with past traumas with the help of appropriately skilled therapists. Although there may be short-term discomfort with such psychotherapy, the long-term gains resulting from such therapy can make a significant difference that can last for the rest of your life. And remember the lesson from the Vietnam vets—time alone does not heal PTSD.

Second, many veterans assume, at least initially, that therapists or group leaders who were not in combat cannot really understand what the veterans are going through. As a result, they refuse to engage in treatment with that therapist. No matter how they feel at the beginning, however, most veterans eventually come to understand the real truth of the matter: It is not the biography or personal history of the therapist that is most important. It is through the training, experience, and empathic personality of the mental health professional, rather than the professional's own combat service, that a therapeutic *alliance* between the patient and the therapist is created.

If you do seek care from a therapist who has not personally been in combat, take care to avoid the assumption that he or she cannot understand what is happening to you or be of help in treating you. Your therapist should be given a fair shot at being of assistance to you. Your most important goal should be to seek a therapist with whom you feel you are in a *safe, open, caring, and compassionate relationship*. If these factors are not present, there is little good that will come of therapy no matter what method of psychotherapy is chosen. If, however, after giving the therapy a fair chance, you cannot get past the belief that the non-vet therapist (or any other therapist for that matter) cannot understand or help you, I strongly urge that you be open and honest with the therapist and request therapy from someone else. Otherwise an opportunity to improve may be lost as "the baby is thrown out with the bathwater."

CHAPLAIN P:

I'm glad that Dr. C has touched on this subject. I am a female, civilian, non-combatant who not only serves as a pastoral counselor to military personnel, but who also designs programs of pastoral care and pastoral counseling for the assistance of PTSD-affected soldiers. Despite the fact that I am a contract provider in the service of the military rather than an active duty service member, I am nevertheless very much accepted and embraced by the military forces I serve. Admittedly, the fact that I am knowledgeable about military life and affairs, including military language and the down-and-dirty aspects of deployment, certainly doesn't hurt. But I am an example that even someone who isn't a soldier can, nevertheless, help a soldier, if he or she has the needed skills to do so. What is important is the ability to empathize, *LISTEN* with a caring heart, learn as much as possible about the life circumstances of the person seeking help, and finally, to think like a soldier even if you aren't one.

STEP SIX: CHOOSING AMONG METHODS OF PSYCHOTHERAPY

Individual or group therapy

I personally feel that individual therapy is generally the best *initial route* with traumatized veterans. Group therapy can be helpful in allowing them to be around other vets and to come to understand that they are not alone in their suffering; however, group therapy can pose problems for some vets, especially early in treatment. Group therapy can, in some instances, expose veterans to other people's "stuff" in ways that can become overwhelming and even retraumatizing to them. One problem is that different veterans in a group may be at very different stages of recovery. One member may want to appear to be very tough, which may cause feelings of shame or exclusion to another, whose psyche is still in fragile condition. Members also vary in the type of medication they are on. Some members may be extremely anxious and reactive, while others are very chilled out, depending upon what other co-occurring conditions they suffer from and what drugs they do or do not receive.

In general, I find that putting vets into a group setting too early in therapy is, in some ways, very much like sticking them back in the foxhole, where they feel they must bear each other's burdens rather than concentrate on their own. Nevertheless, I feel that vets with PTSD need group interaction. It is inaccurate to assume that all groups are for the same purpose or operate in the same way. Many vets assume, mistakenly, that just because one group was not successful for them, no group will be. This is not the case.

One way I navigate around this difficulty is by combining individual therapy with group support. A support group is different than a therapy group. It exists primarily to provide socialization, group interaction, support, and validation. A supportive group can take many forms. It can be a formally organized group, such as at the Vet Center or a church or community center, or it might take the form of an informal, makeshift group that meets weekly over coffee at the local coffee shop. Being part of a support group is, in my experience, an excellent way of combining individual and group interaction for the recovering veteran. I personally encourage all vets to find a support group, especially if they are not in a therapy group. As individual therapy, education, and group support progresses, there may then be an appropriate place (and time) for group psychotherapy to be introduced.

There are many benefits from group therapy, including the opportunity to see in others what we cannot see in ourselves, as well as allowing others to help us see our own issues more clearly. Sharing our thoughts and feelings with others can be a powerful tool in letting go of issues that have plagued us. So group therapy can be useful for the veteran if used at the right time in the overall therapy process, with the appropriate vet, and with a group of vets who are compatible. Most of all, to be most valuable as a treatment method, the vet must feel comfortable with the group leader and the group members as well as fully understand the reason for the therapy and the process that will be used for the group therapy. If this is the case, group therapy can be of great value to many veterans.

Methods of psychotherapy used with PTSD

<u>Cognitive-Behavioral Therapy (CBT)</u>: The type of psychotherapy that has been found in research studies to be most helpful in the treatment of combat-related PTSD is called cognitive-behavioral therapy or CBT. There are two types of CBT that are used most commonly: cognitive processing therapy (CPT) and prolonged exposure therapy (PE).

In CPT, which can be done individually or in a group, veterans are asked to question and challenge the distorted thinking patterns that may result from stressor experiences and that perpetuate themselves in the form of continued, imprinted misperceptions about danger in the here and now. These misperceptions in the brain trigger, in turn, the activation of the stress/alarm response that causes PTSD symptoms years after the end of the initial trauma. For example, a vet may believe that by thinking of the traumatic incident or going to places that remind him of the trauma, he will go crazy, lose control, or die. The result of these distorted beliefs is that the veteran avoids any thoughts of or places associated with the trauma. CPT enables the veteran to look more logically at these distorted thoughts, question them, and change them. CPT teaches the vet to understand the difference between remembering the *thought* of the trauma versus having to actually *re-experience* the trauma itself. This opens the door for the vet to consider and explore other more realistic options.

In the same way, as vets recall incidents that occurred in a combat situation, many begin to feel guilty or angry. Often these feelings are based on distorted thinking. A vet may harbor terrible guilt about having watched the killing of a child. Another may be eaten up with guilt over accidentally killing a fellow soldier or having inflicted civilian casualties even when rules of engagement were observed. In all of these situations, CPT can help in terms of putting the experience in the context of war and combat. The vets who have done these things come to learn from CPT that often tragic and unfortunate things occur in the heat of combat, when it was not the intention of the soldiers to produce the outcomes that arose. By clearing up distorted thoughts, the veterans can become more realistic in understanding feelings resulting from past memories and present events.

The second type of cognitive behavioral therapy (CBT) is called prolonged exposure therapy (PE), which has also been shown in research studies to be very effective for soldiers and vets with PTSD. In PE, veterans are asked to talk about, visualize, and intensely focus upon emotionally traumatic experiences they had in the past. Often they are asked to write down their experiences. Sometimes, audiovisual material is also used, so as to immerse the soldiers back into the traumatic event by means of virtual reality. This recalling is repeated over many sessions (usually twelve) until the traumatic stimulus no longer provokes anxiety, guilt, or other unwanted reactions.

The idea is that by recalling the trauma(s) that initially caused the PTSD and mentally reliving them in a safe environment and with proper guidance from the therapist, the powerful negative emotions experienced when talking or thinking about the incident will decrease in intensity and frequency over time, and the symptoms that accompany the recollections will also decrease. PE requires that the veterans learn and practice relaxation techniques to reduce unwanted anxiety when it occurs in the process of therapy or outside of the therapist's office. Proponents of this method contend that, because it is conducted in the supposed safety of the therapist's office, the method is safe and effective.

Yet, many of the vets who have been exposed to either CPT or PE said it caused them to have worsened symptoms (nightmares, flash-backs, thoughts) *and they refused to continue and complete the process.* In thinking about what went wrong for these vets, it became clear that it was not the method itself, but rather how, when, and on whom it was used. My knowledge of and clinical experience with CBT (either CPT or PE) has convinced me that it can be very useful for warriors and veterans, *if* it is inserted into the therapeutic process at the right time and explained and understood well so that the vet feels confident that it is the right method for him. If the patient is not convinced that it is right for him before starting it, the process generally results in a negative, rather than a positive, outcome. Using CPT at a *later,* instead of earlier, point in the therapy process is usually more effective. I know that the VA and military's heavy dependence upon CPT and its broad and premature application of the method has turned many soldiers away from therapy and resulted in their dropping out of treatment for PTSD, when they might otherwise have been helped through this or other methods.

The theory behind both methods of CBT is that by attempting to avoid the memories, the present reminders of that trauma, or misguided thoughts about the trauma, the vet continues to re-experience trauma from the past into the present. As a result, the trauma continues into his present life long after the actual event occurred. In CBT, either by reducing the negative emotional response to the original and ongoing remembering of the trauma or by changing the thoughts associated with it, the vet can overcome many of his present bothersome symptoms. The problem for most vets for whom the methods are suggested is not in the theory of CBT techniques but rather in how they are actually used in practice.

The first problem is utilizing the techniques too early in the recovery process. CBT is a method of psychotherapy that focuses on logic, judgment, and higher-level thinking processes. It also is conducted through talking and the extensive use of language. Therefore, the entire method is dependent upon faculties that are centered in the upstairs brain, the neocortex. These are the very faculties that are most significantly impaired in the returning warrior or those vets who have had little or no prior treatment for their PTSD.

I have been told of many scenarios in which warriors return from combat, report for mental health screening (usually in connection with a Warrior Transition Unit or WTU), and have a clipboard slapped in their hand. Very soon thereafter, they are escorted into a setting where they must begin individual or group CPT.

Embarrassed and confused by their posttraumatic cognitive (thinking) impairment and lacking the words to express their terrifying experiences, these soldiers cannot comply with the therapist's demands, and they emotionally shut down. Therapists who don't understand that soldiers cannot work on processing data that is still locked up in the midbrain (and most therapists are not trained to understand this) may brand the soldier as noncompliant with therapy. This begins a terrible cycle that can quickly lead to a military reprimand, as well as the soldier's swift exit from therapy.

Additionally, the CBT method relies upon the underlying assumption that the soldier's traumatically impacted thoughts, feelings, and reactions are *irrational* and must therefore be changed. With regard to traumatic reactions, this is simply and fundamentally inaccurate. Instead, the soldier should be educated to the fact that his reactions are not "crazy" or "irrational," but that they are the result of unconscious and normal biological processes. Many of these processes have been deliberately trained into the soldier at an intense level because those processes assist in performance of the combat mission. To tell a soldier that he has acted irrationally, when all that he has really done is respond to normal biological signals as well as his military training, can cause confusion at best, and guilt and anger at worst—thus interfering with improvement, rather than fostering it.

SUGGESTION FOR OVERCOMING PROBLEM ONE (using the techniques too early in the recovery process): I recommend that CBT should be initiated with returning warriors *after* they have had an opportunity to fully process their traumatic recollections through experiential methods that do not rely on cognitive approaches. In addition, I recommend that soldiers should not be told that "their thoughts are irrational" unless they truly suffer from psychosis or thought disorder. If PTSD is their problem, it is more appropriate to advise them that it is possible to reframe their responses in light of the change in their social surroundings, which are no longer life-threatening.

The second problem results from the soldier not being fully educated about both PTSD itself and the method of therapy recommended. Most vets have spent years "trying to forget" about the traumas they experienced. If they cannot understand why they are now being asked to do just the opposite and recall the traumatic experiences or thoughts associated with them, they will not accept the CBT and will either refuse to start therapy or drop out after the first session. I have heard over and over from vets, "Forget it . . . I'm not putting myself through that anymore!" Usually that is due to the fact that the first step of CBT—i.e., educating the client about PTSD itself and the method of CBT being used—is not done at all or is not understood by the client.

SUGGESTION FOR OVERCOMING PROBLEM TWO (soldiers' lack of education): The manual used with CBT for the VA and military notes that, before proceeding with therapy, the vet should be educated about PTSD itself, the manner in which the CBT therapy will be performed, and how it will help the vet deal with his symptoms. It is critical that this step be performed and that the information is understood and accepted by the vet before beginning other steps of therapy. If you are the patient, make certain your therapist explains in detail the rationale for the therapy, the technique, and the goals before you agree to go further with the therapy.

The third problem is that CBT is supposed to include teaching of relaxation and other techniques used to reduce anxiety that results from the therapy (memories and thoughts) itself. Without learning to "de-stress" following a session, vets may find themselves helpless to effectively go on with life's activities and may be even more distraught and incapacitated by symptoms occurring outside of the therapist's office.

SUGGESTION FOR OVERCOMING PROBLEM 3 (failure to teach techniques to reduce anxiety): Not only should stress management/relaxation techniques be taught to the vet, but they should be practiced by the vet until he is convinced that he can handle PTSD-related anxiety in an effective way when it arises.

DR. C:

There are several other reasons why we use caution in advocating for the use of PE without dealing with the problems Chaplain P discussed above. First, the methods assume that the therapist (or veteran) can know and focus upon the precise trauma that initiated their PTSD. In fact, many therapists (and sometimes the vets themselves) do not possess this information before beginning the therapy. They may assume that the PTSD is rooted in one event when it is actually connected to another event or to an entire lifetime of events. As a result, the therapy may have to be repeated several times before the soldier is exposed to the right trauma. Experienced therapists realize that it may take time to know their patients well so they can aid them in understanding the root trauma causing their PTSD.

Even if the root trauma causing the PTSD is known, it is probably best not to begin dealing with the most emotionally "charged" traumatic event first. Rather, it may be wiser to begin with more here-and-now symptoms that are the result of the PTSD (such as the need to sit in the back of the room or to avoid crowded places or driving in certain areas). By having success in dealing with here-and-now activities and symptoms, the vets can gain a sense that they can be successful in using the therapy method to deal with their more emotionally disturbing thoughts, emotions, and symptoms.

PE is usually conducted in a counseling office, without the benefit of the soldier's having learned relaxation or other techniques for dealing with symptoms, should they occur, or having been pre-treated with central-acting medication to prevent traumatic retriggering. As a result, the soldier is intentionally re-exposed to experiences that incite fear, loathing, revulsion, or terror, which, in turn, reactivates the stress reaction, particularly when this method is used in the earlier sessions of treatment. As a result, the soldier may emerge from such therapy feeling physically and emotionally sickened and as terrified as when the incident actually occurred. The aftermath of such an experience is often that the veteran makes a decision to avoid future sessions, "I'll never do that again!" Again, experienced therapists can enable their patients to avoid these emotional experiences or teach them how to deal with them before they get out of hand for the vet.

THE BOTTOM LINE ABOUT CBT PSYCHOTHERAPY: So while we have concerns about CBT, they are less about the technique itself than about when, how, and with whom it is used. If CBT (either CPT or PE) is used correctly, at the right time, and with the appropriate patient who is adequately prepared for it, it can be of great value in helping with PTSD. Most importantly, if this type of therapy is recommended for you, be certain you understand the technique to be used and its goal and make sure you want to engage in the therapy. Don't engage in it just because someone recommends it. Also, as with any type of therapy, periodically assess whether it seems to be working for you.

<u>**Eye Movement Desensitization and Reprocessing (EMDR)**</u> involves the veteran thinking of the traumatic event and at the same time moving his eyes rapidly following the movement of a pencil or finger of the therapist. It is believed by some that the rapid eye movement in EMDR creates brain activity similar to rapid eye movement (REM) experienced during sleep and thus can help the vet work things out and neutralize the negative stimulus, while other experts are not certain how the eye movements help. With EMDR, vets are able to process their thoughts and experiences in such a way that they remember the event without the emotional pain. EMDR is a treatment method in which US Army Family Life Chaplain therapists are formally trained. If you are interested in pursuing this method, you may wish to contact your military chaplaincy office for details.

Many civilian counselors are EMDR therapists, as well. Although research studies about EMDR are mixed in terms of which parts of the technique are essential at this time, clinical investigation of the method continues and will, doubtless, yield more information in the future about its exact mechanisms. Meanwhile, it is broadly used, and many find it very helpful.

Other Psychotherapeutic Methods: There are other therapeutic methods that are used with PTSD, such as client-centered therapy, pioneered by the psychologist Carl Rogers. It is based on assisting the client to process his or her events while providing validation and unconditional regard for the patient's responses instead of negative judgments. The patient/client is helped to over-come shame and alienation.

Narrative therapy has also been helpful in PTSD. Though utilizing some of the theory and technique of CBT, its purpose is to dislodge the data about trau-matic events that is randomly triggering reactions in the midbrain and to trans-form the data into an organized informational narrative that the upper brain can wrap its head around. When this occurs, the skills that are accessible only in the upper brain—such as judgment, planning, and coping—can be brought to bear on the traumatic issue. The result is that the midbrain stops hijacking the upper brain, and the client is able to attain greater mastery over the traumatic event through cognitive thinking processes rather than through stress/alarm reactions.

NOTE TO CLINICIANS FROM Dr. C: I believe the simplest and most effective method for encouraging narrative processing of traumatic events is "Looking at the Hand Life Deals Us©," a method designed by my colleague, Chaplain P, for use with warriors in the combat zone, as well as before and after deployment. It works safely and rapidly to thoroughly ventilate soldiers without resorting to questioning them and often leads clients to rapid acquisition of insights they did not previously have. In addition to lowering levels of perceived stress for warriors, it can assist in case and therapeutic planning, as well as clinical assessment for qualified personnel. The system is very inexpensive, simple to use, and avail-able in both civilian and military versions. Information for clinicians concerning the system, and how it can be obtained, is available at the My Back to the Wall website (www.mybacktothewall.com).

CHAPLAIN P:

Psychodramatic Therapy is a powerful tool for trauma. This method, which was designed in the early 1930s by Dr. Jacob Moreno, was the granddaddy of all other group therapies. It allows a patient to explore a trauma experientially, rather than cognitively, and without being exposed to retraumatization. By working experientially, the method engages the structures and processes in the brain where trauma lives so the person can devise alternative means of response. It is the experiential-behavioral type of therapy that can most satisfactorily precede cognitive therapy in trauma. Psychodramatists are certified and undergo years of rigorous training to practice this very effective healing art. You can consult the My Back to the Wall website (www.mybacktothewall.com) for more information about how to find practitioners of this therapy in your area.

DR. C:

Yet another potentially helpful method is entitled **Post Traumatic Scene Examination and Evaluation, or (PT-SEE).** PT-SEE is another very user-friendly experiential approach that was developed by Chaplain P to address the needs that she saw among warriors, burn victims, and other traumatized individuals who needed a way of processing their traumatic recollections other than simply "talking about it." The method allows a client to access many of the same benefits of psychodramatic therapy, but in settings where traditional psychodrama would not be possible or accessible. One benefit of the method that I as a physician find to be very attractive is that PT-SEE allows patients to reencounter and reexamine their past traumas without actually re-entering into them or re-experiencing re-exposure to the traumatic incident. It uses some of the concepts of PE and CPT in such a way that clients are able to attain a bird's-eye view of their total situation, using five levels of sensory-motor and cognitive skills. The therapeutic goal is to allow the client to employ these skills to create new and safer endings to their traumatic situations. It also creates new imprinted experiences, which assist in defusing the traumatic effect of old events while leading to new cognitive insights. Descriptions of these and many other methods will be found on the My Back to the Wall website (www.mybacktothewall.com).

It is important you not merely submit to a particular method recommended by your therapist, psychologist, or psychiatrist, but that you and your provider discuss the matter. You should be told about the method your provider wants to employ and the reasons why it would be a good method for you. This is important for the trauma survivor's sense of control over a very sensitive situation. A good provider will be aware of this and will be supportive of your efforts to be knowledgeable about any therapeutic method in which you are engaged.

TREATMENT FOR PTSD USING MEDICATION

Medication can be useful in treating some of the symptoms of PTSD, but at the time we are writing this book, there is not yet a single, one-size-fits-all medication that is generally successful in treating all of the symptoms of the disorder. Usually, medications are used to deal selectively with symptoms of the disorder, and in this section I will present the use of medication in this way.

Drug classifications

Before talking about more specific treatments, I want to make some general comments about the different classifications of drugs and the means used to decide what class a medication is in. This sometimes causes a lot of confusion because we often use medications for reasons that patients find hard to understand. Perhaps we give an antidepressant to someone who is suffering from anxiety or use a high blood pressure medicine for nightmares. We may use an antipsychotic medicine for someone who is not psychotic (out of touch with reality). We call this *off-label* usage of medications. This is the name given to perfectly acceptable uses for drugs, when the uses appear to be different than the use on the drug's label, and for which it is formally approved by the Food and Drug Administration (FDA).

We categorize medicines based upon what the FDA first approves them for. For example, Zoloft® (generic sertraline) was first approved for the treatment of depression, so we call it an antidepressant. Later, however, it was found that Zoloft® treats symptoms of panic disorder, obsessive-compulsive disorder, and PTSD in some (not all) patients. But because Zoloft® was first approved by the FDA for the treatment of depression, we still call it an antidepressant, even though it may be safely and effectively used for other conditions.

Desyrel® (generic trazodone) was first approved by the FDA as an anti-depressant, but it is often used to treat insomnia in vets. Minipress® (generic prazosin) was first approved for the treatment of high blood pressure but more recently has been shown to help reduce or eliminate nightmares in PTSD. And Seroquel® (generic quetiapine), an antipsychotic drug, is sometimes used to help reduce depression, insomnia, anxiety, anger, and mood fluctuations in PTSD-afflicted vets.

I mention this because often the vets I see look up their medication on the Internet and find out that it is in a category of medicines that doesn't seem to make any sense in terms of why it is prescribed for them. If in doubt, ask physi-cians to explain what kind of drug they are prescribing and why they think it will be helpful for YOU.

Types of medication often used in PTSD treatment

Sleep-Inducing Medications: Insomnia is one of the most bothersome symptoms of PTSD for many vets. Not getting restful sleep can cause fatigue during the day, not to mention how distressing it can be to be awake when you would prefer to be asleep and everyone else in the house *is* asleep. In addition, having nightmares makes the vets frightened to go to sleep, and thus they may become terribly anxious at night when it is time to do so.

If the primary cause of the lack of restful sleep is recurring nightmares, a medication called prazosin (originally used for treatment of high blood pressure as Minipress) can be of value to many vets—especially those whose nightmares have begun more recently (rather than having occurred for years or decades). This medication blocks the effects of the sympathetic nervous system and espe-cially the stress-activated brain chemical transmitter, norepinephrine. Prazosin and medications similar to it have caused some vets' nightmares to go away completely, and in others nightmares are reduced in frequency or severity.

The more traditional sleeping medications promote sleep and sometimes reduce nightmares, but not as often as one might think. This includes the newer ones—with names like Ambien® (zolpidem), Lunesta® (eszopiclone), Sonata®

(zaleplon), Rozerem® (Ramelteon)—and the older ones such as Restoril® (temazepam) or Dalmane® (flurazepam). In addition an older antidepressant called trazodone is now used frequently by the VA for its sleep-promoting properties. Nowadays, a tranquilizer called Klonopin® (generic clonazepam) is also used at bedtime to promote sleep. All medications can have side effects, and they are listed on the website for each drug. Be aware that not all antidepressants are helpful to PTSD sufferers for insomnia. For example, the antidepressant amitriptyline is often used for insomnia; however, in some, it can worsen symptoms of tachycardia (rapid heart rate) connected with PTSD. In addition, some of the more commonly used antidepressants—called SSRIs—such as Zoloft®, Effexor®, Lexapro®, and others can help with depression but actually worsen insomnia.

Finally, with regard to sleep, newer research has shown that sleep apnea (a condition where the patient stops breathing during sleep so that oxygen levels in the blood are decreased) is more common in patients with PTSD than those without it. Sleep apnea is not usually treated with medications but with a special mask called a Continuous Positive Airway Pressure (CPAP) mask device, which requires a prescription.

Antidepressants: The medicines most commonly prescribed for treatment of depression and anxiety-caused symptoms are the drugs called antidepressants, with names like *Zoloft® (sertraline), Paxil® (paroxetine), Celexa® (citalopram), Lexapro® (escitalopram), Effexor® (venlafaxine),* Cymbalta® (duloxetine), Pritstiq® (desvenlataxine), and Wellbutrin® (bupropion). I have seen veterans on all of these medications.

These drugs work in different ways, and their level of effectiveness varies considerably from person to person. The medications listed in italics are the ones most often prescribed by the VA, while the antidepressant Zoloft® (sertraline) is used with particular frequency by the Army among active-duty personnel in combat.

Different varieties of antidepressants have different ways of working (what doctors refer to as their "mechanism of action"). This fact makes it impossible to make conclusive statements about the overall usefulness of this class of medication in the treatment of PTSD. To do so would be like applying the same observations to both apples and oranges. While a detailed examination of each of these drugs is beyond the scope of this book, it is probably sufficient to explain that antidepressants affect levels of neurotransmitters, and this is the reason they are often used in the treatment of PTSD.

Specific medications can be extremely helpful to some people, while in others they can induce very serious side effects. Some of these known side effects can even include "paradoxical reactions," in which the drug causes a worsening of the very symptoms it is intended to improve. Certain antidepressants, however, pose special risks for young adults, including suicidal behaviors early in treatment. Others elevate the same neurochemical (e.g., norepinephrine) that is already elevated in some PTSD sufferers, which may create a compounding effect for some. The FDA also warns about the possibility that antidepressants used without mood stabilizers can potentially bring about mania (periods of agitation and severely increased activity) when given to patients who, along with PTSD, are also sufferers of known, or undisclosed, bipolar disorder. For this reason, their administration to patients with PTSD should always be monitored with extreme care by competent psychiatric medical professionals.

Atypical Antipsychotic Medications: More recently, medications in the *atypical antipsychotic* class; such as Seroquel® (quetiapine), Abilify® (aripiprazole), Zyprexa® (olanzapine), and Risperdal® (risperidone); are sometimes used, either alone or with one of the antidepressant class drugs, to treat depression and anxiety. Please note that simply because you are prescribed an atypical antipsychotic medication *does not mean that your doctor thinks you are psychotic.* The reason these drugs are used is that, in addition to helping improve the action of antidepressants prescribed for anxiety and depression, they may have a positive side effect, in that some patients find they reduce anger and irritability. Sometimes these medications are prescribed for this purpose as well, often in conjunction with anger management therapy. Attention should be paid to the negative side effects of any medication, as virtually all drugs have them.

These medications are also used in patients with co-existing psychiatric disorders such as bipolar disorder, panic disorder, and substance use disorders. As previously noted, the selection of medications should be made and monitored very carefully, since some medications (such as SSRI antidepressants) may cause a "kindling effect," a steady increase in the symptoms of bipolar disorder, in some people.

Drugs That Decrease Sympathetic (Adrenergic) Activity: The drugs in the class known as *adrenergic blocking agents* (medications that block the effect of norepinephrine and epinephrine) were originally designed as antihypertensives, to control blood pressure. As it happens, these drugs work within the parts of the brain and central nervous system where traumatic stress is signaled. They are often very useful to PTSD patients because they, in effect, short circuit. or interrupt, the stress/alarm signal that causes PTSD symptoms.

The drug Inderal® (generic propranolol) is a medication known as a *beta blocker.* It works by blocking norepinephrine receptors located directly on the heart and can make a significant difference in some PTSD patients who experience the panic associated with a racing or pounding heart rate. Since the mind does not experience the symptoms of anxiety (i.e., rapid heart rate), it "thinks" that no danger is present, and the patient does not experience a posttraumatic stress reaction. It has thus been used for decades as an effective drug to reduce anxiety. For this reason, it counteracts two of the major symptoms of PTSD, from which most other symptoms flow. It is most effective in patients who experience the Locked and Loaded presentation of PTSD.

Clonidine (Catapres®) is another sympathetic acting agent called an *alpha 2 partial agonist,* which has a unique method of action. It is very effective for individuals whose hypertension is occasional or *episodic.* By the same token, it is frequently and safely used for PTSD to block or suppress the stress response in those patients whose blood pressure may be *low to start with*, including those who display the Hunkered in the Bunker profile. It does not act to reduce blood pressure below a certain level; however, it sticks around in the bloodstream, where it remains available to work in the event that the person experiences a triggering episode that might cause the stress response to suddenly spike. It is also a drug of choice in the treatment of withdrawal symptoms when medical patients who have experienced trauma and extreme pain (such as the burned) or who have a co-occurring substance abuse problem are being gradually removed from opiates like morphine. As a result, it is often useful in the treatment of PTSD patients who have co-occurring conditions.

The drug prazosin is another sympathetic blocking drug, called an *alpha 1 agonist.* It is used to control not only elevated blood pressure, but also off-label to help with nightmares and night terrors in patients with PTSD.

The anti-hypertensive (blood pressure) medications that we've discussed in this chapter are known as "central acting" medications. This implies that they are highly targeted medicines designed to regulate blood pressure by acting directly within (I) the brain and (2) the nerves encased within the spinal cord. These two parts comprise the central nervous system; hence, the drugs that work in these areas of the body are known as "central acting." Like all drugs, they have side effects, most of which are temporary.

Tranquilizers: One other class of medications used to deal with the anxiety of PTSD is the tranquilizers. Drugs used in this category include Xanax® (alprazolam), Ativan® (lorazepam), Klonopin® (clonazepam), and Valium® (diazepam). While these drugs lessen anxiety that is already present, they do not prevent the development of anxiety. It is for this latter reason that, more typically, we use other medications (e.g., the antidepressants) instead. In addition, research has shown that the tranquilizers can interfere with higher thinking and can get in the way of psychotherapy (like CBT). As a result of this problem, physicians generally do not use tranquilizers in those veterans with PTSD who are undergoing psychotherapy. Finally, for some the tranquilizers can be overused and, in some cases, cause problems with habituation and addiction.

ALTERNATIVE/COMPLEMENTARY THERAPIES

DR. C AND CHAPLAIN P:

Psychotherapy and prescription medication discussed above are generally considered more traditional professional therapies. But some vets have received great benefit from prescribed and/or professionally administered alternative therapies as well.

Acupuncture, part of Traditional Chinese Medicine and one of oldest healing arts, involves stimulating anatomical points of the body. A variety of techniques are used, frequently penetrating the skin with thin metallic needles. The goal is to achieve balance within the body. **Acupressure** applies pressure to the body's pressure points rather than using needles.

Therapeutic massage can reduce anxiety, enhance sleep, improve concentration, and help restore emotional balance. Some massage therapists are trained to work with trauma survivors.

Biofeedback therapy, also known as neurofeedback therapy, changes your patterns of brain functioning, using the power of your own brain. You are hooked to an electroencephalogram (EEG) machine to read the electrical waves transmitted by your brain and send an image to a computer. The image moves on the screen as long as your brain waves remain within the desired frequencies. The brain interprets the movement of the image as a reward and strives to stay within the desired frequency range. Vets have been able to change their brain waves and gain better control of their symptoms.

Neurotherapy is a form of EEG-driven biofeedback in which the neurotherapist identifies areas of imbalance in brainwave patterns, makes slight corrections, and feeds them back to your brain through light waves. During repeated treatments, your brainwave patterns are "nudged" back into a healthier pattern, resulting in improvements in attention, anxiety, mood, emotional control, and cognitive function. For more information, see *The Healing Power of Neurofeedback* by Stephen Larsen, PhD (Healing Arts Press).

Hypnotherapy can help vets come to terms with what happened to them and develop a new perspective on the situation. The therapist will guide you through the process to reprocess the experience and change your perspective and psychological reactions to the trauma.

Nutritional supplementation is often recommended by a professional during the treatment process. Chaplain P has worked in collaboration with physicians since 2003 in discerning medically appropriate and helpful courses of nutritional supplementation for trauma survivors, emphasizing the use of essential fatty acids and certain amino acids. It is very important to stay away from fads or unproven vitamins and herbs. Just because things are described as "natural" does not automatically make them helpful or safe. For the latest data on nutritional supplementation, go to mybacktothewall.com and click on the "Nutrition" tab.

Homeopathy is an alternative form of medicine that uses natural substances diluted repeatedly so only a small amount of the original substance remains. Though controversial in traditional medicine, it has been of value to some PTSD sufferers. The therapy is individualized so if this is a therapy that interests you, you will need to search out and find a practitioner.

All of the therapies listed in this alternative/complementary section may be helpful to some with PTSD. However, you should talk to your PCP or mental health practitioner before using them as sole treatment for your condition. The National Institutes of Health have a center known as

National Center for Complementary and Alternative Medicine (NCCAM) that can be found on the web at www.nccam.nih.gov. The site gives up-to-date research on the alternative treatments for medical conditions.

Relaxation and self-help techniques you can use on your own

Throughout this book, we advocate that you take responsibility for your own recovery. In addition to working with your treatment providers to ensure you are receiving the best and appropriate treatment, you can be proactive in finding ways to deal with your PTSD symptoms by learning to relax and reduce stress.

The most effective sequence of techniques for stress reduction is movement first, then breathing practices, and finally relaxation/meditation. The movement practice should be calming.

Movement practices are important, especially for vets who are used to physical activity, as a way to reduce physical tension and ease into the other practices.

Yoga, a mental and physical discipline that originated in India, may provide you with benefits from both the physical and mental aspects. There are a number of different types of yoga, some of which relate to specific religious traditions, such as Hinduism and Buddhism. Other styles are guided meditation without the religious component. Many vets find that yoga helps reduce tension, improve sleep, and give them a sense of control.

QiGong (Chi Kong), an ancient Chinese and Korean practice, uses movement and breathing to circulate energy and strengthen both the inside and outside of the body. One form of QiGong is called **Tai Chi,** a Chinese martial art that uses slow, continuous, circular forms to maintain a sense of mental and physical balance. Breathing control and relaxation are important elements of Tai Chi, and veterans who practice the martial art report that they feel less anger, anxiety, and depression.

Breathing Practices can help you relax. The following breathing techniques can be learned easily to rapidly reduce stress and, if practiced daily, can restore the balance of the stress response system over time.

(1) Slow breathing through the nose at five or six breaths per minute with the eyes closed is called Resonant or Coherent Breathing. This can be learned from a CD entitled Respire-1, which you can find by following the links at www.mybackto-thewall.com.

(2) Deep breathing exercises help you to breathe properly—from the belly and not the chest—and consequently help you to relax.

(3) Advanced training is available for other breathing techniques, such as Victorious Breath, Alternate Nostril Breathing, or QiGong Breathing, to name a few.

Relaxation techniques can help release tension and reduce stress. In focused relaxation, you choose a small object that means something to you. Focus all your attention on that object as you breathe in and out deeply. Try not to think of anything else; if thoughts intrude, turn your attention back to the object you're focusing on. After several minutes, you should feel calmer and more relaxed. Another relaxation technique is progressive muscle relaxation, in which you tense a major muscle group and hold the tension for several seconds. Then you suddenly release the tension and feel the deep relaxation. Move from one muscle group to another until you have tensed and relaxed all the major muscles in your body.

Meditation can also help you relax. You can simply sit quietly, slowly breathing in and out and saying a calming word, such as "calm," "peace," "relax." You can also meditate following a particular spiritual tradition. However, you may need to go slowly in following traditional meditation techniques to avoid being overwhelmed with thoughts and feelings. Meditation should be a positive experience, not a difficult one.

These self-help relaxation and stress-reduction techniques do not take the place of the traditional therapies described above, but they can help you be better prepared to benefit from treatment. More information about them can be found at www.mybacktothewall.com.

STEP SEVEN: ADVOCATING FOR YOURSELF IN THE SEARCH FOR EFFECTIVE TREATMENT

DR. C:

People respond to medications differently, so knowing that a medication really helped another vet does not mean that that same medication will work for you. The reverse is also true. There may be unique circumstances that caused a friend of yours to react negatively to a medication, whereas that same medication may be just what you yourself need.

Therefore, you should talk to your treating physician openly and honestly about various medications. If your doctor prescribes a medication for you, avoid making the mistake of not even starting to take the medication simply because you are convinced that the drug won't work based upon what friends or relatives tell you or what you may read on the Internet or what you see in a TV commercial. The selection of medication should always be between you and your physician and must be based upon your individual circumstances, as well as the biological characteristics of your own body—and no one else's.

You may experience side effects from a medication. If that happens, don't stop taking the medication before it can do any good. Often, side effects are temporary, and the doctor knows they are likely to rapidly go away or decrease in severity as you continue to take a medicine. Sometimes, a doctor can make changes in the prescription (e.g., taking the medicine in smaller doses several times a day instead of all at once, reducing or increasing the dose, or taking the medicine at a different time of day) to reduce or eliminate the side effects. But if you stop the medicine without talking to the doctor, he has no chance to deal with side effects, and you lose the opportunity to gain maximum benefit from the medicine.

I see many vets who seem either overmedicated or undermedicated for their condition. I cannot stress enough the importance of talking candidly with your physician about how you are doing on your medications. If you are always feeling "drugged out," "zoned out," or unable to do normal activities of daily living while on a medication, your doctor should know. Likewise, if you don't feel any change in your condition after giving a drug a fair try, then don't just continue to feel bad . . . *say something!* Your doctor may want to change your dose, switch your medication, or use a combination therapy instead. Also, take the medications as prescribed, and, as a general rule, do not stop medications abruptly (as they may cause discontinuation symptoms). If you decide to discontinue prescribed medications, do so after talking to and working out a plan to discontinue with your physician.

STAY THE COURSE UNTIL YOU GET THE RESULTS YOU SEEK

DR. C AND CHAPLAIN P:

If you have decided to enter treatment, you are to be congratulated. It is virtually never too late to make this decision. There are soldiers who have been back from the Vietnam War for over forty years who are only now seeking treatment—and benefiting from it. Do not, however, stop being proactively engaged once you enter treatment. That is the point at which you should become most actively involved. Continue to educate yourself. Read, listen to, and learn everything you can about PTSD and therapies used for it. Utilize reputable websites—including our own, wwwmybacktothewall.com; those sponsored by large universities with research departments; or the PTSD website from the VA itself, the Center for PTSD, which can be found at www.ptsd.va.gov.

You can also be of help to your physician or therapist by recommending information presented in this and other books, as well as recommending the excellent PTSD references found in Colonel Charles W. Hoge's book, *Once a Warrior—Always a Warrior: Navigating the Transition from Combat to Home—Including Combat Stress, PTSD, and TBI.*

Most of all, never stop asking questions, and never resign yourself to accepting the status quo until you really do experience improvements. Remember that "bad (embracing the suck) is never good enough."

CHAPTER FIVE:

V_IEWING YOUR ISSUES IN A NEW LIGHT

"People say that I 'lost' my legs in the war . . . as if I had misplaced them. I didn't lose my legs. I willingly offered them up in the service of my country."
~ Iraq War veteran

APPROACHING ISSUES FROM A NEW ANGLE

DR. C AND CHAPLAIN P:

One of the most important things we can learn to do in life is to *reframe* negative events that have happened to us. To reframe life events is not to deny them, sanitize them, or mask them. It is, instead, to view them, almost like a painting on a wall, which changes as your viewing angle shifts. Sometimes, when even an ugly picture of life is viewed through a different perspective, one sees new meaning, new possibilities, and new solutions.

Research has shown that those veterans who—despite the hardships they encountered—looked back upon their combat experiences as a period of growth and purpose did far better in life and were much more resilient. Holocaust survivors who saw meaning in their determination to overcome and survive their sufferings had similar experiences.

Just as viewing the combat experience through a different lens can change the meaning of the experience and our response to it, so can viewing PTSD in a new light change your perception of your illness. A new view can minimize shame and self-blame, and, instead, encourage sufferers to take a proactive approach to what is a treatable medical condition.

Now that you have read a good deal of this book, we hope that the angle through which you are starting to view your own PTSD or that of a loved one is starting to shift. You now know the following things:

(1) That millions of people have this disorder, and that you are not alone.

(2) That you weren't born with PTSD, but acquired it because of something you experienced, either in the service of your country or in the course of a terrible event you did not ask for.

(3) That PTSD is a psycho-neuro-endocrine disorder, which means that it is a real medical illness with a real biological basis.

(4) That PTSD is as real a war wound as any physical injury, and one for which you deserve to receive treatment.

Viewed in this light, PTSD sufferers and their loved ones can begin addressing their issues in a new way. They can start by describing their symptoms and behaviors more accurately. The father back from the war can say to his children, "I am so sorry that my brain seems to be irritable today. It sometimes gets confused and thinks it's back in Iraq. But it isn't about you. My heart loves you very much."

When a stop by the local gas station makes you uncomfortable, you can put a name to the feeling by saying, "The smell of diesel triggers my nervous system," and by using language to identify your trigger, take the first step toward gaining mastery over it. Instead of giving up on yourself and your relationship to your family, you can say, "I have a medical illness. But just as if I had diabetes or cardiovascular disease, I can and should take responsibility for finding ways to better manage this illness."

GAINING NEW PERSPECTIVES IN YOUR VIEW OF THE WORLD AND YOUR PLACE IN IT: PTSD RESPECTS NO WAR ZONES

CHAPLAIN P:

It's important to remember that PTSD is bigger than any single person or any single war. While the suffering that it causes anyone should never be minimized, it is helpful to look around you and see that you are not the only one dealing with the problem. Your problems may not seem so overwhelming if you enlarge your perspective and take a larger world view. Statistics show that a full 50% of people in the US have experienced at least one serious traumatic event in life and that approximately 20% go on to develop PTSD symptoms. Warriors experience PTSD at a much higher rate—from an average of 25% to as high as 50% among some soldier populations that have been studied—but they, nevertheless, don't claim a monopoly on this problem. In any situation or place you find yourself, it's not uncommon to find someone in the room who has had an experience as harrowing as yours. But people can, and frequently do, survive these events intact.

In a given type of situation, there are almost always "odds," or percentages, that get tossed around about whether people recover or not. And in all these situations, there is also a number that is usually "calculated" to "predict" an individual's supposed chances. For example, someone might say that the odds of achieving recovery from a particular trauma are "50/50." I don't believe that such numbers are, in fact, what determines people's odds. Instead, I find that people's *reaction* to such numbers is, in fact, the most interesting indicator. For example, the usual reaction is for people to view the number as a statement of what they *cannot* recover, rather than a statement of what they *can* strive to attain. If the odds are stated to be 50/50, most people will think of all the reasons why they will be among the 50% who succumb. Well, what about the other 50%? *Somebody* has to be on *their* side of the equation. It may as well be *you*!

Alice, for example, is a female vet who has had terribly traumatic experiences, but whose capacity to reframe her experiences and maintain resilience is striking. She combines acceptance of those things she cannot change with a strong internalized determination to change those things that she can. "It seems to me," she said, "that my life is like a high-crime ghetto area, riddled with shattered windows. But, you know, in every one of those ghettoes, if you look carefully enough, you will find at least *one* window, in which someone has made geraniums bloom. I am determined to *be* that window."

Alice is an example of what researchers call a *dispositional optimist*. This optimism is a quality in human beings that science has credited with lowering mortality, increasing recovery, and extending life expectancy of the ill far beyond the limitations of what modern medicine can attain. It exists through the making of an internal, personal choice: to learn from every situation (even those that are traumatic), to act upon the belief that we can continue to learn new ways of coping with even severe setbacks, and most of all, to exercise a commitment to continue showing up for life. We encourage you the reader to read Dennis Prager's book, *Happiness Is a Serious Problem: A Human Nature Repair Manual*, in which he writes about how changing our view of a problem can help us go on with our life despite the existence of a potential problem.

Many people with PTSD have stopped showing up for life because they think, or have been told, that they are worthless individuals or "crazy" for having the illness. They no longer show up for themselves, their spouses, or their children. Such a waste of human potential is, quite simply, unacceptable. Let's take a look at some common issues affected by PTSD and how a new view can affect ways in which *you* show up for life.

TAKE A NEW VIEW OF YOUR MARITAL AND FAMILY INTIMACY

Many relationships fall apart when one or both parties have PTSD, simply because one partner doesn't understand the other's state of mind, and therefore cannot help the partner adapt. For example, many wives do not have a clue as to why their husbands react as if the war were still going on after they return home. What you have read in this book about how the brain imprints traumatic stimuli and recycles them thousands of times, long after someone is out of danger, explained a lot that you may not have known before.

Wives: When your husband continues to pace the floor and guard the house instead of cuddling up with you on the sofa, imagine what would have happened if he had not been on guard in the war zone. Remember that in war, constant vigilance kept him alive. Even a momentary distraction, let alone a ninety-minute movie, could have been deadly.

After the return home, many warriors transfer that vigilance over to the home. Here, biology rears its head again and places spouses in conflict. One spouse (typically the wife, although not always) wants to resume the kind of interpersonal connectedness that we refer to as romantic love, which pairs emotional and affectionate expression with gratification that is merely physical. The phenomenon of romantic love demands that lovers focus all of their attention on one another and virtually ignore everything and everyone else around them. Biologically speaking, it has the effect of actually turning off the threat/alarm response mechanism in the brain.

This means that for the hypervigilant redeployed husband, romantic love may come at a cost. His brain has to disable the very same mental circuitry that has helped to keep him and others alive for many months. Ask yourself if, during wartime, your partner could have ignored his battle buddies, as well as everything in his environment, just so that he could focus on what gave him pleasure. It's not likely that he could do so then. Therefore, it is difficult for him to do so now, and it will take time.

It may hurt you terribly if he overreacts when you make any kind of a sudden move to hug or kiss or simply play around with him. Remember that he may have come out of an experience in which the slightest gesture, as seemingly innocent as a civilian reaching for a cell phone, might have been intended to detonate a bomb and kill our troops.

In addition, many of the vets with PTSD with whom we have spoken say that their interest in sex has decreased considerably and that often, even with interest present, they find that sometimes the "equipment just doesn't work right." Without understanding the reason for the lack of desire or the problems "with the plumbing," many male vets become embarrassed, frustrated, or guilty, and thus begin to avoid intimacy all together. The answer is in the changes brought about by the physiological and emotional effects of their PTSD.

Husbands: Remember that intimacy and fear do not mix. If your partner fears that you will unconsciously make a hostile move, she isn't likely to relax enough to make real intimacy possible. Think carefully. Is it possible that her fight-flight-freeze reactions are being triggered by *your* overreactions and volatile temper? Maybe it is time for you to go on meds designed to control anxiety or dampen aggression, for the benefit of both of you.

Remember that the definition of what constitutes great sex can be very different for men and for women. For men, the satisfaction of sexual desire is often the prime agenda, and men can often go there directly, willingly bypassing all those little rituals like cocktails and dinner, romance, and foreplay.

But women don't function in the same way. They have to become prepared for sex in their heads before they get fully in gear in their bodies. So for women, the rituals of romantic love constitute an important part of the pregame warm-up for sexual encounter. Relaxing, and taking the time to actually make love, rather than just have sex, means that a warrior husband has to temporarily disable his vigilance switch. He has to quit walking point in his environment long enough to be fully engaged in the moment (and hopefully, much longer than that) with his wife or partner. This is no small order.

To do this, you will need to experiment with what makes both of you feel safe enough, and sufficiently separated from danger, so that he can mentally come off guard duty. Some possibilities include changing the time you make love from the night (in which we keep watch for hidden dangers and intruders) to the morning or daytime.

Try having sex when children aren't in the house; this relieves you of having to be hypervigilant about their safety or wellbeing while you're trying to concentrate on your love life.

Going on vacation so that you are in a totally new environment, like a safe and beautiful hotel that you are not responsible for defending, might be an option.

Remember to turn the power of smell (our most vigilant sense) to your advantage: work with your wife or partner to find a scent that you both love, that makes you both feel good, and that isn't associated with the war. For many, this is the smell of vanilla, but the choice is up to you. Go together to a candle shop and sniff until you've found the right smell. Then light candles in your bedroom. Candlelight enhances romance and provides the safety of light, while the smell reassures your brain that it's safe to get involved with one another.

Finally, get involved in stages. While it may seem like a chick thing, it can actually also be good for a returning warrior to just engage in holding, touching, and stroking for a while. This way, he can experience some intimacy, even though his danger switch isn't completely disengaged. Once a warrior's brain gets accustomed to the idea that the house won't burn down and the enemy won't begin lobbing mortars as soon as he lets his guard down, it will be time to move on to more heavy-duty involvement that requires less attention to danger and more intense attention to the love in your life.

If you have problems with "the equipment" and are experiencing erectile dysfunction (ED), talk with your physician about medications and other treatments that are available for this condition. ED is a common complaint of vets with PTSD and seems to be related to the chemical changes that occur with the condition. It is not an indicator that you are less of a man, and there is no reason to feel guilty about it. Treatment is generally available if you ask for it.

Has your wife gained weight and complained of insomnia, exhaustion, infections, soreness, bloating, and other symptoms? These are stress responses, not necessarily a lack of desire for intimacy. Have you considered the degree of fear she experienced as she waited for your return, holding her breath as she watched every news report? How much stress has she been subjected to as she held the family together during your tour? Is it possible that this added stress has triggered a resurgence of traumatic stress that she may have experienced in her early life, possibly as a result of abuse or assault? Instead of criticizing or expressing disappointment at her physical changes, view them as a reflection of what she has sacrificed and the stress she has undergone so that you could continue being a soldier.

You both need to view the issue in a new light. Both parties need to mentally role-reverse with their partners in order to see things through the other's eyes and experience. Reframe your perspectives by considering what factors are influencing the other person's behaviors instead of taking those behaviors personally. Remember that many of those behaviors are not under the conscious control of the person with PTSD but are reflexive reactions rooted in having been in a life-threatening environment.

In working with married veterans with PTSD, I often find a wife who is also traumatically stressed. Often the husband is the Locked and Loaded type, and the wife is the Hunkered in the Bunker type. But the Army only looks at his condition and does not evaluate hers. Wives are highly unlikely to realize that they, too, may have traumatic stress or even full blown PTSD. Viewing marital conflict in this new light may be very helpful.

More effective for this than any pill is a simple, hefty dose of honest communication that will help each party walk a mile in the other's shoes. Wives often say to me, "You're right. I don't think about what he's been through or how things look to him because he refuses to tell me anything about his experiences! I feel I need to know."

Husbands, in turn, say, "I don't want to tell her. If I told her the horrible things I've seen and done, it would do her more harm than good." One sixty-year-old Vietnam vet on his fourth marriage recently told me, "My new wife is only thirty-four. She wasn't even born until years after the war. How could she possibly understand the things I saw?"

All are right, to a degree. And that is the key word: degree. Simply letting the most gruesome details of one's last tour spill out over the kitchen table may not be helpful. But neither is it helpful for spouses to feel shut out of the warrior's experiences, especially when they continue to witness bits and pieces of those experiences emerging during their partners' nightmares. A compromise is needed.

The assistance of a good family counselor, such as an Army Family Life Counselor or VA family therapist, can really be helpful in this situation. With the consent of both parties, a counselor may serve as an intermediary to explain to family members, in edited and less gruesome terms, the general nature of the experiences that have most seriously affected a warrior. This may be easier for the warrior than attempting such a conversation himself or herself. It is certainly better for a spouse to receive the edited version than it is to continue operating in total ignorance.

Another method I have found is helpful in promoting the sharing of difficult experiences is for a warrior to find a movie that communicates the feel of what he went through, even though the events may have been different. *Saving Private Ryan, We Were Soldiers, Brothers,* and *The Patriot* are examples of movies with scenes that may serve as a representation of the kind of trauma a warrior has experienced but cannot speak about. There are probably many more such movies that may serve as an entry point into a discussion of combat, trauma, loss, and the resulting thoughts, feelings, and behaviors that we have talked about in this book.

Asking the spouse to watch the movie as a symbol for what happened, rather than as a verbatim description, can be very helpful. (I recommend that the spouse watch the film in private, without the veteran-spouse in the room.) The spouse doesn't have to know every grisly detail. Getting just enough information may be exactly what the partner needs to view a difficult situation through the lens of a warrior's experience. However, marital counseling without an individual grasp of one's own PTSD illness is probably not going to be very successful.

Restoring intimacy in marriage after combat often takes time, understanding, and gradual adjustment. Here are a few simple suggestions.

(1) Expectations need to be kept to a minimum so that partners don't feel that they are failing to measure up. Sometimes, especially when a spouse is very hypervigilant, it's important to begin with intimate contact other than intercourse. Simple holding and caressing is important and less likely to be interrupted if a momentary distraction occurs.

(2) One vet I know is fearful of sleeping inside the house and camps out in a tent in the yard, much like the hooch he occupied in the war. I said to his wife, "Companion him. View this in a new light, as an invitation to sleep out under the stars together once in a while. If you exhibit a willingness to follow him outside, he may eventually be more willing to follow you inside."

(3) If your husband needs to check the locks, say, "Let's check them together." You will validate rather than ridicule his fears,

and at the same time you serve as a witness to the reality that all is okay and his fears are really unfounded, after all. If this process repeats many times, his brain may learn that the fear response is no longer needed. It's a very gentle, loving kind of therapy.

(4) Instead of reacting angrily or with rejection, offer to help your spouse make a posttraumatic diary that will calendar when he or she is affected by triggers, as well as the times and circumstances in which they are experienced. Now that you understand how triggers work, offer to help him unravel their mystery together.

Viewing trauma and children differently: minimizing emotional damage

In my work with families affected by trauma, I have seen many children become PTSD patients, simply because they were so seriously secondarily affected by a parent's untreated PTSD. For normal growth and development, all children require a sense that their parents are safe, loving, and consistently trustworthy. When children are exposed to chronic episodes of ballistic adult behavior or aggressive and volatile reactions, their own flight-fight-freeze responses kick in.

They live in constant fear of when the other shoe will drop. They learn to avoid and hide from a parent. When they need love and support and receive irritability and anger, they learn that a parent cannot be depended upon and feel betrayed. To a child's brain, this constitutes a threat to their emotional and biological survival, resulting in pediatric traumatic stress.

Children whose parents are Hunkered in the Bunker suffer equally. A parent's withdrawn behavior signals intense emotional rejection to a child and can lead kids to feel inappropriately responsible for fixing Dad or Mom. They may think, "Dad wouldn't be this way if only I were better." This leads to children feeling they are never good enough, and to their making constant, herculean efforts to be little adults who must earn their parents' love by holding everything in the family together. It's a prescription for a seriously damaged childhood.

Viewing your issues in a new light means recognizing the serious lifetime damage that can be inflicted upon your children if you fail to seek treatment. If you have PTSD, you have a responsibility to address the situation so that your children will not develop long-term mental illnesses or emotional disorders.

If you are a spouse, you have an equal responsibility to insist on proper intervention. Simply telling your children, "Dad doesn't really mean what he says. Just ignore it when he's like that," is *not* adequate or appropriate. It is a way of avoiding the problem and, worse yet, of enabling it to continue out of fear of confronting it. You must have the courage to act, for your benefit and that of your children.

Equally as harmful, however, is the situation in which the spouse who remained at home encourages an emotional split between the children and the military parent who deployed. Sometimes parents at home have grown accustomed to the power they have gained by being the one to whom the children constantly turned for guidance and permission. It may make them feel good, and, rather than relinquish some of their authority to the returning parent, they may encourage the children to continue this practice, instead of bringing Dad (or Mom) back into the picture after redeployment home.

Military marriages are falling apart in increasing numbers because of the difficulties partners experience in readjusting to each other, to their respective roles in marriage, and to their children after a tour has ended. Some husbands want to simply import their military rank into the home by occupying an authoritarian role. If they have PTSD, they may become over-controlling and, at times, even tyrannical. Others are the opposite and feel excluded from any authority role in the home after the wife has exercised it all the time they were deployed.

Some wives who may have had to pick up the entire burden of parental responsibility during a spouse's deployment may be reluctant to return to the way things were, especially if they know that in a year or less, another deployment will roll around and they will need to readjust all over again.

Still other wives may have been so overburdened by having to single-handedly parent a family that they can't wait to relinquish the reins, and wind up dumping all responsibility on a traumatized returning warrior. The warrior who said farewell to younger children may return, a year or more later, to a houseful of rambunctious, rebellious adolescents who aren't ready to adjust to two disciplinarians instead of just one.

The time warp caused by the rapid growth and change of children can, under the best of circumstances, make a warrior feel deeply depressed and out-of-sync over what he or she has missed of a son or daughter's childhood. Nowhere is this more apparent—or more painful—than when deployment has caused a parent to skip a major event in a child's life, such as first steps, first word, a graduation, a first communion, or some other milestone. Under the worst of circumstances, it can make some households feel more like a war zone than the one the warrior left.

When this happens, it's definitely time to view issues in a new light—one that emphasizes the opportunity rather than the conflict these situations present. You owe it to your children to seek family counseling. MFLAC counselors are independent counselors who set up offices on post, where their services are provided by the military. They are highly qualified and very helpful. Even though the time period that a specific counselor may be at your particular post or installation and available for sessions may be limited, MFLAC's are nevertheless a great way to jumpstart short-term, solution-focused therapy. Army Family Life Chaplains are well-trained counselors specializing in helping couples address the challenges that military life imposes on a family. Similar counselors exist in other branches of the military. The VA has similar counselors, and you may also be able to access counseling for your children under the TRICARE program of care for military dependents. Finally, you can access counseling help through some of the resources in this book, on our website, or through nonprofit organizations that provide veteran services.

With the help of a counselor, both parents can learn about and appreciate the skill sets that each has acquired when they were separated by deployment. Instead of becoming threatened by the other's areas of competence, they can consciously decide to divide responsibilities in new ways that capitalize on those skills. She may have become a crack lawnmower jockey; he may have become a pretty good cook. Expanding upon and changing roles can really enliven a marriage and allows children to see their parents as more interesting people who aren't in a rut and aren't afraid to learn new things. After all, risking oneself on Dad's lasagna once a week could be pretty scary, but it could also make for a new family dinner ritual that draws the family closer.

Children need to be brought into the process and allowed to participate in helping the warrior reintegrate back into the home. Let little children create a play about all the things they have done during a tour; let older kids put photos and music together into a PowerPoint diary of their lives as a gift to a returning parent. Be creative. Rethink. Reframe. Bring your kids into the picture.

Now you (the partner with PTSD) know that you have a real medical illness that is nothing to be ashamed of. View your condition through a new lens, explain it to your children (simply, of course), and take steps to get treatment, for their sake. Drop the shame; you don't need to bear it. Ditch the fear of being called "crazy"—you are not.

If you are aggressive, get on medication to dampen it as you learn behavioral ways to manage it. If you react to triggers when with your family, learn to identify the triggers and responses openly and without embarrassment. "Whoops! There goes my alarm again. Sorry, kids!" tells children that things are okay and that you are not reacting to them. By all means help them understand that it is not about them—it is about an illness that you have and are determined to make better. In doing so, you will teach them the invaluable lessons of hope and persistence in the face of difficult situations.

Don't be afraid to attend family activities for fear some stranger will call you "crazy." "Crazy" is not nearly as bad as the epithets your kids will use to describe you years from now if you let your illness rob them of a relationship with you. Neither emotional unavailability nor unrestrained emotional volatility ever won a child's heart. Both of these things leave children both helpless and hopeless. Instead, help children to see your situation in a new and more positive light. Let your children see that you are honestly encountering a problem and are taking responsible steps to manage it. It's a lesson they'll profit from and respect you for as they get older.

VIEWING TRIGGERS IN YOUR ENVIRONMENT AS MANAGEABLE EVENTS

Probably the most difficult thing for soldiers and families to deal with is the recurrence of PTSD-related *triggers*. Defined simply, a trigger is a stimulus in the environment that is intercepted by the amygdalae and hippocampus in the downstairs part of the brain. If the amygdalae recognize the stimulus as being both (1) familiar and (2) threatening, they will set off the alarm that activates the posttraumatic stress response.

If you are a Locked and Loaded type, your experience of a trigger is likely to involve rapid breathing and heart rate, a rush of energy that makes you feel wired, a feeling of anxiety and irritability, and the need to do something physical in response to that feeling. If you are a Hunkered in the Bunker type, your experience of a trigger is more likely to involve a feeling of being smothered, trapped, or claustrophobic. You may experience a scared-stiff feeling that leaves you unable to move or help yourself or a feeling that you need to hide or erase yourself. You may even feel yourself unable to speak. Although you may feel your heart rate increase, it is likely to be felt more as a flutter or palpitation than as a pounding big bass drum.

The stress/alarm response that is activated in the brain and body occurs internally. But the triggers that activate it occur externally where they can be seen, touched, heard, or smelled. This means that they can be identified. Once you begin to identify your triggers, you can begin to manage them so you won't be at their mercy all the time.

This chapter includes a simple four-step process that I created and teaches my patients to help them deal with triggers.

The I Am Able Method©

The I Am Able Method (IAAM) (Copyright 2010, Chrysanthe L. Parker, All rights reserved) is quick and easy to do. It reinforces the concept that the person who is grappling with the challenges of PTSD is a *proactive person of ability* and not a helpless victim. It forces your downstairs brain to begin reporting in to your upstairs brain so that your CEO can begin regaining a measure of control over your behaviors.

The method requires that you use pen and paper, each sheet divided into four quadrants or sections, which you will process through *in order*. You can also use the form provided on the My Back to the Wall website, which you can download and print multiple copies, from which you can assemble a *trigger diary*.

The four quadrants of the IAAM are as follows:

(1) I Am Sense-Able: Write down the feelings and sensations that you experienced when you felt triggered or uncomfortable. This is information you derive from *inside* yourself.

(2) I Am Observe-Able: This means that you are capable of gathering objective intel from *outside* yourself. Write down the time of day, place, weather conditions, and activity you were engaged in, plus anything you saw, touched, felt, smelled, or heard when you first noticed you were uncomfortable. Add any other observations you have about the incident.

(3) I Am Reason-Able: You are able to use your upstairs reasoning skills to compare the inside data (#1) with the outside data (#2). Are they alike or are they different? What knowledge do you derive from this? Specifically, consider the following:

(a) What were you most afraid of, or what bothered you the most?

(b) What feelings were in your body when you felt uncomfortable?

(c) When and where have you felt this way before?

(d) What thoughts do you have that go with the feelings?

(4) I Am Response-Able: You are able to begin making use of your upstairs brain to start crafting reason-based responses to your environment, instead of always relying on your primitive reflex-based reactions. Using your executive thinking skills, you can determine how often you experience a trigger, if there is a pattern to your experience, and how it may be related to a past traumatic event. With that information at hand, you can ask yourself the following:

(a) Am I experiencing now the actual degree of danger I experienced then?

(b) Is it actually necessary for me to fight, run, or hide?

(c) Am I physically okay?

(d) If so, write down and then verbally speak the following message, in its entirety:

"I recognize this trigger (name it) as being from the past.

I no longer need to react to it in the present.

I give my brain permission to relax because I know I am safe."

On the My Back to the Wall website, you'll find a form that you can print and take to a local shop like Kinko's or the UPS Store for laminating. It is conveniently sized to fold and fit in your wallet. Whenever you feel yourself triggered, get it out immediately and go through the exercise. Then, later in the day or evening when your feelings of panic have subsided, go through the written exercise. Do this each and every time you have a triggering episode. Enlist the help of your spouse also to identify when you appear to be triggered. After you have done your written exercise, sharing it with your spouse can help bring him or her in the loop and increase the level of understanding and support for your situation.

Now, you may be wondering why it is necessary to go through this process. There is most definitely a reason. In Chapters Two and Three, you learned that the downstairs brain is responsible for creating triggers. What you now must learn is that the upstairs brain is responsible for defusing triggers. The key for engaging the upstairs brain is the use of written and spoken language. When you both write and speak about a trigger, it serves as a key that unlocks the power of your upstairs brain to begin taking over responsibility for dealing with it reasonably, instead of defaulting to your primitive survival centers. Do not sidestep any part of this exercise, even if you think it will take a lot of time and trouble. The truth is that in actual application, it takes seconds or minutes. And isn't getting more control over your life worth that? Over time, if you perform it faithfully, it will help you train your upstairs brain to kick into gear more and more quickly.

<u>Remember that triggers aren't necessarily an exact match; they serve as symbols.</u> Try to look beneath the surface of what makes you uncomfortable. For example, one Vietnam veteran would become very triggered when he would see black socks on the floor of his kids' rooms. He would become overwhelmed by the desire to vomit and would start screaming. What in the world was so awful about black socks? After careful thought, the vet remembered an incident when he was packing up gear in the dim early morning light in the jungle. As he was preparing to move out, he saw several black objects in the brush that looked like socks. Thinking they were his, he went to retrieve them. To his horror, they were not socks, but the black feet and lower calves that had been blown off of an African American soldier who had stepped on a mine.

The association between the black socks and the black legs and feet was close enough for the brain, which looks for surface similarity when identifying threats to survival and doesn't always strike an exact match.

Suggestions for Spouses/Partners: If you see your spouse or partner flare, go ballistic, or freeze up, and the response is inappropriate, disproportionate to the situation, or just plain for no reason, *stop before you speak*. Instead of reacting negatively (e.g., "I hate it when you go off on me for no reason!"), use your own reasoning powers to evaluate what the situation is telling you. Even though there seems to be no reason that you can see for the response, that doesn't mean there is no reason at all. Rather, it is an obvious indication that the cause is something that only your partner's brain is aware of. After all, only his brain—not yours— holds the data about the past trauma.

Respect the fact that his unreasonable behavior may be exactly that—not a product of reason, but a product of a trigger that is activating his primitive stress response. Wait a few moments for things to subside and say, "I know you were really bothered back there by something I don't know about and probably shouldn't take personally. My gut is telling me you were triggered by something. Can we work on it together and see what it might be?"

Handling triggers in this way may seem awkward at first. Stick with it. Like all skills, this must be learned until it eventually becomes second nature. If you start constructing a trigger notebook and read it over and over again, you will imprint messages in your upstairs brain that will assist you in gaining mastery over those things that cause you to default to survival mode. It also helps to appreciate that **remembering** an event in the now does not have to be the same as **re-experiencing** the trauma of that event when it originally occurred.

If your doctor feels it is appropriate, you can also use this method in conjunction with central-acting medications or nutritional substances which help interrupt the alarm response. The most important thing to remember is that you do not have to remain helpless. Triggers can be managed.

VIEWING RISKY BEHAVIORS—"HIGHER, FASTER, FARTHER"— THROUGH A DIFFERENT LENS

Something that spells the end to both the relationships and careers of many active-duty and former soldiers is their increasing drive to engage in risky behaviors when they return home from downrange. It takes many forms but is almost always a "guy thing," associated with the Locked and Loaded profile. Locked and Loaded warriors often feel a need, or even a deep-seated craving, for danger that leaves both family members and commanding officers aghast, not to mention infuriated.

"What is with him?" I hear wives say over and over again. "Is this some sort of midlife crisis or what?" These wives are referring to a pattern of behavior that involves increasingly higher levels of risk, is often expressed through activities engaged in at increasingly faster speeds, and puts soldiers farther and farther outside the boundaries of acceptable behavior. These behaviors are distinguished by the fact that they don't seem merely recreational and they're not relaxing—the men engaging in these activities seem driven. Wives, family members, authority figures, and employers often do not recognize the relationship between such behaviors and PTSD.

From what I have observed, risky behaviors generally fall into one of three categories: things that are (1) physically risky, (2) relationally risky, or (3) socially/professionally risky.

Physically risky behaviors in PTSD include a sudden interest in extreme sports (e.g., motocross, skydiving) or extremely fast vehicles, usually motorcycles or fast cars. I hear many tales of the family minivan that suddenly gets traded in for a Harley. Actually, the number of motorcycle crashes in which returning vets have been killed after redeployment has reached such astronomical numbers that motorcycle safety has become the object of a major public service announcement campaign, seen often on the Pentagon Channel. These announcements, however, only address the vehicle operational safety issue and do not clue vets into the biological reason why many of them feel so driven to come back from war, only to become crash dummies at home.

Relationally risky behaviors include unsafe sex, extramarital affairs, porn, and gambling, all of which can become highly addictive. These behaviors are almost never pursued merely for their own sake. Instead they are a way of walking the line in ways that the warrior knows can really spell disaster in his relationships.

Socially and professionally risky behaviors usually involve a refusal to comply with rules (including truancy) in school or the workplace or insubordination or disrespect of a commanding officer in the military. These behaviors are virtually guaranteed to bring the soldier into a dangerous confrontation, including the threat of expulsion, loss of a job, loss of a career, or possible criminal penalties and incarceration. So why on earth would soldiers court such disastrous consequences?

If you ask a warrior why he engages in these kinds of behaviors, he's likely to tell you that it makes him feel "alive." He's also likely to tell you that he felt more "alive" downrange than he does back home and is in search of that feeling again. These warriors may think that they are rebels without a cause, harmlessly searching for the meaning of life. In fact, they are usually in search of a particular kind of chemical rush associated with their PTSD, and their quest can, and often does, cause significant harm.

In Chapter Three, we discussed the chemical profile of Locked and Loaded personalities. It includes high levels of noradrenaline (which super-stimulates the heart) and dopamine (an internal combination of an opiate and speed that acts as a feel-good painkiller, similar in function to an opiate and stimulant drugs). The continual reengagement of the HPA Axis in Locked and Loaded individuals can place huge physical demands upon the body and can be very exhausting. When Locked and Loaded warriors' fight-or-flight responses are triggered, the sudden rush of noradrenaline gives them a super-charged feeling of energy that overcomes this exhaustion. In addition, a rush of dopamine affects the body like the administration of an addictive drug. It feels good now but wears off quickly. Over time, getting the same feeling again requires more and more. A cycle very much like drug dependency sets in.

When Locked and Loaded warriors redeploy home, some (not all) find themselves becoming numb and disengaged from life, which is a symptom of PTSD. They unconsciously search for ways to overcome this and feel "alive" again. Usually by trial and error, they learn that engaging in risky behavior gives them the rush they crave, much like engaging in, and surviving, a firefight. As their relationships begin to deteriorate, and their nightmares, hyperarousal, and re-experiences of trauma continue to intensify, they often feel deep-seated emotional pain and seek something to soothe it. Again, usually by trial and error, they subconsciously learn that behaviors designed to place them at maximum risk result in their feeling a mellow kind of high. This is a sign of their dopamine level on the rise.

Without realizing it, these warriors use risky activities as a means of virtually *"self-scaring" their brains and bodies* in order to elicit a biochemical response that feels uplifting or soothing to them. Since they no longer have an enemy shooting at them, they manufacture the needed risk themselves. In other words, they develop the intense need to "self-scare." In the process, they become their own worst enemies. They can cause serious damage to themselves and the people around them. Sometimes, risky behaviors are potentially lethal, lending a new, and literal, meaning to the term "scared to death."

Viewing the issue of risky behaviors in a new light means understanding what drives it biologically and then taking appropriate action. Most soldiers don't understand what they are doing to themselves, their bodies, their loved ones, and their employers. They need to be confronted with their behaviors and educated to the biological connection that their conduct bears to PTSD. When PTSD behaviors get this risky, it's definitely time to seek treatment.

PTSD AND SUBSTANCE ABUSE

DR. C:

So, which comes first: the chicken or the egg? Combat or cocaine? Abuse or alcohol? While there are as many different stories as there are trauma survivors, one thing is certain: trauma and substance abuse often go hand in hand. This issue, too, deserves to be viewed in a new light that leads to less shame and more insight into the circumstances and histories that shape—and dismantle— peoples' lives.

The entry of substance abuse onto the life stage of many trauma survivors begins in childhood, long before their lips have touched booze or their hearts have been jolted by crack. Children of substance-abusing parents are more likely themselves to become substance abusers, and three times as likely to become the victims of childhood trauma. Sometimes, the trauma inflicted by substance-abusing parents is meted out in violent forms that result in broken bones, ciga-rette burns, and trips to the emergency room where fanciful stories are told about how little Johnny "fell down the stairs again."

In other cases it occurs in the dark, in the hushed silence of little girls who lie frozen in terror while their bodies are exploited by sadistic adults. The substances consumed by these parents numbed their senses, unleashed their inhibitions, and make them more than willing to treat children as objects, or worse.

When survivors of childhood trauma begin to grow up, they have only rarely known the healing power of love, trust, and competent treatment. Their pain is unceasing. Often the only "doctor" making house calls on them is the local pusher. Many begin with booze and quickly move on to street drugs, which turn them into juvenile replicas of the parents who abused them to begin with.

Some of those abused as children (if they are lucky enough to survive their childhoods) look for escape from their surroundings by seeking a life in the mili-tary. To them, it appears to be a haven, in which the prospect of facing combat seems no worse than the drug-fueled chaos of an abusive household. But their central nervous systems are already scarred and imprinted by trauma. They gain a foothold in a world of military opportunity, only to lose that footing more quickly when exposed to the traumatic stress of combat or deployment. When that happens, the siren of substance sings a familiar lullaby to them, offering comfort and consolation from nightmares and flashbacks. This possibility becomes even more likely if a parent is himself a substance abuser. Genetics certainly can play a part in the development of substance abuse in children, but only a part. Not all children of substance-abusing parents become substance abusers themselves, and some substance-abusing children come from families that lack substance-abusing parents.

Still other young men and women enter the military as fresh-faced young-sters of promise or as family men and women, determined to make the Army their home. For them, the pain of untreated PTSD may open a door not only to emotional illness, but to the terrible social and relational destruction which booze and drugs rain down on soldiers, as well as entire families.

> *"I used to drink a fifth of whisky every day," said the wholesome, clean-cut Iraqi Freedom vet sitting across from me. "I tried to get treatment from the VA, but time after time my appointments would get cancelled. I finally gave up and didn't go back. At least the booze was one thing I could depend upon to not cancel on me."*

The difference between engaging in chronically risky behaviors, on the one hand, and the abuse of substances, on the other, is only that they are two different routes to the same goal: self-medication of emotional and physical pain. Risky behavior is as much a "drug of choice" as alcohol or cocaine. It may take the form of a compulsion to engage in extreme sports, to gamble, to do things which could place one's own wellbeing or that of another at risk, or to engage in conduct or relationships that are illicit, and therefore perceived by the brain as dangerous. This includes things such as consuming pornography or engaging in extra-marital affairs. All of these things serve to stimulate the brain in various ways. Practitioners of "risky business" use danger and risk to jump start the body's own manufacture of soothing neurochemicals. It is a way of getting a high that is not much different than buying one's chosen substance over the liquor store counter or from the pusher down the street. In each instance, the element of danger is consistently sought out as an avenue of escape.

Alcohol is the choice of those looking to chill out from the pain. A central nervous system depressant, booze is a one-way ticket to self-induced depression. Marijuana is a favorite with those seeking to retreat into an avoidant fog. Opiates, such as prescription pain killers—hydrocodone, Oxycontin (oxycodone), as well as street heroin become useful for those attempting to "numb out." Cocaine, methamphetamine, or prescription ADHD medications like Adderall (mixed amphetamine salts) jumpstart the heart rates of Locked and Loaded types, who became so accustomed to existing outside the wire at mach speed that anything less feels like slow motion.

PTSD has a high rate of co-occurrence with other illnesses, including alcohol and substance abuse. Co-occurring substance abuse magnifies and complicates PTSD, making it more difficult to sort out symptoms, diagnose underlying problems, and prescribe effective treatment. Finally, but very importantly, the use of alcohol in combination with other drugs that a warrior may be receiving for PTSD, for an injury, or for another health condition can be deadly.

If you or someone you love is suffering from co-occurring PTSD and substance abuse, it is critical that you ensure prompt treatment from caregivers skilled in the management of dual-diagnosis patients—those who suffer from substance abuse *and* PTSD (or other psychiatric illnesses). If PTSD is not treated, those who seek to self-medicate against its pain will continue to do so. If alcohol and substance abuse are not treated, these addictions destroy entire families, and, for some warriors, become the instrument of suicide.

Research shows that it is important to treat *both* disorders, because treating only one of the illnesses (PTSD or substance abuse disorder) without dealing with the other makes it more likely that neither will be permanently improved. Making a choice to seek treatment for yourself or to stage an intervention to ensure that it is available for another takes courage. Do not hesitate. Take the step toward treatment. In every instance, it is a risk worth taking.

VIEWING your present symptoms and life situation in the light of what you have learned about PTSD can be of great help in starting to initiate changes in your life that can decrease suffering and increase meaning and wellbeing. But, as we will talk about in Chapter Six, change is not something that you have to do alone. A support system can be invaluable.

Chaplain P and soldiers shoulder-to-shoulder in Iraq . . .
the power of human connection

CHAPTER SIX:

EMPOWERING YOURSELF THROUGH STRONG SYSTEMS OF SUPPORT

FAMILY SYSTEMS OF SUPPORT

CHAPLAIN P:

Although families are the very social systems that prove to be most vulnerable to attack in the wake of trauma and PTSD, they are also the most important resource to which we turn for badly needed support. Dealing with family after having experienced service-connected trauma can be both helpful and difficult. I want to explain some of the reasons that family support can be vital to recovery from trauma, without shying away from or glossing over the difficulties that may arise.

The first and most important thing about families is the simple fact that the greatest portion of our emotional investment lies with those to whom we are connected by ties of kinship and marriage. This is true both socially and biologically. As we've already discussed, incredible acts of sacrifice are willingly performed by people every day for the protection of family members or in the interest of their welfare. As anyone who has lacked a healthy family or suffered abuse at the hands of a family knows, the love and support of a well-functioning family is the most critical factor influencing every aspect of our growth, development, and emotional wellbeing. At no time is this more important than after a trauma.

Among the most important characteristics of a healthy family is its capacity to provide its members with a source of unconditional love and positive regard. When people have returned from combat in a traumatized state, they are often drained of self-esteem. They may have witnessed buddies killed in ways they could not prevent. They may constantly second-guess every minute of every battle, wondering what the outcome would have been if they had acted differently. They may feel guilty about actions they had to take in the midst of combat. They may wonder why they survived, when others died. In short, many people feel that they no longer deserve to be loved or cared for. To know that one is loved for oneself alone, without the need to perform at a certain level, is critical to the reestablishment of self-worth and self-esteem. Few systems can provide this support as well as a family.

Families are also the visible reminder of why we willingly go to war. When soldiers look at their wives, husbands, children, and loved ones living in a free society, they are confronted with the concrete evidence that gives human shape and feeling to their willingness to risk their lives if called upon to do so. Understanding that there are things greater than ourselves and of ultimate value, such as the continued freedom and safety of our families, is an essential element of the meaning of life. To sacrifice on behalf of these things is part of the very reason for our being.

Since trauma and war have the capacity to stress all human beings to the breaking point, they are as likely to reveal not only the best, but also the worst qualities within us. No one is likely to know more about both our dark and our light sides than our families. As human beings, we cannot avoid the reality of our own flaws and frailties; it is a great gift to know that we can be loved in spite of them. It is an earthbound reminder of the way in which God loves us.

I am convinced that it is essential for every soldier to know in his heart why he or she needs to go to war. I am equally convinced that it is essential for every soldier to know to what, and to whom, they are driven to return from war. Life is full of being apart and of coming together. The power of love to exist and persist, even in the absence of those we love, is truly a divine gift that only man enjoys. Like religious faith, it binds us to those whom we cannot see or feel or touch, but who are an absolutely real presence in our lives. It bears witness to the fact that love is not only more powerful than the circumstances that surround us, but that it can totally transcend time and place. I am often moved to tears when I think of the power embodied by the love that connects soldiers in distant lands to loved ones half a world away. The power of love that kept soldiers in WWII connected to loved ones with whom they might not communicate for *months* or *years* at a time is almost beyond comprehension. But it is, nevertheless, real.

The great contemporary theologian Henri Nouwen wrote eloquently about the importance of "going" and "returning" across the continuing cycle of our lives. He said that one of the most important things in any person's life was the knowledge that someone awaits our return. In the current epidemic of suicide in the military, it becomes increasingly clear that those who end their lives at their own hands are those who believe that no one awaits them. Often, they feel betrayed by spouses or partners whose affections have turned elsewhere during or following deployment. Or they may have gone to war as the product of dysfunctional homes that left them without meaningful attachments in the first place. In either event, we are coming to understand more and more that the value of family support may spell the difference between life and death for many soldiers.

Some of the new and emerging research on human behavior, especially within the family unit, sheds additional light on why familial ties are so important to the management of PTSD. Recent studies reveal that certain kinds of human behaviors—including caretaking, touching and embracing, and compassion—are not only social aspects of family life, but also serve to biologically increase our potential for survival.

One reason appears to be because these innately human behaviors increase levels of the hormone oxytocin in our bloodstreams. Oxytocin may be called one of the body's prescriptions against the ravages of PTSD. Its effects include interrupting the HPA axis response to stress-producing situations that leads to PTSD (referred to in this book as the "stress/alarm" response), lowering high levels of neurochemicals (such as norepinephrine) associated with panic and anxiety, calming and stabilizing blood pressure and respiration, and disengaging posttraumatic hypervigilance. Similar effects seem to result from the stimulation of the vagus nerve, which occurs when we perform acts of compassion and caregiving for others. In short, the kinds of behaviors that supportive and loving families provide to warriors are powerful healing medicine.

DR. C:

Unfortunately, however, not all veterans are lucky enough to have loving or caring family systems. The question then becomes how and where to seek the type of support you need when you do not have a supportive and emotionally healthy family. While each individual must seek and find the answer, several things are true.

First, we know that the Beatles were right—the love we get is equal to the love we give. If our hearts remain open to others, there are many places and ways in which we can offer love to others in our community. The inevitable return on this investment is that we receive an even greater love than we give, along with a renewed understanding of the purpose that our own lives serve in the lives of others.

Second, we know that as human beings, we are not necessarily limited to finding love within the confines of the families into which we are born. We are capable of loving, and of being loved, by virtue of *emotional adoption*. The possibility of finding and receiving the supportive love of a *family equivalent*—whether that is from a group of people or from one single individual—is never foreclosed to us.

OTHER SYSTEMS OF SUPPORT

Whether we have a supportive family or not, we all need the help of others—a support network. Strength on the battlefield comes, in part, from the knowledge that there are others who will help, understand, and "have your back" when needed. For many, the concept of "a band of brothers" is a primary factor that drives behaviors during combat deployments. After you return from combat, that type of support system is just as important as well. As Chaplain P said, a supportive family is ideal. They can be the linchpin you need most to R-E-C-O-V-E-R. Even if past experiences and pent-up feelings have led to a lot of mistrust and misunderstanding, you may find it worthwhile to try to rebuild the relationships, as described in the previous chapter. Many vets who have worked with their families to patch up their relationships have told me that this made "all the difference" for them in improving their PTSD symptoms. And this patching up can be done even years later—it is never too late.

However, you can also receive support from others who understand, such as other veterans and members of veterans support organizations. Talking to other vets about military stuff is easy for most of the vets I see, but talking to them about how you are really feeling—the thoughts you have, the feelings you are experiencing, and the behaviors you are engaging in—is much harder. Many say it is just too difficult to talk to others because it forces them to "face the demons inside." Yet most vets who improve find this is the very activity that ultimately brings them emotional peace. Talking openly and honestly with others who understand can be the very thing that begins to break the PTSD cycle of negative feelings, withdrawal, and self-destructive behavior. This support network can be a single veteran or a group of vets who get together regularly or periodically—for example, meeting for coffee or a meal at a local restaurant. Or it can be one of the many veterans organizations that exist. This belonging to an organization can be in person or even now on the Internet.

Many vets don't know about the various organizations that exist to support and help them. You will find links to many such organizations listed in Appendix B to this book, as well as at the My Back to the Wall website.

As mentioned earlier, veterans of recent conflicts haven't always felt welcome in some of the more established veterans organizations, but that has changed. In fact, these organizations give a chance for older veterans to help or mentor younger ones. There are also organizations dedicated to veterans of recent conflicts.

Remember that your perception of these organizations may be developed based on the personalities of people who are at the particular meeting you attend. At some meetings, you may find no feeling of belonging or comfort. It might take time to develop such feelings, or the mix of attendees at that particular meeting may not be to your liking. In that case, don't give up. Try another meeting or a different group.

I've learned about vet reunions held in different parts of the country at various intervals. As mentioned early in this book, I personally was privileged to attend one of these reunions held in Indianapolis. More than 200 Vietnam vets and their spouses attended. Many said that they had initially been very reluctant to attend. Most said, "That is putting it mildly—when I first heard of the reunion, I thought NO WAY am I going!" And yet to a person they said they were grateful that they had decided to come to the event.

I attended an event held at the reunion called a "talk around," where one by one each vet who desired to do so stood up, picked up the microphone, and began to talk. Some talked about their experiences *in country*, others talked about their present experiences, and some about the thoughts, feelings, and behaviors caused by their PTSD over the years. They renewed friendships with their Vietnam vet "brothers" with whom they had served decades before.

Some learned for the first time that a fellow soldier they had believed to be killed in action many years ago was actually alive and well. For many who attended, it was the first chance to rid themselves of anger toward a member or leader of their group who they had blamed for tragedies. Often they learned they didn't know all the facts involved in decisions made all those years ago, and when those facts were opened to them, their feelings changed.

I saw the tears and the smiles and relief experienced by the vets, many of whom had not previously let go of their pent-up guilt, anger, and frustration. Some who had been to more than one of these reunions told me how valuable the events had been in improving their lives and relationships with their own family members.

I personally am familiar with two of the leaders of this movement: Lt. Lee Alley and Hector Villareal (Captain V). These men and many others contributed to the book *Back from War* by 1st Lt. Lee Alley, a book I wholeheartedly recommend to all vets and those who care about them. The book gives information, stories, phone numbers, and email addresses for helpful organizations, as well as other indispensable information that can be the start of the turnaround for the Vietnam vets.

Back from War presents information about the reunions and leads the vets toward those agencies that can be of help. It teaches the veterans how to find on the Internet those who they served with (and who many lost contact with when they left or were taken from the battlefield). Reuniting with those fellow brothers-in-arms has been life-changing for many of the Vietnam vets who have done so. Most of all, the book shows the Vietnam vets that they are not alone and that there is, indeed, help available for them.

Many states offer the help of personnel called State Vet Counselors who can help the vet effectively navigate the highways and byways of the VA to get the help they need. The DAV also offers help for vets in this regard as well.

I hope that in the future we will see more groups for veterans with PTSD similar to groups for alcoholics and substance abusers to help them recover from their condition (e.g., like Alcoholics Anonymous or Narcotics Anonymous). Some vets have had great success with such programs, but there are not many available. I hope that these groups will develop throughout the country, and perhaps in each community, so that vets experiencing similar life problems from their condition can get together, mentor, help, and be helped by others. It is important that these groups focus on improving the vets' lives despite their PTSD and not just be a vehicle for storytelling or complaining. I hope these groups or others with similar goals will be formed in the near future.

Also, do not forget the power of just getting together daily, weekly, or periodically with a group of other vets to talk with, share, and help each other. Many vets I have seen tell me these early morning "coffee clubs" have been tremendously valuable for them.

An increasingly important source of support for warriors and families impacted by PTSD is the constantly expanding community of nonprofit organizations (NPOs) in this country. These nongovernmental agencies represent a welcome resurgence in citizen involvement in response to the needs of warriors that has not been seen since WWII. But whereas citizen involvement in WWII was often in response to the request of the government and was focused on the support of the war effort in general, the current coming-of-age of nonprofit agencies supports a different agenda. No longer are citizens focused on providing help to the government, as they did in WWII through materials rationing, scrap drives, and Civil Defense. Today's nonprofits are focused upon providing specialized assistance to the individual warrior or family member in almost every conceivable area of need.

This model, in which individuals voluntarily reach out to provide support and service to others, is in keeping with the highest ideals of our citizenry and is emblematic of its compassion and inherent generosity. Today's nonprofit warrior support agencies convey the message to soldiers and families that they have served the American people, and it is in turn, the obligation of the American people (not just the government) to respond to their needs. This is an extremely important way in which our society, like ancient Native American societies, can validate and take responsibility for its role in both sending warriors forth and in serving them upon their return.

CHAPLAIN P:

In my work with warriors here at home and downrange, I have become very aware of the extent to which soldiers and veterans' needs have changed radically in the midst of the wars in Iraq and Afghanistan. Warriors survive injuries that, in prior conflicts, would have resulted in death. As a consequence, more warriors live with disabilities and the unique needs for support and assistance they create. Unlike the families of soldiers who were drafted as teenagers while their families stayed put, contemporary military families volunteer as a unit, to pursue a life which involves constant moving; reassignment; and uprooting of homes, children, and spouses. Repetitive cycles of deployment, as well as activation of National Guard and Reserve units, have subjected military families to difficulties not previously experienced by the dependents of career soldiers. And whereas the eyes of the nation were formerly focused upon those whose combat wounds were visible, we are increasingly aware of the anguish suffered by those who return as mental and emotional casualties of war. No governmental agency or department can hope to satisfactorily address such a broad spectrum of human need. It is natural, then, that nonprofit agencies should have sprung up throughout the nation, with the capacity to draw upon individuals' skills and resources in the meeting of unique human problems.

Although veterans of present conflicts are aware of the vast array of mental health and related services, we find that veterans of past conflicts may not be as aware of what is available to them. If you have a need or problem related to mental health, PTSD, or social support, there are several steps which you can take.

Your first step is to get online and conduct two different kinds of searches. If you are a veteran or active duty serviceperson, you can start by doing a web search through sites organized under "Warrior" or "Veterans" headings with mental health as a subtopic. Wikipedia lists more than sixty different organizations in which you can find support. Each of these, in turn, lists multiple other organizations that provide support. You may want to scan all of them to see which ones offer services you are interested in. You can narrow your search by isolating keywords that describe your need and location. Don't limit yourself to one search engine—search them all. Then you can do a web search organized by your specific topic or need, such as "PTSD Support Groups" or "Mental Health Care." You will find hundreds of nonprofit agencies, many of which offer mental health or supportive services for veterans with mental health needs.

Your next step is to access the United Way community hotline in your area (dial 211 in most locations). United Way can direct you to organizations, which will either serve the specific need you are facing or direct you to agencies that act as clearinghouses and referral centers for other organizations that can provide the needed help.

A third resource that you should access is the Warrior Transition Office of the military installation nearest to you. The WTO (or WTU, Warrior Transition Unit) can provide you with resources that include both private and governmentally sponsored services.

Finally, even if you are eligible for, or are currently receiving, assistance from the VA, you should still contact the VA facility nearest you to obtain information concerning sources of nongovernmental help. The VA can also refer you to your local Vet Centers, as described in Chapter Four. You will find lots of valuable information at the VA's National Center for PTSD (http://www.ptsd.va.gov).

GET SUPPORT BY GIVING SUPPORT TO OTHERS

CHAPLAIN P:

Although it surprises many, compassion is not merely a trait that we learn by cultural, family, and social custom. In fact, research has shown that compassion is actually part of how we are biologically wired. As UC Berkley Professor Dacher Keltner explains in his book *Born to Be Good*, old belief systems about man's survival through superior capacities for cruelty against his fellow are, in fact, not true.

"Compassion," says Keltner, "is a biologically based emotion rooted deep in the mammalian brain, and shaped by perhaps the most potent of selection pressures humans evolved to adapt to—the need to care for the vulnerable. Compassion is anything but blind; it is finely attuned to vulnerability. It is anything but weak; it fosters courageous, altruistic action often at significant cost to the self."

I often treat soldiers who have a distorted vision of themselves as either having become, or needing to remain, "cold and heartless." This often obscures the fact that warfare, which certainly involves acts of violence, also gives rise to some of the most extraordinary acts of compassion of which man is capable, often performed under fire or at significant personal jeopardy. Such acts of compassion are not only performed for the benefit of one's battle buddy, but also for civilians. And recent conflicts in the Middle East exemplify the American military's capacity for compassion even toward enemy or indigenous populations.

US military rules of engagement reflect the extreme care that is exercised to protect such people, often at greatly increased risk to our troops. US soldiers are known worldwide for their capacity to respond to disaster, extend a hand to defeated former enemies, and provide humanitarian aid and medical care. In the chest of virtually every soldier I know beats a compassionate heart.

So what does your moral and ethical self have to do with managing your PTSD? Quite a lot, as it turns out. Compassion is an emotion that is associated with the activation of the vagus nerve. As Keltner points out, the stimulation of the vagus nerve is what produces that "feeling of spreading, liquid warmth in the chest and a lump in the throat." But the vagus nerve does more. When stimulated, the vagus nerve causes our heart rate to drop, and it reverses the processes in the brain that trigger the posttraumatic threat/alarm response. What this means to you is that by performing acts of compassion for others, you may interrupt your own traumatic stress in a way that no drug ever could.

The ways in which you can support others are virtually endless. You can start by helping other vets, if you feel drawn to do so. Volunteer at a vet center, serve in a program that feeds vets who are homeless, offer to build ramps for wheelchair bound or disabled warriors . . . The list is virtually endless. You can contact local organizations in your area that serve returning veterans, as well as the VA and your local United Way, to learn more about the hundreds of ways in which your compassion can be put to the service of others and, in the process, help to heal yourself.

DR. C:

Hector Villareal, known as Captain V, is one of the contributing authors of *Back from War*. He and others also advocate volunteering as a way to get support. Volunteer to talk to vet groups, civilian groups (Kiwanis, Rotary, etc.), churches, schools, and whoever wants to listen. You may be surprised at the amount of interest there is among the general public. You have information that others do not, and nobody knows about your experiences better than you. The best part of volunteering and talking to others is that you may benefit yourself. Teaching and mentoring others can bring to you a sense of self-worth and meaning.

Hector Villareal and Vic Luebecker have started two organizations, the National Coalition for Veterans and Hope 4 Heroes, which may become the prototypes for other such volunteer groups. These volunteer groups also give the vets a chance to become part of a support system that, in the long run, can be the help they need to restructure their lives. Giving to others can be one of the key elements in getting the emotional boost you need to overcome the impact of your PTSD. For some, this may include volunteering to speak at church, mentoring children, or becoming involved in activities benefitting others, and thus indirectly benefitting the vets themselves.

SPIRITUAL SYSTEMS OF SUPPORT

"Man is never helped in his suffering by what he thinks for himself, but by revelations of a wisdom greater than his own. It is this which lifts him out of his distress." ~ Carl Jung (20ᵗʰ century psychologist)

CHAPLAIN P:

In his landmark book *War and the Soul,* psychologist Ed Tick put words to what generations of soldiers have known, but up to then had no words to voice: that the malady that afflicts them after their experience of combat may rightly be termed "PTSD: Post Traumatic <u>Soul</u> Disorder." Any warrior or veteran who does daily battle with the symptoms of PTSD understands the meaning of this concept. PTSD does not merely affect our biological and intellectual selves; it may go beyond that. It strikes at that core of what each of us is as a unique human being. For many, it is a wound to the very <u>soul</u> of the person.

If we are to examine what it means for our souls to be wounded by PTSD, we need to give thought to what the soul is. In his book *The Care of the Soul,* Thomas Moore says that:

"Soul is not a thing, but a quality or a dimension of experiencing life, and ourselves. It has to do with depth, value, relatedness, heart, and personal substance."

Every individual with PTSD is a person, whose identity must stand apart from the illness from which he or she suffers. To define a person's identity solely in terms of his or her illness is something like describing a donut in terms of the empty space created by its hole, rather than by the positive space occupied by its whole. PTSD is never exactly the same from one person to the next; it exists in the totality of what each person is, in body, mind, and soul. In this sense, PTSD causes us to reexamine and redefine the *personal substance of who we are.*

This impact upon our very personal substance is what makes PTSD a wounding to the soul. It stands to reason then that recovery from PTSD is a journey of the *spirit.* And because spirituality has been found to be such a critical element of strength after trauma, we want to devote some space in this book to discuss how and why spiritual support is known to make a real difference in posttraumatic recovery.

What is spirit?

To understand why spiritual support is, for many people, an essential component of their personal empowerment, we must first understand what spirit and spirituality mean.

The word spirit, as I employ it, refers to the part of every human being that cannot be seen or touched, but which we, nevertheless, know exists. It especially refers to that part of us that serves as a bridge or connection to God or a divine Higher Power.

Like a breeze, the human spirit makes the power of its presence or absence felt, despite its invisibility. In fact, the same Greek word, pneuma, was used in the Bible interchangeably to describe any or all of three things: wind, breath (e.g., the breath of life), and the invisible spirit of God. In ancient times, these three things—both visible and invisible—were all considered to be aspects of the same whole. But for many years, the physical, emotional, and spiritual aspects of human crisis have been artificially divided.

Today, we are becoming increasingly observant of the role played by the spirit in every aspect of life. When the non-visible spirit of a person is active, it can actually empower the visible, physical aspect to do or survive many things that would otherwise be considered impossible. Likewise, when the human spirit has become broken, a person may become incapable of doing much of anything, even though they might, strictly speaking, have the physical ability to do a great deal.

When our expectations of life are quantified according to the norms and measurements of the physical world, our assets may appear to be quite limited. In the spiritual world, however, cause and effect relationships are not limited by what can be seen, touched, felt, or measured. The upper limits of what we can achieve are not necessarily limited by our visible capacities. Whereas our physical potential may appear to be limited, our human potential may, in the spiritual sense, become limitless.

To begin, then, I like to simplify spiritual concepts in the following ways:

Spirit is the part of each person that transcends, or exists above and beyond, the confines of our physical bodies and links us to the source of creation.

Spiritual is a word which we use to describe things having to do with this invisible, yet very real, part of ourselves.

Spirituality is the collection of beliefs, attitudes, and practices that people employ in order to acknowledge, validate, nurture, and sustain the spirit. In so doing, spirituality nurtures our active relationship with God, creation, and the universe.

As a pastoral counselor and trauma chaplain, I am impressed by the extremely important functions played by *both* individual spirituality and religious beliefs in the process of survival and recovery from trauma and crisis. Scientific studies conducted during the last twenty years on this subject demonstrate conclusively that spiritual practice lengthens life expectancy, increases health and wellness, and helps fight disease.

Personal spirituality and post-traumatic empowerment

Personal spirituality, an enormously important force, can empower individuals because of the way it allows people to experience themselves as having a personal connection to and a relationship with something more powerful than the chaos that exists around them. Being caught in the grip of circumstances they don't control, especially in the midst of events that make human beings feel weak and insignificant, the idea that they can depend on and receive strength from a source far greater than themselves can bring great comfort, reassurance, and the courage to endure. It means that they are never entirely alone.

The belief that a higher power sees what is going on in the world and may serve as a witness to our own tribulations helps to reassure people that even when they are physically alone, they are not necessarily suffering anonymously. People of faith take a measure of comfort in the belief that, from a distance, God *is* watching. The hope that the intervention or assistance of a higher power can, at some point in time, ensure that some degree of justice will eventually be done is very important in helping people to deal with the senselessness that often accompanies traumatic events.

Perhaps the most important way in which people are empowered through personal spirituality has to do with the *meaning* it lends to each human life. If I as an individual believe that my existence is connected to a higher power, by which I have been created and am loved, I am in essence in a relationship of kinship with the Divine. This, in turn, influences the degree to which I place value upon my own life.

Despite having experienced horrific events which left them injured, traumatized, and despairing, many people report to me that respect for the spiritual value of their life, as creations of a God "who makes no junk," precludes their committing suicide. In addition, spirituality helps these people recognize that the *scope* of their lives, as well as their power to cope with life, is above and beyond those things that we can see, hear, touch, feel, and objectively measure. Sometimes, it's very important to hold onto the belief that what you see is not necessarily all you get.

The idea that one's capacity for life and wellness is not necessarily subject to the physical limits of the body operates as a wellspring of strength and determination. It is that indefinable force that allows many people, including wounded warriors, to transcend the limitations posed by their physical injuries and exceed others' expectations about whether or not they can recover. When the body has been injured or material and physical resources fail us, the knowledge that there is still an invisible and empowering force within us that can be brought to bear on any situation often determines personal survival.

When people believe that this non-visible internal force can be consistently replenished by a higher power, it is like having access to an inexhaustible spiritual fuel rod. Personal spirituality empowers many people to not only survive, but to thrive, in trauma's wake. It does this by creating a channel through which people feel they are able to access the higher power of the divine, and through this, the best of what is inside themselves.

The personal empowerment that comes from individual spirituality can be nurtured in countless ways. Prayer; music; meditation; the reading of sacred scriptures or inspirational writings; journaling; the appreciation of nature; positive visualization and breathing exercises; the paying of conscious attention to the ways in which body, mind, and spirit speak to each other and to God; and pursuing habits of daily living that instill peace or joy are just a few of the many routes to the enhancement of individual spirituality.

I have become keenly aware of the way in which individual spiritual practices may help people to overcome feelings of helplessness, hopelessness, and loss of control that are at the root of all traumatic response. When people knowingly and intentionally pursue individual spiritual practice, they are engaging in a very powerful form of choice-making behavior. This means that they are in control of their decisions and are accessing both the emotional and rational spheres of the brain.

It also means that they find these practices helpful to themselves and possibly to others. This implies that the individual gains a sense of awareness that his or her actions have an effect upon life and play a role in determining the way it is lived and experienced. We call this capacity to make a difference in one's own existence personal efficacy. When people experience personal efficacy through their practice of spirituality, they are, by definition, counteracting the forces of helplessness, hopelessness, and loss of control that are at the very root of PTSD. Viewed in this sense, it becomes more apparent why personal spirituality is among the most powerful weapons that one can wield against posttraumatic symptoms.

Religious support and posttraumatic empowerment

People often ask me if one can be a *spiritual* person, and yet not be a *religious* person. Since both individual spirituality and organized religion involve a personal connection to God, I believe the answer to that question is "yes." But I also believe that spirituality and organized religion serve equally important purposes in life. It is not so much a question of which wellspring one chooses to draw from, as it is a consideration of why one would limit oneself to one, when he or she can have the benefits of both.

Human beings are, optimally, like a well-built house. For maximum strength and endurance, they benefit from being engineered with both internal and external sources of support. Individual spirituality, like interior studs and beams, helps to create a strong internal core. Even when one is cut off from others by traumatic events and must dwell alone in one's house, its internal structural integrity is maintained by individual spirituality.

But a strong external structure is equally important. A strong foundation keeps a house well-grounded and connected to the world of which it is a part. A sound roof helps shelter an individual from the dangers of the outside world. The strength of a building's exterior walls is significantly increased by the adjacent walls of its neighbors.

Religion operates as a powerful external source of human support, which is created in the course of worshipping and honoring God. It both strengthens, and is strengthened by, individual spirituality. Religion, however, serves to address needs that the exercise of personal spirituality alone may not address.

The first and most important of these needs is the capacity of religion to address our basic human need to exist in some form of community. Humans are born to exist in communal society. Infants left alone after birth will inevitably die. Children abandoned in foreign orphanages where they receive virtually no human interaction suffer profound deficiencies in mental, physical, and immune development and frequently die of the condition labeled failure to thrive. Elderly people who live in seclusion without benefit of human connection become severely mentally and physically depressed and increasingly disabled.

The development of specialized cells in the skin (called Langerhans cells) that activate our immune responses to disease is totally dependent upon our being in contact with, and touched by, other human beings. Lack of human warmth and touch makes us, literally, more susceptible to disease. Existence in community is, quite simply, necessary for life. For many, a faith community helps answer this fundamental need to exist in community. For others, it may become an important form of surrogate family.

Religion, however, answers far more than our physical need for belonging. It addresses our higher emotional and moral needs. It is a method through which human beings share of themselves, in the material, emotional, and ideological senses of the word. Making a decision to share of time or resources through service to a faith community literally signals to the brain that survival is no longer in danger and that other endeavors can now take a front seat for a time. This is a profoundly anti-traumatic message.

Similarly, material sharing is an outgrowth of compassion for others, which most religions teach and advocate. The development of compassionate behaviors has been found to stimulate oxytocin, a hormone that triggers sensations of bonding, happiness, and peace and counteracts the stress levels initiated by trauma. Ideological sharing not only helps us to build common bonds of thought and belief, but it also ensures that we are listening responsibly to others and not merely to the voices in our own heads, thus helping to ensure that we are on the right path when war and trauma overwhelm us with confusion. While the survival-based reactions involved with PTSD are usually all about saving ourselves, the sharing of resources and ideas engages our higher and more socially governed thinking processes and expands our world vision to include the welfare of others. In promoting this pro-social behavior, faith communities are actually helping trauma survivors to

(1) overcome the intense isolation that often accompanies PTSD,

(2) place their own situation in larger perspective by recognizing the sufferings or needs of others, and in so doing

(3) counteract both the self-focused and tunnel-visioned effects of trauma.

These are not the only positive benefits that faith communities confer on the trauma survivor. There are many more. Faith communities are designed to act as an oasis or "safe house" for their members. They are like a place to which trauma survivors can safely and strategically retreat in times of trouble or intense despair, thus providing an important external resource to help meet the essential human needs of the traumatized. They witness to the existence and uniqueness of each person, exhibiting supportive concern when a person is ill, injured, or observed to be missing from the flock. For many people, their most beloved house of worship embodies a certain combination of sights, smells, sounds, and feelings that are like positive triggers, which exert a calming effect on both the spirit and the body, helping to overcome the negative triggers that bombard the PTSD sufferer.

In addition, most faith communities are designed to preach, and extend, forgiveness and toleration. They tell us that we are "good enough" in God's eyes—a message that people who have returned from war badly need to hear. They act out that message by treating and embracing their members as worthy of belonging to the community. Since ancient times, expulsion from one's community has acted like a psychological or, in some cases, a physical death sentence.

The reverse is also true. The assurance that one is assured of a place in the faith community counteracts this primal fear. This message of moral, theological, and social acceptance may be very important to trauma survivors who feel stained by their experiences, by their PTSD, or both. For the rape or sexual assault survivor, for example, the religious message that our bodies are not rendered unholy by the crimes of others may be essential to renewed self-acceptance.

For soldiers who have returned from a war in which they may have been called upon to kill or injure others, self-forgiveness may become difficult or impossible. I have often spoken with warriors whose greatest traumas are spiritual and are centered upon the thought that they will never be forgiven for what they have been called upon to do in combat. It may be vital for such warriors to hear a religious message that reminds them that even gruesome acts, done by virtue of necessity in defense or for the protection of self or others and in performance of a higher duty, are forgivable by God, as well as by the larger community that dispatched them to war in the first place.

Our nation's houses of worship often provide the closest thing to a public homecoming that society currently offers. In contrast to earlier conflicts, our soldiers no longer parade down the streets of the towns from whence they were called to war. While there is, of course, a reuniting with family and immediate friends at the time of redeployment, there is rarely, if ever, a public acknowledgement of the warrior's return on the part of a broader segment of society. The same society that sends its young men and women to war does not always complete the circle by welcoming them back into the communal fold when they return.

Ed Tick pointed out the critical nature of this contemporary omission in our culture by comparing it to the approach taken in Native

American cultures, in which the war dance was performed to acknowledge not only the return of the warrior, but also to symbolize society's reaffirmation of public responsibility for the conflicts warriors were called upon to fight. This public acknowledgment served as a ritual cleansing. It helped the warrior expiate burdens of guilt and shame and reinforced the warrior's place in society. In the Vietnam era and the four decades that have followed it, we saw the damage done to warriors when society called them to war and subsequently disavowed them.

Today, religious communities play an important role in ensuring that similar spiritual and emotional wounds are not inflicted upon the veterans of current conflicts. A church, synagogue, or other house of worship may be the only civilian group setting into which warriors may be welcomed home and reassured that their service strengthens, rather than severs, their relationship to other members of the community.

Searching for new sources of spiritual support: Looking forward

When spiritual and religious support systems fail, it is often because belief systems will never suffice to explain all aspects of God or human existence. Religious and spiritual belief systems are least effective when they are used as tools for looking backwards in an effort to retroactively explain historical events. Sometimes, this attempt to explain events in retrospect leads to men voicing their own prejudices and purporting to lend God's stamp of approval upon them. This was recently seen when some individuals attempted to "explain" Hurricane Katrina by voicing the conclusion that the storm was evidence of God's wrath against the people of New Orleans. The application of religious or spiritual belief systems in such a judgmental way serves only to divide human beings, and never to uplift them.

By contrast, religious and spiritual belief systems function most effectively by supporting people as they focus forward—on what is to come. In other words, the question that religion may best be able to answer is not, "Why did this event happen?" but rather, "How can I look to God to help me cope with what has happened?"

241

For those readers who have become disillusioned after a trauma and are tempted to turn away from spirituality and faith, I encourage you to do just the opposite. With competent spiritual guidance, people can use periods of disillusionment as positive opportunities to ventilate their anger at God, ask tough questions, seek new answers, and connect to new systems of support that feel genuine and authentic to them.

One of the great blessings of our society is that there are many different belief systems and religious communities open to people. Often, our past religious affiliations were established in childhood, less by conscious choice and more by the connections established by default as a result of family or cultural tradition. But if these past associations do not feel supportive to you, then I encourage you to investigate and explore other faith communities that are in harmony with your personal spirituality. In this way, the combined benefits of individual spirituality and a faith community can help you focus on the future and remain centered upon the ways in which God serves as a source of sustenance and healing, even in the midst of events we do not entirely understand.

Locating pastoral counseling and spiritual support

If you are in the midst of a spiritual crisis, finding the right kind of pastoral counseling is essential. Of course, having a personal relationship with a clergyperson trained to help trauma-impacted persons work through their posttraumatic issues is ideal. But this kind of help may not always be immediately at hand. Some people have no clergy. Some clergy are not trained to provide pastoral counseling. And even among clergy trained in the art and theology of pastoral counseling, many are not trained to provide this kind of care in connection with severe traumas.

There are, however, several resources that people can turn to for referrals or for qualified spiritual counseling, if it is not already available. Keep in mind that these resources provide assistance that is additional to, and not in conflict with, your relationship to your personal clergyperson:

(1) The American Association of Pastoral Counselors (AAPC) is the official organization of professionals whose extensive education and training spans the disciplines of both mental health and theology. AAPC counselors are available throughout the United States. Some practice privately and accept insurance, while others are affiliated with churches or non-profit organizations. You can call the AAPC or consult their website to locate a pastoral counselor near you.

(2) The National Center for Crisis Management (www.nc-cm. org) and its subsidiary organization, the American Academy of Experts in Traumatic Stress (www.aaets.org), confers board certification upon chaplains who are specialists in providing support and intervention to trauma survivors and who can be located through the organization.

(3) The Chaplaincy Corps of all branches of the military service are available to serve active duty personnel and their families. Military chaplains provide confidential pastoral support. They do not seek to impose their personal faith perspectives on individuals, but rather are specifically trained to support persons of all faiths in their own search for spiritual support. Military Chaplains are not only providers of spiritual and faith support, but are also highly skilled and fully educated and credentialed counselors.

(4) Check with your local hospital, where you may be able to access a professional chaplain who is a clinical member of the Association of Clinical Pastoral Education (ACPE). You may also locate an ACPE chaplain through the organizational website (www.acpe.edu). ACPE chaplains are trained clinicians who provide spiritual support in hospitals and pastoral education training centers.

(5) Check with large churches in your area. Many large churches conduct programs of spiritual support and pastoral counseling for their parishioners as well as members of the outlying community.

In addition to pastoral counseling, PTSD sufferers can benefit from connecting to one or more sources of spiritual support in many places in their communities, beginning with local churches and synagogues. Many provide not only religious worship services, but also programs of education for spiritual education, enrichment, and fellowship that can serve as tremendous sources of support and guidance in difficult times.

Check out an adult scriptural study class or lecture series, at your own house of worship or another. Or consider a weekend retreat, such as Marriage Enrichment, ACTS, Cursillo, or Emmaus. "Strong Bonds" is a superb retreat format used among military personnel. Any or all of these can be truly enjoyable as well as life changing. Your local Jewish Community Center is likely to have a great array of superb programs of interest, accessible to Jews and Christians alike.

Larger cities maintain community websites that include many resources for spiritual and religious enrichment. Similarly, most colleges and universities have active campus ministry centers with programs and study groups you can attend. These can be very helpful because campus ministries are especially geared to the needs of people who are searching for faith, who may question their faith, who find themselves in a period of transition in faith.

Your local library is likely to have a central database of events, programs, or groups that are geared to people interested in spirituality or religion. Even your local bookstores (including religious bookstores) may be a treasure trove of resources for your own personal spiritual education.

Investigate the large number of spiritually-oriented smartphone "apps" available in both Apple and Droid formats. Be sure to look for a "preview" before you order one that must be paid for to be sure you will like what you get. But even among the ones that are free, there are some superb resources that include daily scriptures, meditations, and even audio sermons.

Last, but certainly not least, consider downloading some of the hundreds of fantastic audio and video programs that are available for free in the "spirituality and religion" section of iTunes, NPR (National Public Radio), PBS, and other similar websites. If you are like me, you will soon become a podcast junkie who enjoys receiving education and inspiration through your ear buds while you walk, jog, or power-lift your way through yesterday's donuts. And don't forget the My Back to the Wall website (www.mybacktothewall.com), where you will find still more helpful resources and strategies for developing and maintaining a healthy spiritual life.

Chaplain P posing the question: "Are you ready to get out of your bunker and gain control of your life?"

CHAPTER SEVEN:

Redefining THE MEANING OF YOUR LIFE:

POSTTRAUMATIC GROWTH

"The world is full of suffering, and the overcoming of it."

~ Helen Keller

DR. C AND CHAPLAIN P:

One of the reasons that we elected to write this book in different literary "voices" was our belief that sharing two professional perspectives on a variety of topics, instead of just one, would give our readers double the advantage. But when it came to writing the concluding chapter of a book which had taken us almost two years to craft, the need to maintain our separate identities as writers and professionals just didn't matter to us. That's because we both felt that the "R" with which we were to end the R-E-C-O-V-E-R system needed to be about redefining what brings meaning and satisfaction to one's life. And, quite frankly, we realized that both of us had been forged out of the same internal, philosophical, and spiritual "stuff." And this "stuff" has nothing to do with what has previously kept our literary voices separate in this book. It doesn't have to do with our respective training or degrees or professional specialties. It has to do with only one thing, and that is why we both feel humbled, joyful, and overwhelmingly grateful to be alive. And so we determined that it was fitting to end this book exactly as we began it—IN ONE VOICE.

When we are born, our skeletal systems may appear to be fully formed, but that is far from the case. Throughout our bodies are found growth plates—those gaps in our bones where bone is less dense in order to accommodate future growth and expansion, as well as the gradual acquisition of increased strength. Interestingly, the strongest point of any bone is where it has previously been broken and repaired itself.

We like to think that we all have two kinds of growth plates: the kind we are born with and the kind we acquire throughout life as a result of challenging experiences, which leave us feeling brittle, devoid of internal strength and support, as if we might fracture at any moment. But while fracture may on the face of things seem to be the worst case scenario, nature itself has given us the potential to turn our breaking points into our greatest strengths.

ESCAPING THE TRAP OF "TUNNEL VISION"

After a traumatic event, people often see life through tunnel vision, in which their own acknowledged hardships serve to obscure their view of others in their community, their nation, or their world. Managing PTSD calls upon us to open our eyes, view the circumstances of others, and place our own in proper perspective. To look at others who have experienced as bad or worse than we ourselves have endured is critically important, not only because we should appreciate the sufferings of others, but even more importantly, because we have a vital need to observe and appreciate their *overcoming* of that suffering.

For years both of us, in our respective professional capacities, have worked among some of the most horribly afflicted people in our society. People who ask us about our work in trauma often say, "However do you keep on doing that kind of work? Isn't it depressing?" Both of us, in our own way, usually reply, "Are you kidding?" or words to that effect. We always reply that life among the suffering is not depressing, but exactly the opposite. The mission of helping others improve their lot in life fills our own lives with meaning and purpose; the perspective provided to us by our intimate view into other peoples' sufferings ensures that our own hardships are always of lesser consequence than theirs. The people we serve do not inspire pity, but rather always command our admiration and respect. They serve as our greatest teachers, for they put a real human face upon the qualities of endurance, determination, and faith.

If you want to empower yourself to exercise management over your PTSD, you can begin by opening your eyes and expanding your view of how others around you survive and, in many cases, thrive. Not all survivors of trauma go on to develop PTSD, and many people who have suffered PTSD are able to recover and experience what is known as *posttraumatic growth*. So what spells the difference between these people and those who are never able to rise above their misery? Is there a formula for resilience after trauma?

As it turns out, there is. And although the road to posttraumatic growth bears the individual stamp of every human being who walks it, we have learned that some paths are more consistently productive than others. In this chapter, we will discuss some of the ways in which you, yourself, can use these strategies to help redefine your life and reshape your own wellbeing.

WHO YOU ARE VS. WHAT YOU DO

In our view, the starting place for every trauma survivor is the clarification of his or her own identity as a "human being," rather than as a "human doing." Many trauma survivors, especially warriors, tend to fuse their personal identity into the occurrence that wounded them. In doing so, they label themselves as part of the problem and begin to define themselves as synonymous with a horrific event from which they can never mentally detach.

Instead, it is vital that you nurture and maintain a sense of personal identity that is separate from the traumatic event or period and that does not become fused with it. You yourself are not the war— you are one person who went to war at society's request. You are not the battle—you are one person who experienced a certain part of it as one or more life events. You, personally, are not the foreign policy of an entire nation—you are one person who has performed a duty. Do not artificially expand your role in a trauma beyond that which you actually played or for which you were actually responsible.

Why is this important? Because when people search outside themselves for answers about why traumatic events happen, they seldom find that convenient explanations are at hand. Human beings, however, have a seemingly incessant need to continue seeking explanations for things, because with explanation of an event often comes control over preventing its recurrence. Lacking any other convenient explanations for things, many trauma survivors (through the lens of their tunnel vision) come to the mistaken conclusion that they and their own actions are the underlying reason for traumatic events. This results in much self-blame and second guessing.

As an example, many family members of persons who were tragically killed in the World Trade Center on 9-11 were interviewed after the terrorist attack. Not surprisingly, many could not wrap their heads around what had happened. In order to try and impose some orderly cause and effect upon the event, many began blaming themselves for their loved ones' deaths, even though they were not involved. Nevertheless, they reached for and grabbed hold of responsibility that was not theirs to own—e.g., "I should have called and told my daughter not to go to work that day"—and self-blame—"It's my fault she died, because we didn't go shopping that day, as we had planned. If we had, she wouldn't have been in the building." They enlarged their traumatic role, and with it, their posttraumatic suffering.

Warriors need to remember that they and the war are *not* one and the same. Soldiering is something one does. A war is something that happens. Nevertheless, over and above what one *does* as a soldier (what we call "human doing") and what one *experiences* in a war that happens, there remains the intangible but defining quality of what you are as a human being. Every soldier is, at the same time, many other things: a son or daughter; a spouse; a partner; a parent; a friend; a compassionate spirit; a lover of humanity, nature and—if you are a person of faith—a lover of God.

It is an indisputable fact that wars are fought and nations are protected by military forces that require obedience from their officers and enlisted personnel. If you serve the military, you do not have free choice about a great deal of what you DO. But you always have free choice to determine the kind of person you ARE. The human "doing" part of you may belong to the government, and it is certainly enhanced by strong values and character. But in the end, the human "being" part of you belongs to you and you alone. Nurture your inner self and your interior life. When you feel as though you have lost nearly everything else, it will remain as the one thing that belongs, first and foremost, to you.

Helicopters do their work well, in part because they are able to hover over a scene. This affords them different access and different perspective. Even amidst a battle in which they are engaged, helicopter pilots are a part of the battle, yet able to step out of the scene and maintain a view that transcends, or hovers above, what happens below. Trauma-impacted people can do the same.

Extract yourself from the tunnel vision that may have trapped you. Instead of fusing yourself onto one or more events, develop the capacity to stay connected with your emotional identity as if it were a craft with the ability to hover over your life. Define yourself by those intangible qualities, beliefs, and value systems that reside in you and that float over the events you have experienced or may continue to experience. What were these qualities before your trauma? What were they after? What are they now? Allow the human-being part of you to float free from the constraints of any given event in which the human-doing part of you was, or is, involved.

Science shows us that staying connected to others is critical to posttraumatic growth and recovery. Being connected to others actually helps to encourage the secretion of hormones that counteract posttraumatic stress. In other words, interpersonal connection is actually a form of good social medicine. To help you identify your level of social connection when you are feeling isolated, here is a simple exercise to make those connections easier for you to identify. Think of your personal being as a large parachute that hovers above the earth, over your life events.

You can choose where and how and to what and whom your chute is to be tethered. For example, it can be tethered to positive qualities, emotions, or relationships with others. These are all a part of finding meaning in life. Visualize the strings or ropes that are attached to your chute and follow them to the things they are connected to. Is it to love? Service? Compassion? Joy? Laughter? Awe? Curiosity? The feeling of being a part of a community?

Consider also in what direction your chute is tethered. Do your guidelines go only downward? Do they extend laterally to become collaterally anchored to others? Do they extend upward to God or Creator? How many lines extend from your chute and in how many directions? Give each one a name, because they all reflect the sources of meaning in your life. After doing this exercise, you may discover you are not as alone as you think you are.

When we choose to anchor ourselves according to the qualities of our being in life rather than anchoring our identity to specific events, we can begin the process of transcending (rising above) life's traumas. While we are busy extending our tethers downward toward others, we can also remain tethered upward toward a Higher Power that is greater than us and greater than all that is below us. Becoming tethered, or grounded, from both above and below lends a great deal of stability to life. For many, it allows them to remain spiritually suspended over life's crises and connected to life's positive meanings, without fear of falling or drifting away.

MEANING MAKING AND POSTTRAUMATIC RESILIENCE

Increasingly, science is learning that the most important pivotal factor that determines an individual's resilience in the wake of trauma is the ability to make meaning in one's life. Dr. Norman Anderson, who was in 1995 appointed as the first associate director of the National Institutes of Health, became the founding director of its Office of Behavioral and Social Sciences Research (OBSSR). In this capacity, Dr. Anderson facilitated pioneering research in the late 1990s that led to the creation of what he termed "new health science." In his book *Emotional Longevity*, Dr. Anderson recounts his journey down exciting pathways of discovery, which revealed that where we are spiritually, emotionally, relationally, and communally has everything to do with how we make meaning in our lives. He discovered that the process through which we make meaning in life has absolutely everything to do with our capacity to survive trauma, illness, and disease.

Many kinds of people, the research found, had the ability to search for and find meaning in life. These were not people whose lives were charmed or easy. Quite the opposite, these were people who suffered greatly from cancer, stroke, bone marrow transplants, and HIV, to name only a few of the life-threatening crises investigated. Finding meaning in life was not dependent upon life's experiences being pleasant, for they were not. Rather, meaning resulted from the capacity of individuals to permit their life experiences to open them up to new aspects of themselves and others that they had not previously fully appreciated.

Among a broad variety of studies, people have reported that negative events had propelled them toward a greater appreciation of life itself; toward a new philosophy for living life; and toward the adoption of new values, such as greater compassion and less selfishness. They reported actually experiencing improved relationships within their families and a greater sense of support from friends. Armed with a new and increased appreciation for life, they adopted healthier lifestyles designed around a conscious respect for their bodies, paid greater attention to caring relationships, and were more attentive to the needs of others.

The health benefits of finding meaning in life were found to be beneficial across the entire spectrum of human experience, even war. Researchers at the University of California at Davis, for example, studied the relationship between the capacity for positive meaning-making and the vulnerability of combat-exposed veterans of WWII and the Korean War to posttraumatic stress symptoms. It was found that men who continued to associate a positive meaning to their military service were least likely to suffer traumatic stress, regardless of their degree of combat exposure.

THE HALLMARKS OF POSTTRAUMATIC RESILIENCY

In addition to spirituality, there are other characteristics identified by Dr. Anderson that lay the groundwork for resiliency and posttraumatic growth. As mentioned earlier, **dispositional optimism** is the willingness to assign positive expectations and explanations to life events, rather than to continually go back to the negative. It appears that what we expect out of life is, more often than not, what we receive. Daring to expect goodness out of life, other human beings, and the world despite our past experience of traumatic events has the effect of opening us up to positive possibilities that actually or potentially exist, but that a negative attitude would otherwise cause us to overlook or exclude from our lives.

Clinical psychologist Wayne M. Sotile, Ph.D., a specialist in resilience, is the coauthor of *Letting Go of What's Holding You Back*. He reminds us that resilient people believe in themselves and that life has a higher purpose and meaning. Suffering for its own sake is pointless, but when suffering is unavoidable (as in a trauma), then finding meaning in the experience makes all the difference between the person who is a perpetual victim and one who transcends, or even triumphs over, his unfortunate experiences. Resilient people refuse to let trauma define their life. Rather, they choose the attitude that "this is a difficult passage in a long and meaningful journey that is my life. I will get through this."

Self-revelation, or the willingness to open up to others about one's trauma rather than keeping it concealed, is another critical quality of the resilient person. The increased levels of stress, isolation, and fatigue that figure into the concealment of one's pain are, quite simply, exhausting to both body and mind.

Developing and maintaining social ties often spells the difference between the person who recovers from trauma and the one who dies or suicides in its aftermath. Social isolation deprives the individual of the benefits from human relationships that we know to be not only emotionally, but also biologically, powerful in relieving the symptoms of posttraumatic stress.

Lifelong learning and the pursuit of a goal give us daily reminders that our lives count for something and that we are not merely marking time on the planet. Each and every human being has a destiny—including the destiny we choose to create for ourselves—and the potential to achieve it. Every human being can make a positive difference in his or her corner of the world, regardless of how broad or limited that proves to be. Every time we positively influence another's life, we change not only that person's existence, but also the existence of others connected to him or her, including their significant others and their descendants.

Over time, our individual capacity to change the world is far greater than we realize. Maintaining a belief in our ability to pursue a goal, an aspiration, a skill, or a dream is known as self-efficacy. It helps us to go through life with confidence, instead of fear.

VALUE SYSTEMS: REMEMBERING WHO (AND WHOSE) YOU ARE

The experience of trauma often leaves the warrior questioning his or her worth. Some vets erroneously believe that they, personally, are of little value in the world. This often leads to a temptation not only to give up seeking anything from life but also to give up on one's responsibility to offer anything to life. Neither is an acceptable option. All human beings are bound in a circle of giving and receiving. The rules we adopt in life, and which tell us that which it is permissible for us to receive as well as that which we are responsible to give to others, are called *core value systems.*

The individual with a strong core value system is far more likely to recover from trauma. This is because strong core value systems recognize both our own worth and the worth of others. The reality of our own human worth gives rise to ethical and moral obligations to project that worth into the world through right action toward our fellow men.

The person who chooses to live life in accordance with his or her core values declares, in essence, that no past traumatic event will excuse their opting out of their responsibilities toward either self or others. The person who acknowledges and abides by these responsibilities has made an essential life choice. And the person who makes such an essential life choice has, at some level, ceased to live as a victim of trauma.

Every human being has an opportunity to construct and live by a code of core values that reflect his or her individual spirituality and concepts of right action. Core values are expressed in countless ways. Some are embodied in lengthy codes of conduct, or rules for living. Others are very brief. We appreciate the words of the first century teacher and founder of modern Judaism, Rabbi Hillel:

"If I am not for myself, who will be?

If I am for myself only, what am I?

If not now, when?"

Or, one could structure one's whole system of core values around the simple statement of Mahatma Gandhi:

"Be the change you wish to see in the world."

The Rotary Club has crafted a statement of core values that has worked for millions of men and women. Entitled "The Four-Way Test of the Things We Think, Say, and Do," it is an excellent value system that one can incorporate into daily living:

"FIRST: Is it the truth?

SECOND: Is it fair to all concerned?

THIRD: Will it build goodwill and better friendships?

FOURTH: Will it be beneficial to all concerned?"

For many vets and returning warriors, posttraumatic growth may occur if they reexamine and consciously apply the core military values of "Duty, God, Country" beyond the confines of one's military service. Remembering that duty includes one's duty not only to the military but also to oneself, one's own health, and one's family can help restore perspective. Reconnecting to one's individual spirituality and relationship to God is at the core of making meaning in life. And understanding that our country, although an imperfect place, is becoming increasingly conscious of the meaning and value of the sacrifices made by its military men and women may help you to reframe the meaning of your own service. When you can take even one or two important principles from your military experience that can help clarify, inform, and guide you in the process of daily living, then your life in the military has not been a waste and you are no longer a victim. You will have become a true survivor and a vessel of resilience. You will have become a pilgrim on the pathway to posttraumatic growth.

DO NOT SURRENDER TO THE ENEMY OF SELF-DOUBT

In our work with traumatically impacted warriors suffering from PTSD, we are amazed at the number of cases in which the major factor that stands between the warrior and an abundant life boils down to one thing: self-doubt. Self-doubts crop up everywhere, causing us to question everything, up to and including the very meaning of life. Warriors doubt their skill, the sufficiency of their actions in combat, and the correctness of the life-and-death decisions they have made. They doubt the value of what they themselves have sacrificed and whether it will ever be enough to somehow equal or atone for the sacrifices of others. They doubt whether it is right to go to war, and they doubt whether it is right to stay out of the fight. They doubt whether they have acted properly by firing their weapons or by not firing them. They doubt their roles in their own families, their communities, and their units. They doubt their very acceptability before God.

If we could both ensure that everyone who read this book could take just one thing away from it, it would be this: DO NOT DOUBT. Do not doubt that with even a modest amount of support and some faith in a higher power you DO have the capacity to survive the struggle of today, the right to live a better tomorrow, and a purpose for having been placed upon this earth. Whether the reasons for your existence are clear to you or not in the fleeting moment, you can be sure of one thing. You matter.

Never take yourself or your life for granted. On days when you may find yourself questioning whether life is worth living for, remember the hundreds of thousands of American servicemen in present and past generations who considered it worth dying for.

Like most people, there are times in our lives when each of us questions our own purpose for being. At such times, we are lifted up by the words of Marianne Williamson. Known to countless millions, these words speak to everything that we believe and hold sacred about our fellow man, and especially about the warriors whose sacrifices have made our own lives possible: And so we end with these thoughts:

Swapping stories of hope,
FOB (forward operating base) Kalsu,Iraq

Our deepest fear is not that we are inadequate.

Our deepest fear is that we are powerful beyond measure.

It is our light, not our darkness, that most frightens us.

We ask ourselves, "Who am I to be brilliant, gorgeous, talented and fabulous?"

Actually, who are you not to be?

You are a child of God.

Your playing small doesn't serve the world.

There is nothing enlightened about shrinking so that other people won't feel insecure around you.

We were born to make manifest the glory of God that is within us.

It's not just in some of us; it's in everyone.

And, as we let our own light shine, we unconsciously give other people permission to do the same.

As we become liberated from our own fear, our presence automatically liberates others.

Listening and learning with soldiers; Mosul, Iraq

EPILOGUE:

LET`S CONTINUE THIS DIALOGUE TOGETHER

We humbly thank you for the time you have spent reading this book. In doing so you gave us, its authors, a gift of something beyond price, that is, your time, which once expended will never come again. The fact that we have exchanged our thoughts for your irreplaceable time links us in some small but indelible way.

We hope that in the pages of this book you have heard at least some small measure of your own past, received some validation of your present, and seen a glimpse of the possibilities that might lie ahead for your future. We hope that, through our writing, you may come to see yourself through a new set of eyes—eyes that are more encouraged, more self-aware, and more self-forgiving.

Do not turn the last page of this book, as if it were the ending to something, but rather as if it were the beginning. Please honor us by continuing to share your stories, your experiences, and your insights. We promise to learn from them and put them to good use. We have no aspirations of seeking material wealth from this book, but if we are brought into meaningful relationship with our readers as a result of its having been written, then we will consider ourselves rich beyond measure.

The words in this book began with a friendship, and that friendship began with a single word, "hello." Then friendship led to the sharing of ideas over simple food and black coffee. We look forward to the day that we read to one another the emails and letters you may have written to us while drinking your own morning brew. The "My Back to the Wall Gang" . . . We like the sound of it! It might just become the world's largest breakfast club and, in the process, may help thousands.

May your journey toward wholeness never cease. May you never lose hope that life can be better for you and those you love. May those who have helped fight our wars one day receive peace of heart and mind and spirit. And may the service that you have contributed to the liberation of others be ultimately rewarded through a more abundant life and the unshouldering of your own burdens.

APPENDIX A:

PROTOCOL FOR CONDUCTING YOUR OWN

PTSD SELF-INVENTORY

What follows is a simple step-by-step guide for monitoring yourself over a period of three to four weeks, for the purpose of giving more accurate information to your medical or mental health caregiver. Do not be surprised if, in some cases, you find yourself feeling better just from having performed this method. It is based on sound principles of emotional processing, which are beneficial in their own right and which you can provide to yourself.

What if you believe you cannot follow the protocol for the full three to four weeks? Then I suggest you do it for two weeks, including two five-day work weeks plus a weekend in between. You owe yourself and your doctor or counselor that much.

The reason that we suggest that you follow this method for three to four weeks, if possible, is twofold. First, PTSD presents very differently from day to day. To be sure that what you have is actually PTSD, and not something else, you need to observe yourself over time and pass your observations on to your care provider. Second, if you had the benefit of the very best quality mental health care obtainable, your therapist or counselor would do exactly the same thing, i.e., track you over the course of several visits and observe how your symptoms change or remain the same. If it helps you to maintain your motivation, consider doing this with a buddy or with the help of your spouse or partner.

Do not be discouraged when you read these instructions. Describing exactly what you need to do takes several pages. However, actually doing it, in practice, should not take more than about fifteen to twenty minutes a day total and can spell the difference between receiving correct treatment and a lifetime of frustration and misery. After all, if warriors complain that their clinics take too little time with them and do not reach accurate conclusions as a result, then here is a chance to do better on your own behalf.

FIRST: GATHER YOUR SUPPLIES

You will need a few simple supplies. We strongly suggest that you use bound notebooks or ring binders, as loose sheets almost inevitably get lost, and your information gets lost with them. Even 9 x 12-inch blank sketch books available at almost all dollar or office supplies stores make really durable notebooks.

- Five-subject spiral notebook or sketchbook (blank). If the notebook does not include five tabbed dividers, then purchase the kind that one can self-stick to create your own sections

- Pens and highlighter

- Personal wrist cuff that measures blood pressure and heart rate (available at your local drugstore; CVS, Walgreen's, and other chains have their own inexpensive store brands; also look at discount chains such as Big Lots in small electric section. Available for between $25-60.)

- Self-inventory forms (which you can download from www.mybacktothewall.com), including:

  (a) PCL-M for the *DSM-IV*, which is a screening for PTSD (download free; make 6 copies)

  (b) PHQ-9 (Patient Health Questionnaire) or QIDS (quick inventory of depressive symptoms), which are screening tools for depression (download free; make 6 copies)

  (c) Vital signs record form (download free)

(d) Food Intake and Exercise Record form (download free)

(e) Cumulative Assessment Rating Record form (download free)

(f) Calendar of Stressful Occurrences form (download free)

(g) Digital camera (cell phone camera works fine), with data card, if needed

(h) Tape/audio recorder (you can use the one in your cell phone or smart phone if you wish, or you can purchase one for less than $30)

(i) Weight scale: any kind will do, or you can weigh yourself at the drugstore or local gym

(j) Plain #10 (business-size) envelopes

NEXT: PREPARE YOUR SUPPLIES FOR USE

- Put data cards in camera or phone, if needed

- Install batteries in blood pressure cuff and learn to use it. Be careful to keep your wrist level with your heart. Do not move or talk while taking your reading.

- Label sections in spiral notebook:

  (a) Thoughts, Feelings, Behaviors (abbreviated TFB)

  (b) Physical

  (c) Triggers

  (d) Meaning Making

  (e) Diet/Exercise

You are now ready to begin a multi-modal self-inventory. You will do some work in all five parts of your self-inventory book on most days. This will only take a few minutes, usually about fifteen to twenty, per day. If you keep your notebook with you during the day, you can accomplish this protocol as you go through your day, with little effort.

Notebook section 1. Self-inventory of thoughts, feelings, and behaviors

- Using two of the six copies that you have downloaded or copied, honestly and thoughtfully answer the PHQ-9 (QIDS) and the PCL-M assessment forms on Day 1 of your self-inventory period. Give the other copy to your spouse or domestic partner and request that the form be filled out as if he/she were you. (This is important and helpful. Don't avoid it. Family members may see things that we ourselves don't, especially if we are avoidant, detached, or numb.) Sometimes, the things they see, and that you don't see in yourself, could save your wellbeing or even your life.

- Following directions, each of you should score the inventory, using scoring materials found on the My Back to the Wall website. Remember that this is not a test, and your answers will not make you "crazy." DON'T DISCUSS OR COMPARE YOUR FORMS. Instead, put each one in an envelope and mark the date and type of form. Do not seal the envelope. Simply tape each envelope, with its form inside, to a page in section 1 of your notebook. Put the flap side of the envelope against the page you're taping it to. Don't even bother to look at the forms until the end of the month.

- Repeat your own inventory form once each week for three additional weeks. Each time, put the form in an envelope, label it, and tape it in your notebook. Your spouse or partner will NOT need to repeat the form until the fourth and final week. This accounts for a total of six sets of forms (twelve in all): four sets for you and two sets for your significant other. At the end of four weeks, retrieve your forms from your notebook. Record the ratings for each question on the Cumulative Assessment Rating Record that you have downloaded. Ask your spouse or partner to do the same. Tape this, too, into your notebook. See how the ratings have either varied or stayed consistent from the baseline inventory to the ending inventory. You can also compare your self-ratings to your spouse's/partner's observations to see how your self-perceptions differ from the perceptions of your spouse and family.

- Return the forms to the envelopes and keep them in the notebook.

- Do not destroy or alter them.

CONGRATULATIONS! You've now taken a baseline PTSD and depression measurement on yourself.

You are not helpless. In fact, you have now empowered yourself to start taking charge of your own care. You should bring the forms that you have completed to your doctor's appointment to assist you in giving accurate information to your provider. These forms are your property. DO NOT LEAVE YOUR ORIGINALS WITH YOUR PROVIDER. KEEP THE ORIGINALS FOR YOURSELF.

- Throughout the month, make a daily record of anything you experience as stressful—including blowups, fights, or arguments with friends or family; times you feel angry, rageful, or "P.O'd", etc. Formal journaling isn't necessary—just a phrase or two about what happened. As the month progresses, use a highlighter to note themes or words that seem to reappear. Assign a rating from 0 to 5 to indicate the amount of stress you feel each day (with zero being the least amount of stress and 5 being the greatest) and include this in your daily record.

- Tape the Calendar of Stressful Occurrences in your notebook. In each daily block, record the stress rating you assign for that day.

If you follow these steps, by the end of a month, you will have gathered more information than a doctor would be likely to have on you after several months or even years. Your healthcare provider ought to be very pleased to have this information, because it helps pinpoint where your major areas of stress are located and how they manifest themselves. Very importantly, you will be able to see patterns in your life that indicate where your buttons are most likely to get pushed, and you will also see whether there are things in your life to which you are meaningfully attached. This will assist your counselor greatly.

Notebook section 2. Self-inventory of physiological reactions

This is VITAL (no pun intended) and must not be skipped. That is because your behaviors may actually be driven or initiated by your physiological reactions. So you must be aware of them in order to seek proper treatment. Your VITAL SIGNS are an external indicator of your internal stress states, so it is vital to monitor them.

- Using the same measuring device (e.g., wrist cuff) each time, take your vital signs (i.e., heart rate and blood pressure) every day, several times a day, for one month.

- Tape the Vital Signs Record in your notebook and make your recordings faithfully there. Some skips are unavoidable; don't quit just because you don't have a perfect record.

- If you can't avoid a skip, just mark an x, but try to skip as few times as possible.

- Take your vital signs at the following times. If it is a mealtime, take your measurements before eating rather than after:

  (a) After rising (wait a few minutes to allow blood pressure to stabilize)

(b) Noontime

(c) Midafternoon

(d) Evening (around 6 p.m.)

(e) At bedtime

Notebook section 3. Self-inventory of triggers

In this section of the notebook, keep a running record by date and time of any sights, sounds, smells, feelings, or other sensations that you feel especially sensitive or reactive to. If you notice yourself reacting to a trigger that you can take a photo of, do so. Print the photo and paste in the book. If it is a sound, record it on your cell phone or tape recorder, and make sure to keep the recording. If it is a smell or a feeling, write it down, using whatever words you can think of to record the way it makes you feel. Include times that you feel triggered by nothing, e.g., by something which you cannot identify.

For example, as I described in a previous chapter, some people are triggered by silence (the absence of sound) or by simply being alone (the absence of others) or by thoughts of the bomb blast that they thought was coming but didn't. These can be of great use later in therapy. They may also reveal patterns in what is triggering you or simply educate you about what is pressing your sensory buttons.

Notebook section 4. Meaning making

- Using your digital camera, become a highly attuned observer of the world around you. Take photos of anything around you that brings positive meaning to your life. This could be something that brings you strength, such as your spiritual faith. It could be anything that brings you pleasure or joy—including kids, barbecues, a good book, a hobby, your spouse's cooking, a sandlot ball game, or something that you enjoy doing. Include everything that means something to you—your church, your family Bible, or the people whose relationships you value. It will be very helpful for you to concretize these things by photographing them. Print these pictures and paste them into your book. As you do so, you are sending important messages to your brain that can aid in your recovery, so don't feel that this activity is silly or meaningless.

- If there are images or sounds associated with these, you might want to make a video and download it to your computer. These might include sounds of your church service or choir; your favorite MP3 track; videos of your baby sleeping, your children playing, or your best friend on his guitar. If there are things on your recording device or computer, make a written notation of them in your notebook. These notations help to indicate the degree to which you are engaged with the world around you or detached and withdrawn from it.

Notebook section 5. Food intake and physical exercise

- Weigh yourself once daily, after rising and going to the bathroom. Do not worry about looking up calories and fat grams. This is not a diet. It has to do with the way your body may be producing stress hormones that cause you to retain fluid and convert sugar to fat. Your weight will likely fluctuate from day to day. This is normal.

- Record, as accurately as possible, what you've eaten each day. Don't try to change or modify your habits at all. This is not a diet journal. Do the same for all the physical exercise you've gotten, including formal workouts, walks, runs, vigorous housecleaning, playing games with adults or with your children in the back yard or park.

- If you are an exercise junkie, be sure to include that as well, and detail the kinds of exercise you crave. If you run until you feel the runner's high, for example, this is an important sign.

The purpose of this record is to reflect patterns in the way your body expends or stores energy and the extent to which you may feel driven to consume carbs and sugars, as well as retain fluids. We have already talked in Chapters Two and Three about the different PTSD profiles, e.g., Locked and Loaded and Hunkered in the Bunker, as well as the three dominant responses of fight, flight, and freeze. This record, in conjunction with your Stress Record and Vital Signs Record, will create an excellent portrait of you. From it, you may be able to see what patterns are playing out in your life. For further information, consult the "My Back to the Wall" website, www.mybacktothewall.com.

A pilgrimage to "Iron Mike," symbol of the Airborne Corps,
Fort Bragg, North Carolina, 2010

APPENDIX B:

ABBREVIATED LISTING OF ORGANIZATIONS

SERVING THE NEEDS OF WARRIORS AND VETERANS

The following list of organizations is offered as a place for you to start. For the most complete and up-to-date listing of organizations serving the needs of active duty, retired, and veteran service members, readers are encouraged to consult the "mybacktothewall.com" website.

Veterans organizations—a list with links to the sites of each organization:
www.en.wikipedia.org/wiki/List_of_veterans'_organizations

American Legion, www.legion.org

Disabled American Vets (DAV), www.dav.org

Hope 4 Heroes, www.hope4heroes.org

Iraq Afghanistan Veterans of America (IAVA), www.iava.org

National Coalition for Homeless Veterans, www.nchv.org

Purple Heart Society, www.purpleheartsociety.com

Veterans of Foreign Wars (VFW), www.vfw.org

Vietnam Veterans of America, www.vva.org

Wounded Warrior Project, www.woundedwarriorproject.org

Left: Dr C on TV inviting vets to participate in group

Right: Dr. C with Army Meritorious Service Medal

Dr. C teaching on national television

Preparing to serve soldiers in theater as part of a great team; departing Ali Al Salem, Joint Operating Base, Kuwait

Arriving at FOB (forward operating base) Kalsu, Iraq

Touring Victory Base Camp, Iraq

NOTES

NOTES